Open Water Rowing Handbook

— Bruce C. Brown —

INTERNATIONAL MARINE

 PUBLISHING

Camden, Maine

For Gina, who supported me when I needed support,
nagged me when I needed nagging, and had the
wisdom never to confuse the two.

Published by International Marine

10 9 8 7 6 5 4 3 2 1

Copyright © 1991 International Marine, an imprint of TAB BOOKS. TAB BOOKS is a division of McGraw-Hill, Inc.

Library of Congress Cataloging-in-Publication Data
Brown, Bruce C. (Bruce Clifford), 1945–
    Open water rowing handbook / Bruce C. Brown.
      p.   cm.
    Includes bibliographical references (p.) and index.
    ISBN 0-87742-269-9
    1. Rowing—Handbooks, manuals, etc.   I. Title.
GV791.B8425   1991
797.1'23—dc20   90-24860
                                    CIP

TAB BOOKS offers software for sale. For information and a catalog, please contact TAB Software Department, Blue Ridge Summit, PA 17294-0850.

Questions regarding the content of this book should be addressed to:
International Marine Publishing
P.O. Box 220
Camden, ME 04843

Typeset by Watermark Design
Imageset by High Resolution
Printed by Arcata Graphics, Fairfield, PA
Design by Joyce C. Weston
All photos by the author unless otherwise noted.
Illustrations on pages 23, 44, and 65–68 by Larry Taugher.
Illustrations on pages 33, 125, and 146 by Beverly Ann Kelly.
Production by Janet Robbins
Edited by Douglas Logan, Thomas P. McCarthy, Jonathan Eaton

Contents

Acknowledgments

UNTIL you've written a book, you never know how many people become involved in the project and deserve thanks.

Chris Maas, Gordie Nash, and Shirwin Smith helped me immensely with this work. Along with sharing their knowledge of rowing, rowing boats, and boat building, they buttressed me with their enthusiasm and contributed their time. More importantly, they have contributed tirelessly to rowing.

Karen Carlson, John Garber, Bob Jarvis, Kevin Strain, and Betsy Zumwalt-Perez also had a very positive influence on the content of this book.

And, as they say, last—but certainly not least—my thanks to Dave Pyle, who introduced me to the joys of propelling yourself with oars.

Preface

THERE have been many changes in rowing, both in the industry and the sport, since the publication of my earlier books *Stroke! A Guide to Recreational Rowing* (1986) and *Long Strokes: A Handbook for Expanding the Rowing Experience* (1988). This book, which incorporates and revises those earlier efforts, is intended as an update for the present generation of rowers and as a source of accurate information for the reader just discovering the sport.

Despite its accelerated pace of change, rowing remains an individualistic pursuit, permitting a variety of approaches and any degree of commitment from casual to intense. The main division is that between flat-water rowers and everyone else. The former are specialists and the rest of us are generalists, and I intend neither description in the pejorative sense. Flat-water rowers usually belong to college varsity teams or local clubs. They race as singles (one rower per boat), pairs (each rower with one sweep), doubles (each rower with two sculls), fours, quads, or eights (eight-man sweeps). The single-rower shells are 27 to 28 feet long, only 9 to 9 1/4 inches wide, and weigh 30 pounds or less. Their rounded hulls are fast in a straight line but extremely sensitive to misplaced movement from inside or outside the boat. The wave system entrained by a duck landing nearby will be felt throughout the hull. Like Formula One race cars, their specialization is limiting. The term "flat-water" must be taken literally—these are not boats for a wind-induced chop, let alone the open ocean. At $4,000 or $5,000, they're two or three times as expensive as an open-water rowing boat, and they require more maintenance. To the flat-water rower, the leaping acceleration from a single stroke on calm water makes it all worthwhile.

Traditional flat-water rowers insist on calling what the rest of us do "recreational rowing," while most of us who do it refer to it as "open-water rowing." The tag "recreational rowing" offends many who feel it describes how you row, not what and where you row. They also believe there is a certain elitism among flat-water rowers, who "race" and "train" while we row "recreationally." The term "open-water" does not mean that you have to cross oceans, or even row in them, it simply indicates you have chosen to row a boat having the ability to safely traverse unprotected waters. These boats are not all the same. Some are safe in a 10-knot breeze and light chop, while others can be rowed successfully with the wind blowing over 25 and whitecaps breaking around you. They range from single shells 18 to 24 feet long, 20 or so inches wide, and weighing 40 to 50 pounds, to fixed-seat dories weighing 200 pounds or more. There are production-model open-water singles and pairs, but so far all the triples and quads have been custom-built. To this date all open-water boats have been raced with sculls (each rower with two oars) rather than sweeps.

The skills of the accomplished open-water rower are different, but no less demanding, than those of the flat-water rower. I am one of those preferring to call the sport "open-water rowing." As for the boats themselves, we will limit our scope to rowing boats designed and built for use in open water, and refer to them as "open-water rowing boats."

Sculling is a strange sport, one of only two Olympic disciplines practiced while facing backward (backstroke is the other). It requires that you change your intuitive orientation. Your right hand is on the left side of the boat and vice versa. Though it is an equipment-oriented sport, rowing will demand the utmost from your body. No matter how long you row, or how hard you try, you will never fully master the sport, and there are those who have rowed for 80 years yet still complain that their stroke is not good enough. As long as you are willing to learn, rowing will continue to challenge you.

For all its eccentricities, rowing is the perfect sport. It keeps you physically and mentally fit while putting you in touch with the outdoors. Offering a wide range of options to suit individual tastes, open-water rowing draws together a diverse group of interesting, friendly people. It is my hope that by reading this book and becoming involved in rowing, you will experience some of the joys the sport has brought me.

Author's Note

AFTER much thought I've chosen to forgo the gender-neutral term "oarsperson" in favor of the more traditional honorific "oarsman." This is not intended as a slap in the face to feminists (of either gender) or to women rowers—I'm simply more comfortable with the traditional term. Let it be said from the outset that rowing is an egalitarian pursuit, favoring neither gender nor any social stratum over others. A glance through the book will, I hope, confirm that I have written equally for women and men.

Like any sport, rowing enjoys its own specialized vocabulary. If you are using a pair of oars (as opposed to a single oar), you are in fact using "sculls"; you are not "rowing," but "sculling." In this work I have chosen to use the common terms "oars" and "rowing" interchangeably with their more correct counterparts. I hope this will not offend too many purists.

Though I have studied both, I am neither a boatbuilder nor a designer. My comments on construction and design are based on over 30 years' involvement in the sport. They are the observations of an oarsman, not the critical analyses of an accredited builder or designer.

- 1 -
Introduction

ROWING has been with us since man learned the advantages of leverage and adapted them to move a boat more easily through the water. Before that, boats and rafts were propelled by paddles, poles, and rudimentary downwind sails. By devising a way to attach his paddle to a fulcrum point on the gunwale, man incorporated leverage in his stroke and began using longer paddles (oars). By facing the stern of his craft and bracing his feet, he could use his back as well as his arms to increase the power of each stroke. As efficiency increased, so too did the size of boats—boats that could not have been propelled by paddle or pole.

The honor of developing the rowed boat seems to belong to the Egyptians. The first recorded boat with oars appears in a relief on an ancient stone wall erected in that country sometime between 3300 and 3000 B.C. A detailed relief from 2700 B.C. shows Pharaoh Sahure's seagoing war fleet. These Egyptian boats, known to have traveled as far afield as Syria, were equipped with both sails and oars.

For thousands of years, seaborne war, commerce, and exploration were powered by sail and oar. Ancient boats, which could not sail to weather or make way if there was no wind, relied heavily on oar power. The Phoenicians developed the bireme, a galley with oarsmen on two levels. By stacking their oarsmen, the Phoenicians concentrated more power in the same overall boat length, and achieved greater speed. The Greeks evolved the bireme into the trireme, quadrireme, and quinquereme. Finally, with the number of oars at the practical maximum, the Greeks assigned more and more men to each oar.

History was shaped in part by the men who pulled on oars. Cleopatra's barge was propelled by oars. Roman warships at the time of Christ relied on slave muscle power at their oars. Viking longships from the 10th century were powered more by oar than by sail as they plundered Europe and explored the

North Atlantic, discovering Iceland, Greenland, and North America. Saracen dromonds of the 12th century, English warships of the 13th century, and Venetian galleys of the 16th century relied heavily on oar power.

Even when ships grew too large to be effectively propelled by oars, rowing was not abandoned. Eighteenth-century corvettes, a class of warship slightly smaller than a frigate, frequently relied on oar power when all the canvas three masts would support could not find a breeze. At about the same time, whaling ships were putting oar-driven whaleboats to good use, not just in the hunting and killing of their prey, but as tugs, towing the mothership when there was no wind. As late as the early 19th century the United States Congress authorized the construction of 238 Jeffersonian Gunboats, 50-footers mounting a single cannon and powered by a small sail and nine pairs of oars.

But not even the most ardent proponent of rowing could consider any of this "pleasurable rowing."

In the very early 18th century, English bargemen on the Thames began racing their craft as an outgrowth of their occupation. For years they had been racing each other for potential customers; they simply turned the activity into a profitable sport, a sport on which betting thrived. In the early 19th century, English gentlemen came into the sport of rowing. In 1828 the Cambridge University Boat Club was founded, and 1829 saw the first Oxford-Cambridge Boat Race. Early rowing boat races were staged in boats similar to the barges of the previous century: wide, heavy craft with fixed thwarts and gunwale-mounted tholepins. In 1846, Oxford developed the outrigger, allowing its crew to mount the oarlocks outboard of the gunwale. The advance permitted a narrower, lighter hull while still providing the same leverage.

In 1852, the first Yale-Harvard Race was staged in boats similar to English racing boats. Soon Yale out-teched the opposition: In 1870, Yale oarsmen appeared with greased leather pants. Locking their feet in place, they slid back and forth on smooth wooden planks, incorporating leg power into the rowing stroke and increasing the arc of the oars. A year later the rolling (now called "sliding") seat was invented. The racing shell was complete—a narrow, lightly built, easily driven hull; wide outriggers spreading the oarlocks; foot stretchers to anchor the feet, and a sliding seat allowing every muscle in the body, especially the powerful leg muscles, to contribute to driving the oars through the water.

To be sure, the design of the racing shell has evolved over the hundred-plus years since the first appearance of the sliding seat, but these changes have been refinements and the introduction of new materials and building techniques rather than conceptual innovations. In the last century the racing shell has become lighter, stiffer, narrower, and longer, all in the search for

These dories built at Mystic Seaport are faithful replicas of the boats that fished the Grand Banks. They are seaworthy, tough, and capable of carrying heavy loads. Such boats have been rowed great distances in every imaginable kind of weather.

speed. It has been refined to the point that it does only one thing—go very fast in a straight line across smooth water. Through its evolution, the racing shell has become the preserve of the racing elite.

While the racing shell was being developed by collegiate oarsmen and professional racers, another cultural group was taking up rowing as a pleasant diversion. In the late 19th century, socioeconomic conditions provided more people spare time for recreation, and many turned to boating. In England, a variety of gigs were rowed and raced for pleasure. In America, workboats, such as peapods, dories, and Whitehalls were pressed into service as recreational craft. Over the years, these boats developed away from their utilitarian origins, becoming elegant pleasure craft. While they changed, it was more in construc-

The first of the recreational rowing boats, the Martin Marine Alden Single, is 16 feet long and 25 inches wide, and weighs 65 pounds with its Oarmaster aboard. The oars here are Martin's feather oars.

Longer, lighter, leaner, and faster, the Maas Aero represents the new generation of recreational rowing boats.

tion and finish than design concept, and they retained most of the workboat attributes that attracted oarsmen to them in the first place. They were strong and seaworthy, they could be rowed off beaches, and they required no major commitment either to learning the fine art of sculling or to maintenance. Unfortunately, they also retained some of their workboat drawbacks, which made them less than the ideal recreational craft. Though lighter than their progenitors, they were still quite heavy, and with oarlocks on gunwales, they were wide and slow. Fixed thwarts (seats) allowed the new breed of oarsmen to draw power only from their backs and arms.

About 20 years ago, the late Arthur Martin, a naval architect, did a wonderful thing—he combined the sliding seat and outriggers of a racing shell with a light, easily driven, though stable hull, and modern recreational rowing was born. Martin recognized a need and filled it in a brilliant way.

Working both the heart and lungs, sliding-seat rowing is possibly the best aerobic exercise. While a rower's lungs are processing cubic yards of air and his heart pumps oxygen-rich blood through his body, sliding-seat rowing works every major muscle in his legs, abdomen, chest, back, and arms. Unlike cycling, jogging, or walking, sculling is a "complete" workout. It makes demands on the entire body and doesn't require any extra exercise to augment it. Shell rowers have known this for years.

Sliding-seat rowing burns about twice the calories of jogging in the same amount of time, and it does not punish the body. Oarsmen's knees don't give out on them and they don't develop shin splints. I don't know of a rower who has been hit by a car or chased by a dog while practicing his sport. Instead of pounding their bodies, dodging traffic, and breathing foul exhaust fumes, rowers glide rhythmically in a nearly silent conveyance, enjoying a clean environment. A rower finishes his daily workout tired but refreshed. Unlike many people who look for excuses to free themselves from the drudgery of a workout, rowers can hardly wait to get out on the water, and most feel cheated if they are forced to miss a day. The psychological and physiological benefits of rowing cannot be overemphasized—it is a sport that people at any age and any level of athletic ability can take to heart.

- 2 -
Choosing the Right Boat

IN THE PAST, selecting a rowing boat was relatively simple. The choice was limited to flat-bottomed working skiffs, seaworthy though heavy dories and peapods, elegant traditional craft such as guide boats, and racing shells. Each group had its advantages and drawbacks. While most were fine examples of various stages in rowing boat evolution, they did not meet the needs of the average pleasure rower.

Still, for many years rowers made their selections from among these types of craft, and rowing for fun grew slowly but steadily. Flat-bottomed working skiffs, usually stable, slow, and heavy, served as a means of transportation inside harbors. These wonderful load carriers acted as tenders for both pleasure and commercial craft, were used for short trips from dock to dock, and provided a stable platform for fishermen. Dories and peapods, evolving from their workboat origins, became the boats of choice for many traditional open-water rowers. Like their predecessors, the lobster and fishing boats of the Northeast, these new dories and peapods were seaworthy craft that could carry great loads and still move well under a pair of oars. The traditional pulling boats of the late 1800s—Whitehalls and guide boats—were also popular, but they tended to be heavy and expensive and required a regular schedule of maintenance.

All these boats lacked the sliding-seat arrangement of a true shell. To many rowers, the performance gains and extra exercise supplied by the sliding seat were crucial, and if they couldn't enjoy that, they just didn't want to row. Their only recourse was the racing shell. Unfortunately, shells were and still are prohibitively expensive. While fast, they are incredibly unstable and unforgiving, seeming to want to dump the oarsman for the least fault in style or a momentary lapse of concentration. They are lightly built and therefore fragile, and require constant maintenance and tuning. Because their design

Racing shells are longer, narrower, and more fragile than open-water boats.

has been refined over the years for a single purpose—speed in a straight line over smooth water—rowers must adapt to them, not vice versa. Racing shells have always been, and probably always will be, the exclusive domain of a highly specialized racing elite.

For years rowers were forced to compromise. Many bought boats that didn't perform as desired and those boats eventually fell into disuse. Then Arthur Martin founded Martin Marine and began producing boats more suited to the oarsman who wanted to row for fun, and "recreational rowing" was born.

Martin combined modern material—lightweight, nearly maintenance-free fiberglass—with innovative design to produce pleasing, seakindly hulls known as Alden Ocean Shells. Innovative and influential, indeed, but most oarsmen feel his greatest contribution to the sport is the Oarmaster.

Martin's Oarmaster brought the joys of sliding-seat rowing to all those potential rowers sitting on the beach or straining to move heavy boats through the water with only the power of their arms and backs. The Oarmaster was a brilliant concept. Fashioned from aluminum and stainless steel, it is a complete, self-contained unit. It includes seat, tracks, riggers, oarlocks, and foot stretchers. All the stresses and strains of rowing are isolated from the boat's hull. Since they did not have to be stressed to take the rigging, Martin's hulls could be light—nothing more than envelopes designed to hold their hydrodynamically efficient shape and keep out the water.

The fact that the Oarmaster could be lifted in and out of the boats made portability less of a problem than it had been in the past. Suddenly, for the recreational rower, trailers and boat rollers became obsolete. The Oarmaster could be carried as a unit and the boat could be tucked under the oarsman's arm or carried over his head. It took two trips, but neither hull nor Oarmaster was prohibitively heavy. With the riggers detached, the Oarmaster fit in the trunk of a car and the boat rested snugly on a roof rack. This made rowing attractive and simple, even for one person, and opened up waterways previously thought inaccessible.

The Oarmaster's portability and ease of installation soon became obvious to other boatowners and builders, and Oarmasters began turning up in traditional small craft. Dories and peapods with Oarmasters became a common sight. In fact, Martin Marine produced both a 16- and 19-foot pod, the larger boat being fitted with a pair of Oarmasters. Other builders began producing light hulls, in both wood and fiberglass, and equipping them with Oarmasters. Sliding-seat rowing for the masses had arrived!

Martin Marine and several other builders were well ensconced in the rowing boat market when the fitness craze hit America. As joggers injured themselves, many turned to rowing as a safer, more thorough exercise program. Others saw the market potential and new builders entered the marketplace. Many of these new entries were men with long rowing histories who finally saw a way to make a living at the sport they loved. They brought not only new blood, but experience and new ideas to the industry. Today, there are literally dozens of modern, well-designed, well-built sliding-seat boats available at reasonable prices. This plethora of designs has made choosing a boat more difficult than it was in the past. The potential rower no longer needs to compromise; he or she will be able to find a near-perfect boat. Before the consumer can choose in this abundant market, however, he must do two things: Learn something about the different boats and, most importantly, decide exactly what he expects his boat to do for him. All boats are compromises—some do one thing better than others—but none of them can do everything well. Before you make your compromises, know what is most important to you.

■ "RECREATIONAL" OR "OPEN-WATER"?

Originally the term "recreational rowing" was applied to Arthur Martin's boats to distinguish them from true racing shells and trainers—boats more sturdily built and slightly more forgiving than racing shells but still not designed for the average oarsman. Gradually this became the generic term for virtually any sliding seat boat that was not specifically a racing shell or a trainer. As this branch of the sport has grown and become more serious, and the boats have become more high tech, the term "recreational" no longer seems to fit. Obviously any boat rowed for the sheer joy of rowing, be it a 150-pound flat-bottomed workboat with peeling paint and 5-foot ash oars, or a 30-pound Kevlar racing shell with carbon-fiber sculls, is a recreational rowing boat. The term seems to be more a function of how you choose to row, rather than what and where you choose to row. For our purposes, we will limit our scope to boats designed and built for use in exposed conditions, and call them "open-water" rowing boats. The Appledore Pod and Stonington Pulling Boat are at one end of the open-water spectrum, while the Maas 24 and the Little River Pro-Am are at the other. These boats, and all those falling between them, are very different, but more on that later. For now, we are concerned with their common traits, the reasons they are grouped together as open-water rowing boats.

Taken as a whole, nearly all modern open-water boats fall into two distinct categories: racing shell look-alikes and the imitators of traditional craft. The largest, most popular group, the shell look-alikes—the Small Crafts, Maas boats, Little Rivers, and many more—group together quite easily. Though the differences between them are great they have a similar look, and comparisons are relatively simple. The copies of traditional craft are a much more diverse group. They range from 15-foot dories and peapods to 22-foot Viking Whitehalls.

There are modern boats that do not fit into either category, such as the Row Cat, a catamaran with a sliding-seat rowing station; the On Board Rower, which converts a sailboard to a rowable craft; and the California Wherry, which bridges the gap between the two main groups. There are also modern copies of fixed-thwart rowing boats. Some of these are great rowing craft, but since the focus of the book is on sliding-seat rowing boats, we will look at them only briefly.

■ THE OPEN-WATER ROWING BOAT

Traditional rowing craft—dories, peapods, Whitehalls, guide boats and their progenitors—are the first standard we must use when evaluating modern craft. The differences between these traditional pulling boats and modern craft are vast, and though there are many others, construction and driving power are the two major disparities. Traditional boats were wooden, held together primarily with nails and screws. The vast majority of modern boats are molded; most are built from fiberglass and other man-made fibers, but a few are constructed using the wood-epoxy saturation technique (WEST), which combines the beauty and buoyancy of wood with the low weight and minimal maintenance requirements of fiberglass. Modern boats, whether fiberglass or WEST System, are far lighter than their ancestors and require considerably less maintenance.

While racing shell look-alikes are lean boats designed to move one or two scullers across the water quickly, the more traditional designs usually combine at least a portion of their ancestors' load-carrying and rough-water abilities with modern construction techniques. The result can be the ideal boat for many rowers. Beautiful little seagoing craft such as the Martin Appledore Pod and Stonington Pulling Boat can be rowed offshore with confidence. They can carry hundreds of pounds of payload, either passengers or gear, making them the perfect craft for a day's fishing trip or a camp-cruising voyage. Many of these boats, like the craft they're patterned after, can be rigged to carry a small working sail, and are quick when sailed off the wind. With proper planning, and a bit of luck, this sailing ability can make the trip home a relaxing one after a day's rowing or fishing.

While the imitators of traditional boats are not designed for raw speed, some of the best of them come close to the slower shell look-alikes, and what they sacrifice in down-the-line speed they make up for in their rough-water and load-carrying ability.

A word of warning: Some boats today employ the names of well-known traditional designs, yet bear little or no resemblance to their namesakes. These are not necessarily poorly designed boats, but to me the traditional name suggests certain qualities and abilities the modern versions might not share. Fortunately, there are several good books on the subject of traditional boats (see Suggestions for Further Reading). If you are not well informed about the features that make each design unique, it would be a good idea to do some reading before you go looking for a boat. Your research will stand you in good stead while you are shopping, and knowing something about the history of the design you choose will make you a better oarsman.

Today's rower has a better selection at lower prices than ever before. While a classic Whitehall with a hand-carved, bright-finish wineglass transom is still one of the prettiest boats around, all but the most avid defender of traditional craft would be able to list a multitude of reasons why she would not be the right boat for the serious rower of the 1990s. Built in the traditional way, these boats are heavy and require considerable maintenance. Unless you are fortunate enough to have the skills, tools, and time to build your own boat, you would have to find a builder of traditional craft. And then you will learn just how long it takes to get one of these gems, and just how costly it will be. Wood has become expensive, and the craftsman's time to fashion a traditional boat also costs, though not as much as it probably should. And it does take time. If

A wide selection of boats on the shore of Lake Tahoe: a traditional wooden boat with sliding seat and outboard oarlocks, a Vancouver, Aero, and Dragonfly double.

you were to decide today that you wanted a replica of a Whitehall, Swampscott dory, or any other traditional boat built in the traditional way, delivery could be any time from four months to more than a year away.

Conversely, modern boats, both shell look-alikes and copies of traditional boats, are built to be light and practically maintenance-free. Mass-produced, they are relatively inexpensive and almost immediately available. Most of today's boats are off-the-shelf items. If your dealer doesn't have the exact model or color you want in stock, usually all it takes is a quick call to the builder and your boat will be on its way in a few days. Some builders, such as Maas Rowing Shells, offer standard boats for immediate delivery and boats with custom paint and or graphics on a delayed delivery schedule (usually about a month's wait).

The heavy, relatively slow, traditional dories, pods, and Whitehalls are at one end of the rowing boat spectrum. The next genre slips neatly between the traditional boats and their modern, sliding-seat copies. This small group of boats consists of copies of traditional boats with fixed thwarts and gunwale-mounted oarlocks. These boats, usually built of fiberglass with a modicum of wood trim, tend to be rather short and heavy. They range from 12 to 15 feet overall and can weigh between 100 and 150 pounds. Along with their weight, lack of waterline length prevents these boats from being terribly quick—but then they were not designed to race. Lighter and demanding less maintenance than the boats they were patterned after, this genre of small boats could be classed as "elegant rowboats." They serve as yacht tenders for quick trips around the harbor, or as short-range fishing boats, and are a wonderful way to introduce children to the joys of rowing. Taken as a group, they are serviceable, maneuverable, and seaworthy. My own first boat, a Schock dory, came from this group, and I probably had more pure fun in that boat than any other I've owned since. These fixed-thwart boats are at the lower end of the performance and cost scales for modern pulling boats, but they fill a very important niche and, if they suit your needs, you would be doing yourself a disservice by investing more money in a craft with higher performance.

In terms of performance, the opposite of the traditional boat is the racing shell. True racing shells are to traditional rowing craft as top fuel dragsters are to heavy-duty pickup trucks. Each is designed to do a specific job and do it well, but they are hardly interchangeable. Shells, too, are expensive, nearly prohibitively so. They are fragile, requiring very careful handling and nearly constant maintenance. Unstable in the smoothest water, they are nearly unrowable in a seaway. The load-carrying capacity of a shell is nil; in fact, a lightweight shell can hardly support a heavy oarsman. It is interesting that, while in most ways they are exact opposites, boats at either end of the rowing boat spectrum share two features that make them unattractive to the average oarsman: high cost and extensive maintenance requirements.

The vast center of the spectrum was empty until Arthur Martin introduced his Alden Ocean Shell. With this boat, rowers and potential rowers no longer had to choose between speed on one hand and seaworthiness and load-carrying ability on the other.

This ingenious industry benchmark is quite simple in design. She is 16 feet long with a two-foot, one-inch beam. (As with all boats discussed in this book, "beam" refers to the maximum beam of the hull, not the riggers, or unless specifically mentioned, the waterline beam. The oarlock-to-oarlock measurement is generally standard throughout the industry at 60 inches, plus or minus an inch or two.) Lightly built of fiberglass, her hull weighs about 40 pounds. The Oarmaster, which adjusts at the stretchers and the riggers to accommodate oarsmen of different heights, weighs in at about 23 pounds. Assembled, the Alden Ocean Shell weighs about 63 pounds. Granted, that is more than twice the weight of a true racing shell, but it is only a third the weight of many traditional boats.

Though the industry standard, the Alden is not a perfect boat. She is quite wet when rowed in a chop, and her flat bottom tends to flex or "oilcan" in the same conditions. In flat water her lack of waterline length limits her speed, and many experienced rowers complain that the Oarmaster's riggers flex too much, leaching power from their stroke. On the other hand, her stability and maneuverability are boons to the inexperienced oarsman. Her hull is easily portable and simple to store. The Alden is also quite affordable—less than half the price of either a custom-built traditional boat or a racing shell. The proof of the Alden's success is twofold: she's the industry benchmark, and 20 years after her introduction, she is still in demand.

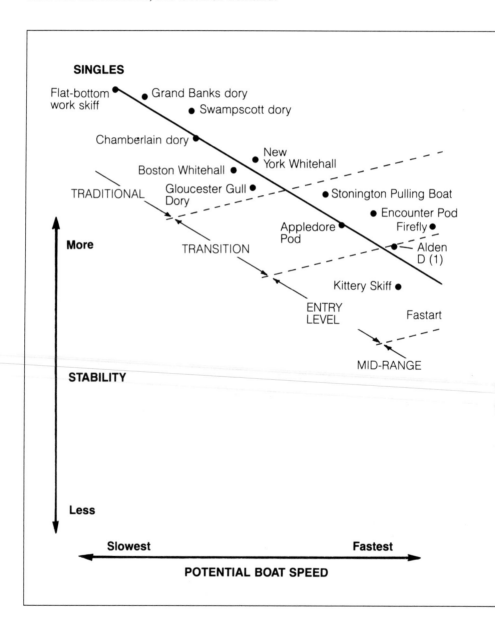

▬ COMPARING SPEED AND STABILITY

The Alden Ocean Shell should not be considered the bottom rung on the ladder of available open-water boats. Take a look at the accompanying chart for a comparison of rowing boats by their two most significant characteristics—

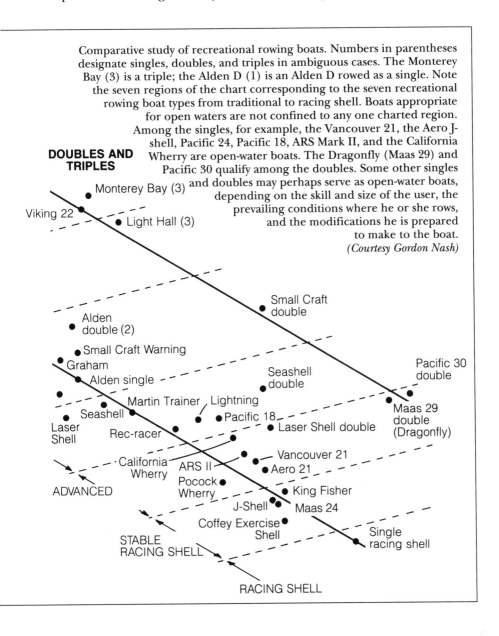

Comparative study of recreational rowing boats. Numbers in parentheses designate singles, doubles, and triples in ambiguous cases. The Monterey Bay (3) is a triple; the Alden D (1) is an Alden D rowed as a single. Note the seven regions of the chart corresponding to the seven recreational rowing boat types from traditional to racing shell. Boats appropriate for open waters are not confined to any one charted region. Among the singles, for example, the Vancouver 21, the Aero J-shell, Pacific 24, Pacific 18, ARS Mark II, and the California Wherry are open-water boats. The Dragonfly (Maas 29) and Pacific 30 qualify among the doubles. Some other singles and doubles may perhaps serve as open-water boats, depending on the skill and size of the user, the prevailing conditions where he or she rows, and the modifications he is prepared to make to the boat.
(Courtesy Gordon Nash)

DOUBLES AND TRIPLES

Monterey Bay (3)

Viking 22

Light Hall (3)

Small Craft double

Alden double (2)

Small Craft Warning

Graham

Alden single

Seashell double

Pacific 30 double

Martin Trainer   Lightning

Seashell

Pacific 18

Laser Shell double

Maas 29 double (Dragonfly)

Laser Shell

Rec-racer

California Wherry

ARS II

Vancouver 21

Aero 21

ADVANCED

Pocock Wherry

King Fisher

J-Shell   Maas 24

Coffey Exercise Shell

STABLE RACING SHELL

Single racing shell

RACING SHELL

speed and stability. This chart was prepared by Gordie Nash, who is eminently qualified to make these comparisons. Founder of Rowing Crafters in Sausalito, California, Nash has built a wide variety of rowing boats and served as a dealer for many nationally marketed craft. A keen competitive rower for many years, he has rowed nearly every boat on the market and all the boats on the chart. At the oars of boats he has built and those designed and built by others, he has set records and won his class in nearly every open-water race on both the East and West coasts. His enviable record includes several class wins and record times in the ultramarathon of rowing, the 32-nautical mile Catalina Island to Marina del Rey race.

As Nash describes it: "The chart starts with the flat-bottom work skiff at the upper left and the racing shell at the lower right. The Alden is very near the middle. All the boats to the right of the Alden are faster and less stable, while all the boats to the left are slower, and most are more stable. Following the graph, stability and seaworthiness are portrayed from greatest at the top to lowest at the bottom. In general, a faster boat is also less stable. This is revealed by the downward slope of the plotted points. Experience shows us that faster boats are lighter, longer, and thinner, and thus less stable. There are exceptions."

While the evaluation of a rowing boat is somewhat subjective—influenced by the rower's size, style, experience, and "feel," I agree with Nash's placement of the boats on the chart. Any single rower given the assignment of evaluating this array of boats would produce a slightly different chart, but I believe, personal and economic considerations aside, they would all line up very

Rower Shirwin Smith demonstrates the stability of an Aero. (Don't try this until you've had many hours in the boat—and don't mind getting wet.)

closely to where Nash has them. Another note about the chart: A few of the boats listed are no longer manufactured. They are included because they are on the used market, and because they provide rowers with comparisons against newer designs.

Speed and stability are not the only criteria by which we judge rowing boats, but they are among the most significant, and are a great place to start the search for the rowing craft that most closely suits your needs. Looking at the chart, we see that the modern copies of traditional boats, the Appledore Pod and the Stonington Pulling Boat, are slower but more stable than the Alden Ocean Shell. We also find that some of the newer racing shell look-alikes fall to the left of the Alden. Two of these, the popular Laser Shell and the Graham Mark I, are both rated as slower than the Alden. On the other hand, a boat that looks very much like the Laser, the Small Craft Warning, is rated equal in speed to the Alden and nearly as stable as the Appledore Pod. To the right of the Alden, we find boats such as the Seashell, Rec-Racer, Maas Aero, Trimline 24, and Maas 24, which trade away stability for greater speed.

The trick for the prospective buyer is to balance speed and stability. For most people, speed is fun; the faster you can push the boat through the water, the more fun it is. Stability, on the other hand, gives the rower a feeling of comfort and confidence. Stability and seaworthiness are not the same thing, though many relate the two. Stability is a boat's willingness to remain upright and level. Seaworthiness is the combination of factors that make a boat safer and more easily handled in rough conditions. Seaworthiness is not factored into the chart, since it is best judged by the individual oarsman.

If speed is your primary consideration, and you plan to row only on sheltered lakes or rivers, or in calm harbors, consider the boats at the lower righthand corner of the chart. If you plan to row offshore in a variety of conditions, you would want to move more to the left. If you want to carry some camping gear and drag a fishing lure, then move back toward the center of the chart. Also consider your own experience and take responsibility for your choice. While most oarsmen of average ability could row a Trimline 24 in calm water, it would take more experience and technique to manage the same boat in rough conditions.

■ WEIGHT, LENGTH, AND EASE OF RIGGING

Of course there are factors besides speed and stability to consider. Along with the prevailing conditions where you expect to row, there are logistical elements to think through before the boat is purchased. Weight is more than a performance consideration; it is also a logistical factor. Weight will determine whether the boat can be cartopped or trailered. Weight will also dictate whether you will be able to launch and retrieve the boat alone. Relying on another person's help getting your boat to and from the water might be necessary, but it puts your rowing at the mercy of their schedule.

Like weight, length is just as much a logistical consideration as it is a performance factor. Most rowers can find a convenient place to store a 16-foot Alden Ocean Shell, but a 24-foot Pacific can be another matter. Human nature being what it is, if you are forced to store your boat in an inconvenient location it will eventually inhibit your rowing program. If your boat is too long to handle easily, and too heavy for you to maneuver comfortably, the drill of getting it to and from the water may become too much of a struggle and you'll stop using it.

Along with weight and length, the rigging can be a logistical nightmare. Basically, there are two types of rigging: fixed and removable. In this instance, "removable" refers to self-contained units such as Martin's Oarmaster and Graham's E-Z Rigger. Of course fixed rigging can be removed, sometimes simply by loosening a pair of wing nuts, but typically the dismantling process is more involved. Being able to pull the entire rowing assembly out of the boat, as with the Oarmaster, can simplify storage and transportation because it both diminishes the maximum beam and lightens the hull. Many rowing boats share slip space with large sailing or power boats, and being able to pull the rigging off easily can be a great help. Even if your boat shares garage space with the family car, the ability to reduce the boat's width from five feet to two feet can be advantageous. Some "fixed-rigger" boats are easier to deal with than others. The riggers of the Laser shell are held in place with quick-release pins, and some boats can be modified simply by replacing lock nuts with wing nuts. On other boats, where bolts mate to captive threaded plates, modification won't be as simple, and many builders discourage changing their designs. If overall beam is a consideration, look very carefully at the boat you've chosen before you write the check.

The more difficult a boat is to get to and from the water, the less it will be used. The more ambitious your rowing program, the more important logistics become. The oarsman who rows his boat three or four times a week, launching off the same beach or dock, may be able to deal with a boat that would give the more adventurous rower headaches. If your boat is heavy and has to be moved about on a small cart or rollers, it might be difficult to drag up on a secluded beach. You will need to think about carrying the cart or rollers with you, or rethink your choice of the boat. Weight is also a factor in open-water shells, where some can weigh half again as much as others. It's one thing to struggle to get a heavy boat from your car to the water on a protected sandy beach, and quite another to land on a rocky beach and get it out of harm's way before the next wave strikes.

■ CAPACITY

The capacity of a boat has little to do with its overall length. The Catalina 14, a 14-foot fiberglass Whitehall replica with a sliding seat, has much more carrying capacity than a 24-foot Pro-Am, a shell look-alike. Capacity also means different things to different rowers. To some it means the ability to carry a wallet and car keys in a safe, dry place, and have a water bottle within easy reach. To others it can mean being able to transport sail bags and ice chests from shore to a larger boat. Others might describe capacity as the ability to accommodate a passenger and a picnic lunch, or a tent and all the camping gear you would need for a two-week expedition.

There is one other thing to remember when you are thinking about a boat's capacity: The term refers to more than just the space available to store gear; it refers to the weight a boat can *comfortably* carry. I don't believe a boat should be loaded to her maximum; there always should be a safety margin. When looking at this figure, remember that you are part of the payload. If your boat has a suggested maximum payload of 250 pounds, and you weigh 200, this means your *maximum* carrying capacity is 50 pounds. There are some very good shell look-alikes available that are specifically designed for lightweight oarsmen. If you weigh near the upper limit of your boat's rated payload, keep this in mind if you're thinking about strapping a watertight bag full of camping gear to the deck. When you take your test row, think about the effect extra weight will have and leave a safe margin for error. Whatever your definition, capacity is a factor that deserves a great deal of thought.

To many scullers, an early-morning row is an experience to enjoy in solitude. It's a time to commune with nature, a period of quiet with which to begin the day, a personal time. The prospect of sharing that private time with another is unappealing. Others enjoy camaraderie and the very different challenges of rowing a double. If a double is attractive to you, but the thought of always having to schedule around your partner is bothersome, there are convertible boats. It's important to note that many doubles simply cannot be rowed successfully by a single sculler; the balance is totally unacceptable. To row a double as a single, you must be able to reposition your weight, properly balancing the boat. The Alden Double can be rowed as a single simply by removing one of the Oarmasters and relocating the other. The same is true of the larger Appledore Pod. Some of the other shell look-alikes, such as Little River's Seashell Double, can also be easily converted.

Open-water boats are no longer the creation of backyard builders. In the Maas factory, singles are built beside the mold for a Dragonfly double.

■ CONSTRUCTION

Since a boat's maintenance requirements, or lack of them, are frequently high on a buyer's list of reasons for choosing a boat, it will pay to take a long, hard look at construction. Most boats today are beautifully finished, but construction is another matter—it is what lies under, and is hidden by, the finish. Construction refers to the materials and quality of workmanship that went into the boat. Your rowing grounds will make a difference in how you analyze the construction of a boat. Some materials that will be acceptable in freshwater regions will deteriorate rapidly in the ocean.

Whether you're buying an open-water shell or a traditional design in either fiberglass or wood, it goes without saying that sturdy construction of boat and equipment will be a top priority. Hull layup requires some inspection before you buy. In their zeal to supply the lightest possible hull, a few builders have produced boats that are too flexible and might not stand up to hard use. In the same size range, you will find boats with hull layups that vary from a single layer each of one-ounce matt, and 10-ounce cloth, to two layers of $1^1/2$-ounce matt combined with two layers of 10-ounce cloth. Then there are the "high-tech" and "state-of-the-art" marvels. Remember, "heavy" and "strong" are not interchangeable; frequently a lighter boat is stronger than a heavier one. When you're thinking of buying a boat, open inspection ports; look and feel inside. Look for extra reinforcement where the riggers attach and under the seat deck. Above all, ask questions.

All things being equal, a lighter boat is better than a heavier one, but strength and stiffness should not be sacrificed on the altar of light weight. If a boat is lightly built at the expense of strength, it is no bargain. Be sure the boat you're looking at is strong enough for its intended purpose. Strength and stiffness should not be confused; there are strong boats that are not particularly stiff. If a boat is limber, it saps power from your stroke by flexing and compressing rather than driving through the water, and it will not carry way as well during recovery.

Don't just accept a builder's or dealer's word that the boat is "high tech" or "state of the art." Look for signs that the builder may have cut corners, using aluminum pop rivets or polished aluminum fittings instead of stainless steel. Ask questions about resins, types of glass, foam cores, wood, glues, and fasteners.

Know that S-glass is superior to E-glass, though at least five times more expensive. Some builders use a lot of S-glass, some incorporate it at stress points, saving weight without sacrificing strength. Know that there are three types of resins—epoxy; modified epoxies, which include vinylester-modified and acrylic-modified; and polyester—and know a bit about the properties of each.

Epoxy resin is by far the best resin on the market today. It is slightly lighter than the others, and it is far stronger, with tremendous bonding ability and high-impact resistance. If flexed, it will not break down over time. It is also the hardest to work with, and costs about three times more than polyester. If a builder goes to the trouble and expense of using epoxy resin, his brochures will advertise that fact.

In terms of strength, the modified epoxies fall between epoxies and polyester resins. They are not as strong or impact-resistant as epoxies, nor do they bond or resist breakdown as well. On the other hand, they perform all these functions better than polyester, are easier to work with than epoxy, and cost about one-third less.

Most fiberglass boats in the world today are made from polyester resins. They are the cheapest and easiest to use, as well as being compatible with polyester gelcoat. They are also the most brittle and least impact-resistant, will break down over time, and offer the poorest bonding. This is not to say you should avoid boats built with these resins—there are plenty of these boats around that have survived the test of time—but there are newer, better resins on the market.

With changes occurring constantly in the chemical industry, it is virtually impossible to provide reliable answers to questions about material compatibility. Some builders and suppliers believe certain resins work better with S-glass, while others are more compatible with E-glass. Some carbon fiber has a binding strip made to be activated by epoxy resins, but that doesn't mean that it will be totally useless if used with polyester. You can't accept blanket statements on compatibility; the information could be several years out of date. Properties of materials change, and builders learn different ways to work them.

Whether your boat is E-glass or S-glass, polyester or epoxy, beware of large concentrations of matt. It contributes some stiffness, but is heavy in relation to the strength it adds. Another weight-adding element is the gelcoat, the bright finish. Gelcoat adds almost no strength or rigidity, but it does add considerable weight. The difference between a thick and thin gelcoat of a 20-footer can be as much as eight pounds. If you're looking at a design you like and it seems a bit heavy, ask about the gelcoat thickness. The builder might be willing to make a slight change, shaving off a few pounds. Be advised, the top builders of advanced boats already know this and are shaving it as thin as they can yet still provide a decent finish.

Foam core (foam is virtually the only coring material used in rowing boats) is sometimes used to add stiffness. When it is used, it is vital to the boat's structural integrity and you should know about its composition and track record.

If you don't understand the answers to your questions, or they seem vague or evasive, it's your responsibility to keep asking until you are satisfied. If the dealer can't answer your questions satisfactorily, call the builder. A long-distance telephone call is cheaper than a boat that breaks down sooner than you expect. Besides, talking to the builder will probably be quite educational.

If you question the way a builder is combining materials, talk to several other builders and listen to what they have to say. See if you can locate owners of boats like those you are considering (the builder or dealer should be able to help you here). Ask them questions: Have they had problems with their boats? If so, was the builder or dealer helpful, or did the relationship end as soon as the money changed hands?

After you've convinced yourself that the hull is strong and sound, sight down it for fairness. You don't have to be a racer to gain advantage from a fair hull. Ripples, or hills and valleys, in the hull will slow the boat through the water, affect her ability to carry way, and make rowing that much more difficult. Be sure the boat you are buying has a smooth, fair hull.

Decking is still another consideration. Most open-water shells have rigid fiberglass decks, but some, such as the Scullcraft and Fastart 21, are open boats. Like racing shells, open boats can be decked over with thin sheets of plastic (similar to garbage bag material), but this is not always satisfactory for rough-

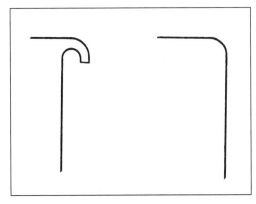

Hull-to-deck joints: rolled lip versus flush joint.

water rowing or the handling some boats receive. If you are going to row regularly on exposed water, you'll need a stiff deck with sealed flotation compartments.

Boats with rigid decks have a joint between the hull and deck, which is an area a prospective buyer needs to inspect. On some boats, this is a narrow 90-degree flange on the underside of the deck just inboard of the edge. The deck is glued to the hull, and the flange covered with a vinyl (or similar) rubrail protecting both the gelcoat and the joint. While the limited gluing surface doesn't seem to be a problem on these boats, the rubrail itself can be. Some builders glue the rail to the joint, and this is far superior to simply heat-shrinking it in place. The rubrail adds weight and may eventually come loose, meaning it must either be replaced or fixed. Of course, the attachment of the rubrail will probably not determine your decision to buy or not to buy a boat, but if the builder has skimped in this final touch, you might want to take a longer look at other, more vital, areas.

A more common method of dealing with the hull-deck joint is a rolled lip. Among others, Maas and Small Craft use this method, which consists of mating together rolled lips on both the hull and deck. The rolled lips provide extra bonding area and improved stiffness in the sheer. Most builders using the rolled flange method of hull-deck attachment don't install a rub rail, so owners will want to be careful not to ding the exposed gelcoat.

Take a good look at the rigging and "engine bed." Riggers are generally constructed of stainless steel, aluminum, and fiberglass (usually strengthened with carbon fiber). But no matter what materials are used, the same three factors are important: stiffness, adjustability, and attachment. A few good strokes of the oars will tell you how stiff the riggers are. All boats flex some—the loads on riggers are tremendous. The question is, how much? On many boats the oarlocks rise and fall half an inch through the stroke, and most rowers accept this. Some other boats deflect as much as three inches fore and aft, and most experienced rowers find this unacceptable. The ability to change the height and pitch of the oarlocks adds greatly to comfort and performance.

Finally, survey the hull attachment points. If at all possible, find a used boat of the type you intend to buy and carefully examine the glass around the rigger mounting points. Are there spiderweb cracks forming in the gelcoat? Has the glass deformed? Of course, either condition could have been caused by the owner's torquing the rigging while transporting the boat, or hitting a dock or buoy. If there's any question in your mind, ask before buying.

In the engine bed—that is, the sliding-seat assembly and the foot stretchers—most problems arise in the area of the stretchers. Beware of aluminum fasteners in the stretchers, especially if you are going to row in salt water. Being low in the boat, the stretchers are awash far more than the sliding seat or the riggers. Rowed in choppy water, all open-water boats take some spray, and stretchers can be constantly wet. Surprisingly, many builders use aluminum pop rivets instead of stainless steel in this vital area. Frequently builders use anodized aluminum cross pieces to mount the shoes or clogs; this is fine, but if there are threaded holes in the aluminum, they can corrode and capture a stainless steel bolt or screw as surely as if the hole was filled with Loctite. You should be able to adjust your stretchers while in the water, and if bolts lock up on you, you won't be able to. I once did a rowing evaluation of five open-water shells; on four of these new, dealer-supplied boats the stretcher locating bolts were frozen and the stretcher placement could only be changed with the aid of a pair of pliers and a bottle of Tri-Flow. If your otherwise perfect boat comes with less-than-perfect stretchers, this doesn't mean you shouldn't buy it; simply be aware that a problem could develop and be prepared to do the extra maintenance required to keep it in working order.

▬ SAFETY

Like stability and construction, the built-in safety features you'll require will depend to a great extent on how and where you plan to row: In a protected harbor or a small lake in warm weather? Long, cold, offshore passages? Virtually all rowing boats on the market have some built-in flotation—sealed air compartments, foam, air bags, or, in the case of wooden boats, the wood itself. These boats will not sink like a stone if swamped; however, some will float considerably higher than others when filled with water.

Most of the open-water shells feature molded-in cockpits. These narrow, shallow indentations will simply not hold enough water, compared with the mass of air trapped in the ends, to sink the boat to her gunwales. These boats are easy to bail and, in fact, can be rowed while the cockpit is flooded. Some earlier designs don't have molded-in cockpits and can fill entirely with water. Their built-in flotation will float them, but they will be more difficult to bail. Self-bailers can be installed in any of these boats, but the Elvstrom-style bailer works only when the boat is moving forward, and an Alden Trainer, when swamped to the gunwales, will not be easy to get underway. If you're thinking about a boat that does not have a sealed cockpit, you should probably investigate a hand-held bilge pump.

The copies of traditional boats are usually open craft with large interior volume—volume that can hold great amounts of water. Most of these boats use either air compartments or captive foam for flotation, and the effectiveness varies with the builder and design. If you have any doubts, ask where the boat settles if she's swamped. If other design aspects fit your needs, but the boat doesn't have the reserve flotation you feel is necessary, remember that air bags, foam, and air compartments can be added to many boats.

▬ HOW SHE LOOKS

After all the logistical and physical characteristics, there are still "aesthetics" to consider. To many, a boat is not a boat unless she has some wood trim. Most of these potential buyers will find the shell look-alikes disappointing. Many have wooden seats and wooden clogs on the stretchers; everything else is fiberglass, stainless steel, or aluminum. Some don't even have wooden seats, and the clogs have been replaced by track shoes. More wood is found in the copies of traditional boats. There you will find wooden sheer rails, transoms, and (in the fixed-seat boats) thwarts. Still others feature wooden decks and half decks. If this is still not enough wood for you, both the Martin Marine Appledore Pod and Hoban Kite Wherry are available in the WEST System. Looking like bright-finish wooden craft of a bygone era, these boats are eye-catchers wherever they're rowed. At any boat show or club regatta, the oohs and aahs are always loudest around the WEST System boats.

If wood is not your thing, then aesthetics will revolve around the boat's lines and colors. Open-water shells are available in a dazzling rainbow of hull and deck colors, many replete with bright graphics emphasizing shape or advertising the builder's logo. While aesthetics can't be ignored, remember that it's the design and craftsmanship that make a boat a joy to row, not the flash of a bright gelcoat. When you're looking for a boat, look beneath the surface. A pleasing finish can enhance a good design; it cannot make a poor design row better.

▬ COST

Rowing boats are not cheap, but unlike equipment in many sports, they are usually a one-time expense. Once you buy a good boat and a good set of sculls, you're set. Unlike sailboarding, you don't have to buy different boards, sails, rigs, and skegs for different conditions; unlike golf, there are no greens fees or carts to rent. You don't even have to buy fuzzy little tennis balls. Open-water shell prices range from about $1,300 to $1,700 with a few a little less and a couple quite a bit higher. Doubles run around $700 more. Quality of workmanship and materials and design are not necessarily factors of cost. If a $1,300 boat is right for you, you won't be upgrading yourself by buying a $1,700 craft. On the other hand, if you let price alone dictate your selection, and you buy a boat that doesn't suit your needs because it costs $200 less, it's no bargain. A boat that doesn't allow you to do what you want is worse than no boat at all because it will be a frustrating experience.

Once you've chosen your boat, take a long look at the builder's or dealer's list of options. You'll need sculls, which will either be carbon fiber or wood (more on scull selection later). Many buyers try to save a few dollars at the purchase, only to spend more later adding or replacing gear. The difference in price between standard and adjustable oarlocks might be just $50 at the time of purchase. If, two or three months down the line, you decide to change over, you could be looking at a price of well over $100. Some builders will install shoes on the stretchers at no cost—if you supply the shoes. A compass or bailer installed by the builder or dealer can be a bargain compared with buying it later and installing it yourself.

▬ BUYING USED

Cost frequently leads prospective buyers into the used-boat market. Buying used can save you money, but real bargains are few and far between. Good open-water boats don't deteriorate or become obsolete, so they retain a high resale value. It's easy to let an attractive price sway you, but be wary. If the boat is not suitable for your kind of rowing, or if it's falling apart, it's no bargain.

Builders frequently know where you might find a boat for sale, and dealers, if they don't handle used boats themselves, may have a bulletin board listing used boats for sale. Races are another good hunting ground for used boats. When you find a boat, don't be afraid to ask questions.

When you're looking at a boat, ask rowers who own the same type if there are any inherent problems. If there are, be sure to carefully inspect those problem areas on the boat you're considering. Ask the seller if you can have the builder (if he is nearby) or a dealer take a look at the boat. In the end *you* must make your own decision. Is the boat the one you want, or are you making a compromise based on price? If you are, will you be able to live with it down the line? Is the boat in good shape for the price? What about the sculls—are they the type you want? Are they in good condition? If you save a couple of hundred dollars on the boat, but have to spend $350 for a new pair of sculls, is it worth it?

■ INTENDED USE

You can learn about design and construction from experts and books. You can study Nash's chart until you can properly place every boat from memory. But none of the knowledge will do you any good until you know one more thing: what you expect from rowing. If you want to spend a day or two each week rowing offshore dragging a fishing line, you will probably not want a Trimline 24. On the other hand, if you plan to row an hour and a half each day in flat water for exercise, you will probably want a more efficient boat than an Appledore Pod.

If racing is your aim, get to know the clubs in your area before buying a boat. There are basically two types of clubs: the traditional clubs, which stage sprints and head races for racing shells, and the newer recreational or open-water clubs, which host races and cruises over open water. If you don't like the idea of traveling to compete, it will be important to know what kind of racing is available in your area.

Before buying a boat, you will need to consider your skill level honestly. If you've rowed any sliding seat, you'll have a pretty good idea of your placement on the learning curve. If you haven't sculled, most rowing clubs and many dealers give beginners' lessons. These lessons are a great boon to the neophyte. They will prevent you from developing bad habits, introduce you to the basics of setting up a boat for the utmost efficiency and comfort, and allow you to row some different boats.

If you have sculling experience, you'll want to try out as many different designs as possible before choosing a boat. Aside from being a learning experience, this can be a lot of fun. Dealers usually have more than one model or brand, and they will be happy to let you compare. Builders frequently bring loaners to boat shows and regattas and are eager to have you row them. The more variety you experience, the better prepared you will be to make your final selection.

You will find that looks can be deceiving: Boats that look very similar can exhibit very different performance characteristics. The subtleties of narrower beams and slightly softer bilges can make one design faster and less stable than a near look-alike. Marginally lighter weight and a slightly longer waterline, along with a few well-placed strands of carbon fiber for added stiffness, can also make one design faster than another.

If you were to walk the aisles of a boat show and look at the Laser Shell and Small Craft Warning, you might think you were looking at virtually the same hull design. The Warning is 6 inches longer and three inches narrower, but out of the water these differences are hardly noticeable. A glance at Nash's chart will show how these small differences, combined with others that are even harder to detect, make the two boats very dissimilar performers. The chart shows the Warning to be considerably more stable and quite a bit faster than the Laser.

There are other examples of look-alike designs turning out to be quite different once you put them in the water. Many design differences that significantly affect performance are so subtle that only a naval architect or a builder could spot them without rowing the boats. Fortunately, you don't have to be a designer or builder as long as you can row the boats. Subtle design differences become obvious as soon as you sit in the boat, strap your feet in the stretchers, and take a couple of strokes on the oars. You may not recognize that the boat has a finer or fuller entry, more or less rocker or firmer or softer bilges, but even the neophyte will know if one design is potentially faster than another, or if one boat is less stable than another.

If you're new to sculling, or have only had a few lessons, don't feel you must limit yourself to entry-level boats. It would not be wise to attempt one of the new 24-foot advanced open-water shells after a couple of hours in a stable entry-level boat, but with a certain amount of caution, a sculler with only a brief introduction to the sport can handle an ARS or Maas Aero. In fact, I've seen people with no sculling experience start their instruction in an Aero. It may take a lesson or two more before they feel completely comfortable in the more advanced boats, but they do well. The beginning oarsman may not be able to get the most out of these potentially faster, less stable boats, but buying an advanced boat will mean not having to move up later.

Some oarsmen seem happier with their boats than other oarsmen. In a few cases, this may just be dumb luck. But in most cases an owner's satisfaction with his boat has more to do with experience and careful study. Many rowers have spent a lifetime searching for the perfect boat, a nebulous concept whose contours change with time. The search for the perfect boat can be an exercise in frustration, or, with an open mind, it can be an exciting and rewarding quest.

- 3 -

Fitting Out Your Rowing Boat

WHILE sculling is an equipment-oriented sport, unlike many other "equipment sports" it won't be a constant drain on your wallet. If you make your first selections wisely, you may never have to spend another dollar on boats or gear. There's not a lot you'll need to choose for, or add to, an open-water boat; some gear you must have from the start, other gear you can add as you see the need develop. We'll start with those pieces you must have.

▬ SCULLS

There's one basic decision here—wood or composite. The battle between users of wooden and composite sculls still rages. Supporters of wooden sculls claim that, because of the deep, more complex curves cut into their blades, they bite and hold the water better. For purists, wooden sculls have three other advantages; they are quieter when they rotate in the oarlocks, they "feel" better, and they are more aesthetically pleasing.

Wooden sculls are usually built of basswood or spruce, and are hollow for lightness. They must be handled with a certain amount of care to prevent chipping and splintering. For transporting and storing, padded blade covers provide excellent protection for the most vulnerable portion of the sculls, but the looms (shafts) also require care in handling. Knocking them on your car's roof rack, for instance, can ding the protective coat of varnish, allowing water to be drawn into the wood. To save weight, many builders of wooden sculls use very thin wood for their loom backs, and this makes them particularly vulnerable to cracking.

You're not home free once you're in the water. If you launch in shallow water rather than from a dock, you will need to keep your blades well clear of the bottom. Buoys and other floating obstacles will also have to be given a wide berth. Your wooden sculls will need to be sanded down and revarnished regularly. But while wooden sculls require more maintenance than their composite counterparts, many rowers still prefer them.

Composite sculls are usually constructed with a carbon-fiber loom, plastic collars and sleeves, rubber-coated grips, and either molded plastic or fiberglass blades. While composite sculls are somewhat tougher than wooden ones, they still should be treated with respect. Blade covers would not be out of place on plastic or fiberglass blades, and the looms are coated with a UV-resistant varnish that will need to be replaced in time.

Proponents of composite sculls assert that their oars are stiffer, lighter, stronger, and require less maintenance. There is no question that they are stiffer. If you watch a rower switch from wood to composite you'll see the difference easily. The wooden oar has much more "whip" in the loom, and a stiffer oar is a more efficient oar. The stiffness transfers power better and you will definitely feel it at the catch—your boat will jump a little more as you feed in the power. Composites are also lighter, though it is impossible to say how much lighter. One cannot claim, for example, that composite sculls are "one-third" or "one-quarter" lighter than wood, simply because wooden sculls vary so much in weight depending on their construction and manufacturer. The difference in weight may not matter over a 2,000-meter course, but if you plan to row long distances, it could be significant.

The real question, as I see it, is not whether you buy wood or composite, but whether you buy good or bad oars, and both are available. Some oars balance poorly, with extremely heavy blades; others will not release well, or will not grab at the catch. If your boat and oars come as a package, and you like the oars, don't change for the sake of changing. The longer you row, the more opportunities you will have to evaluate different sculls, exposing yourself to different construction, lengths, weight, balance, and blade shapes. That way you can see what fits your rowing style before making a change. On the other hand, if you really don't like the oars that come with the boat, or you have the option of ordering any sculls you want, you will have to make a choice. If you are new to rowing, ask more-experienced oarsmen—but be ready for some strongly held, nearly fanatical, responses. The majority of serious scullers now use Concept II composite sculls, though Maas and Latanzo have entered the market. The wooden scull market is dominated by Piantedosi, though there are several other builders.

There is a third type of scull that must be mentioned: those with aluminum looms. They are a lower-cost option to either wood or composite construction, but they are rather heavy. Some dealers will tell you these oars are just fine for heavy basic boats, and they probably are if cost is a major factor in your scull selection. On the other hand, if you are rowing a heavy copy of a traditional design and plan to cover several miles on each outing, you'll want good, light, stiff oars. In the future, developments in aluminum construction may produce an oar on a performance par with composite construction.

Other factors to consider are grip diameter and texture and the sculls' overall length and weight. Some oars come with different-size grips. The grips should fit comfortably within the curl of your fingers, neither curling the fingers too tightly nor leaving them so open that the grip is weak. There are also different textures to the grips. Some are smooth and hard, some are softer and checkered. Try to row with each kind before you make your choice. Most open-water rowers use sculls either 296 or 298 centimeters long, though manufacturers build longer sculls as standard, and custom lengths can be obtained. Longer sculls give a wider, more powerful arc, but they require more overlap and a heavier pull. Longer sculls are coming into vogue with the flat-water shell racing crowd, but remember, they are rowing relatively short distances, where the heavier load may not be a problem. The bigger you are, the more efficiently you will be able to use longer sculls, but for the average person, 296s and 298s seem to be the answer.

Most carbon-fiber sculls come in different weights. The lighter sculls are more high-performance, but like most high-performance gear, they are less forgiving.

The choice between wood and composite may not be critical, but the commitment to maintaining your sculls is. If you choose wood, be prepared to keep the varnish in good condition—it will add years of life to your sculls. The same is true of the UV inhibitor on the looms of composite sculls. On either wood or composite sculls, it is important to maintain the sleeves and buttons. These plastic parts require some lubrication, but avoid the traditional heavy lubricants such as Vaseline and Crisco. Sleeves and buttons of modern sculls require only the lightest application of either a silicone or Teflon spray or liquid. The heavier lubricants will be superfluous and messy at best, and will attract and hold damaging dirt and grit at worst. Gritty dirt or sand is the archenemy of your sleeves, buttons, and oarlocks. Trapped between the rotating oar and stationary lock, sand or dirt will grind away and eventually destroy them. To avoid dirt, never lay your oars flat on any surface. Always prop them up, or lay them across supports (like your gunwales) so sand and dirt won't get on the buttons and sleeves.

The oarsman who chooses a traditional fixed-thwart design will also want to investigate oar options thoroughly. Most traditional designs come with oars, but the package isn't always as well thought-out as it could be. Changing oars can make a big difference in the way a traditional design performs, but it is expensive, so before you select or change oars, be sure you are happy with your oarlocks. If the lock design and placement is not compatible with the oar shape and length, it will not be a successful mating. The loom shape and diameter, including the sleeves, must fit your oarlocks. Then there is the matter of oar length. If your oars are too short, they will reduce your arc through the water and you will lose power and efficiency. If they are too long, they will be out of balance and tire you unnecessarily. Before selecting your oars, make sure you are satisfied with the placement of the oarlocks. A good rule of thumb for determining oar length is the one-third/two-thirds rule: One-third of the oar should be inboard of the oarlock. Therefore, if you know the measurement from the inboard side of the lock to the centerline of the boat, you can multiply that by three to obtain a rough oar length.

Beware: Not all oars are created equal, and that's one reason why the one-third/two-thirds rule is "rough." If your oars have heavy blades, you will have to choose shorter looms or tape counterweights near the grips to achieve proper balance. You will also want to look at blade shapes. There are some short oars (under the standard 296- or 298-centimeter sculling length) with rudimentary cupped blades. The cupped blade will have less "meat" in it than a straight blade, so the lighter end may allow you longer looms and a more powerful arc while retaining proper balance. These are definitely worth looking into, but be aware that the thinner blades will be more fragile than straight blades. These oars will also be direction-specific, which means that to back water efficiently, you will have to roll the oars 180 degrees. If you find a pair of these oars that you're comfortable with, but are worried that the blade ends are too susceptible to damage, you can protect them with a covering. In the past, some oarsmen nailed thin copper sheaths over their blade tips. Nailing can weaken the blades, can lead to splits, and allows water to seep in under the varnish. Instead, I suggest fiberglassing over the blade tip. This is similar to the old practice of protecting the soft wood of the blades with hardwood tips.

■ OARLOCKS

Though there are some outdated styles around, most open-water boats today come with gated composite oarlocks that rotate on stainless steel pins fixed to the sill. Nearly all these oarlocks are adjustable for height, which I consider a necessity. If the oarlocks supplied with your boat do not offer this important feature, find out if you can swap them for a pair that does. Other, more expensive, oarlocks can be adjusted for pitch (controlling the attitude of the blade as it bites, drives through and releases the water). While you can successfully row without this adjustment (and some locks that don't offer a built-

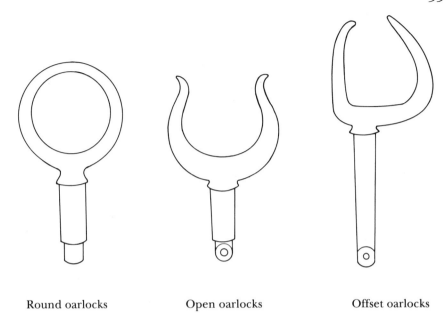

Round oarlocks   Open oarlocks   Offset oarlocks

in adjustment can still be tuned) you might want to look seriously at spending the extra money for the adjustable locks (more on tuning oarlocks in Chapter 4). Some oarlocks are designed and manufactured strictly for freshwater rowing. If you're going to be doing any ocean rowing, be sure the materials in your locks will stand up to the increased corrosion of salt water.

There is a wider diversity of oarlocks available to the rower of traditional designs than there is to rowers of open-water shells. There are also more opportunities to modify oarlock placement to tune your boat. In most fixed-thwart boats you can easily increase the efficiency of your oars' arc by moving the oarlock outboard. The two-man dories lifeguards race are regularly modified by adding wooden spacers between the outboard side of the gunwale and the oarlock socket. This can move the oarlock outboard several inches. Since you can increase oar length (while maintaining balance) by three inches for every inch you move the oarlock outboard, you can see how a minor adjustment will affect the length of your oars. Variations on this modification can be used on most fixed-thwart boats, so if you are considering any change in oarlock placement, make this modification before specifying your oar length.

Whether you change the oarlock socket location or not, what you place in it will make a big difference in how efficiently you row and how much you enjoy it. There are three basic oarlock shapes for traditional boats: the standard horns (or open lock); the almost-as-common round oarlocks, and offset designs where the forward horn is an extension of the shank (or very close to it).

A good set of standard brass horns, say Wilcox Crittenden, are wonderful for a round-loom oar. I've never heard of one breaking, and since they have no forward or aft side, they do not have to be aligned. I do recommend using the lanyard hole at the bottom of the shank to tie the locks to the boat. If you don't want to use a lanyard, put a split ring or a cotter pin through the hole, but attach the lock to the boat in some way.

I don't like round oarlocks—they hold the oar captive between the button and the blade, so they have the advantage of never getting lost, but I feel that advantage is negligible when compared with the disadvantages. In my early days of rowing dories through the surf, I always used Wilcox Crittenden horns on my boats. If I went over a particularly steep wave and dropped down its back, there was a chance one of the oars would bounce out of its lock. With open oarlocks, it was an easy matter to drop the oar back in and pick up the stroke. I once used a friend's boat equipped with round locks; when the oar popped out, it took the lock with it. The lock ended up out by the blade, and while the next wave approached, I had to pull in the oar, place the shank in the socket and start rowing again. I didn't make it, and got well and properly drilled by the next wave. I know several oarsmen who don't row in surf and swear by round oarlocks. They like the fact they can never lose a lock, unless they break an oar. If you like them, great, but be careful if you row in rough water.

I've only used offset oarlocks sparingly on traditional boats, but a variation of the design is standard on the Oarmaster, and I've rowed some distance with that rig. These locks have vertical forward horns, requiring you to use an oar with a D-shaped loom or fit a D-shaped collar to your round loom. They do carry more of your energy into the stroke, but they are direction-specific, so they must be aligned each time you put in the oars. There is at least one company making offset locks for round-loomed oars. I haven't rowed with these, but it's an interesting concept.

An oarlock's construction and compatibility with its oar is more important than its shape. Some marine hardware stores still carry pot-metal oarlocks, which should be avoided like the plague. Not only will they corrode and give your boat an unkempt look, they will probably break. These locks tend to develop cracks in high-stress areas; these cracks corrode and the lock breaks, usually where the shank meets the base or at the bottom of one of the horns.

Oarlocks must match both the shape and diameter of the loom. Remember, if you are going to add leather or plastic collars, they must fit comfortably through the lock.

A boat, oars, and oarlocks—the basics you need to start rowing. I know a gentleman who bought an Aero with just those basics. He has rowed daily for more than five years and sees no reason to add another piece of gear. Some oarsmen, either because they race, make extended open-water passages, or just want to make their boat a bit more comfortable or personal, add some extra equipment. If you know what you want, some of this extra gear is more economical or easier to add at the time of purchase. The rest can be added as the need arises. One note of caution: Extra gear always means extra weight and frequently requires extra maintenance. Avoid adding gear just because someone else has it.

▬ STRETCHERS

Open-water boats come with a variety of foot-stretcher arrangements. Some builders supply leather clogs with plastic or metal heel cups. Others offer wide, Velcro-secured straps and heel cups. There is nothing wrong with either of these setups, but replacing the clogs or straps with a pair of track shoes will give you a more solid feeling in the boat while saving your feet from chafing against the leather or straps. Some builders will make this modification for free if you supply the shoes. Others will even supply the shoes (at an extra cost). Whether you buy the shoes or your dealer does, for safety's sake, get them at least half a size larger than what you would normally wear. This extra room will allow your feet to slip out more easily in case of a capsize. For the same reason, don't lace them too tightly.

Replacing clogs or straps with track shoes provides a more solid feel for the rower. Note also the water bottle, compass, Strokecoach, and flashlight in this cockpit.

If you decide to make this modification yourself, it's simple to accomplish. Use track shoes, the kind with removable spikes. Drill through two of the cleat bases under the ball of each foot and drill matching holes in the stretcher footrest. Two small stainless steel flathead bolts, dropped through from the inside of each shoe, hold them in place. When you tighten the nuts under the footrest, the bolt heads are pulled through the inner sole of the shoe to fetch up against the cleat inserts. Cushioned by the inner sole, you won't be able to feel the bolt heads. The heels will need to be able to lift when you slide aft for the catch, but for safety's sake, they should be tied down with two or three inches of travel. Having them tied down will help your feet slide out in case of a capsize. If you make this modification after you've set up your boat, you may have to slide the stretchers aft a notch to compensate for the thickness of the soles of the shoes.

Some rowers like to have their boats fitted with extra-large clogs so they can wear shoes while launching, then simply slip their shoes into the clogs. This is fine, but be sure you don't opt for running shoes with thick soles. The thick soles lift your heels too high, making it difficult to assume the proper position at the catch.

■ FOOT BRACES

One very basic piece of gear absent on most fixed-thwart rowing boats is a sturdy place to brace your feet. A simple, comfortable footrest that provides good leverage will make your rowing more efficient and comfortable. You don't need to mount clogs or shoes, since you don't need to use your legs to pull you back on the slides, but heel cups and Velcro straps, or padded windsurfer foot-straps, provide a more secure footing, especially in a heavy chop or surf. There are different ways to install foot braces. You can build a wooden module and attach it to the deck. Or you can screw (or fiberglass) brackets or slides to the hull and slide a plank between them, providing a removable brace.

Stretchers and footrests are natural locating points for other gear. Fascinated by rowing-boat performance, Gordie Nash built a unique set of stretchers in his California Wherry. He has since duplicated them in other boats he has rowed, boats as diverse as the Small Craft ARS and his own Pacific 30. Aside from helping him train and set numerous records in open-water races on both coasts, his instrument pod has allowed him to build a unique and exact data base on rowing boat performance. Nash's instruments include a real-time watch, a Strokecoach (which incorporates a time-from-start function along with a digital read-out of stroke rate and count), digital compass, and

Gordie Nash's instrument cluster
aboard his California Wherry.

digital knotmeter. Most oarsmen might feel this excessive, but it shows what
can be done.

Since rowing requires so much of the body, one of the first extra pieces of
gear most rowers start carrying is a water bottle. A bicycle water-bottle cage,
either anodized aluminum or composite to withstand the elements, will hold
the bottle in place. The cage's weight can be measured in grams (the stainless
steel nuts and bolts you use to attach it will probably weigh more) and it can be
attached to the stretchers or the bulkhead. Some rowers solve the problem of
loose water bottles by gluing a strip of Velcro to a bulkhead and another strip
to their water-bottle.

■ BAILERS

A bailer should be considered mandatory. Even though virtually all the open-
water boats with sealed cockpits can be rowed with their small cockpits full of
water, they do not perform as well as when they're dry. Besides, it's cold and
uncomfortable having water sloshing around your feet and up under your
seat. If you stop to use a cup-style bailer in rough conditions, you often end up
with more water aboard than when you started bailing. Stopping also breaks
your rhythm and a cup-style bailer must be tied in so it won't wash overboard

in a swamping. The alternative is the suction-style bailer. The Elvström bailer is an invaluable bit of gear borrowed from sailing, where it is used on many racing dinghies. Mounted in the bottom of the cockpit, it faces aft and sucks water out as the boat moves forward. Bailers can be opened or closed as needed, or left open except when launching or landing on a beach.

While an Elvström bailer will work in most traditional boats, the design functions only when the boat is moving forward. It will not be possible to get a fully awash dory or peapod up to speed and get the suction working. Therefore at least one cup-style bailer, bucket, or bilge pump should be carried any time you're on the water. Be sure you lash your hand-held bailer to something so that it can't wash out in case of a capsizing.

▬ COMPASS

A compass is a necessity for the open-water racer and the long-distance cruiser, but it is also valuable to the beginning open-water oarsman. Not only will a compass get you from point A to point B, it will keep you rowing a straight course. When you begin to row, your journeys will be short, and you can line landmarks up over your stern to keep you on course. With more experience, you'll naturally start rowing greater distances where it may not be as easy to set your course with a particular building, tree, or pier. A compass will allow you to set your course and maintain it, conserving energy that might be spent weaving all over the water, and twisting around to check your heading.

Since you will be facing aft, and most compasses are manufactured to be read facing forward, the direction you read will be 180 degrees off your heading. Back-facing compasses are available but hard to find, so most scullers simply learn to convert the figures in their heads. If you have to make several course changes over the duration of your row, you might plot the compass headings in advance, convert them, and write them beside the compass in grease pencil, or on a piece of tape.

Most compasses used on open-water boats come from sailing; they are tough and designed to survive in the marine environment. Deck-mounted compasses can be through-bolted aft of the cockpit or attached to a custom foot stretcher module. Hand-bearing compasses usually come with brackets that can be attached to the deck or the stretchers, allowing you to read the compass in the bracket and remove it to take a bearing on a distant landmark. In some cases you can cut a hole in the deck and mount the compass through the hole. This mounting is particularly effective in the aft end of cockpits, below deck level.

▬ FINS

Most open-water boats now come with fins, or skegs. A fin will keep you track-ing and, to a certain extent, prevent you from being forced off course by side or quartering winds and waves. Fins, either metal or plastic, usually are re-movable, mounted in receptacles called fin boxes. In most cases different-size fins will fit the box. The smaller the fin, the less tracking you can expect, but it will allow you to turn more easily. Larger fins are handy for crossing choppy water, but you will sacrifice some ease of turning for the extra tracking. Some builders are using surfboard or windsurfer fin boxes. This allows you to select from a wide range of fins, but remember, surfboard and windsurfer fins are designed to give lift, like the keel of a sailboat; look for low-aspect-ratio fins designed for directional stability. It would not be out of line to keep a pair of fins and choose the proper one for the day's conditions.

▬ LIFE PRESERVER

There will be more on life preservers or personal flotation devices (PFDs) in Chapter 7. For now, it's enough to know that you should carry one every time you go out on the water. There are inflatable PFDs that can be tied or taped to the stretchers, and standard life preservers, which can either be stuffed be-tween the stretchers and the rear deck or taped or tied to the deck itself. If you are rowing a traditional design, storage space is not a problem, but be sure you secure the PFD so it can't float away if you swamp.

There are other items you might want to take with you for safety and per-sonal comfort, but we'll deal with those later. Now its time to get to the water, set up the boat, and start rowing!

- 4 -

Getting Started

Despite the natural urge to take your new toy and get out on the water, there are a few details to attend to. Dealing with these before your first row will make your introduction to the sport far easier and less traumatic.

▬ TRANSPORTING THE BOAT

Transporting an open-water boat on your car will expose the craft to more potential damage than it would normally experience on the water—a little extra thought, time, and caution will be well spent. Fortunately, automobile roof racks have improved greatly in the past few years. Both Yakima and Thule produce racks that are tougher, more secure, less subject to corrosion, and far more efficient than their predecessors. Both companies sell "rack systems" that will mount on the new aerodynamic cars and trucks (no rain gutters) or on the traditional rain gutter mounts. Their systems include either thick, nylon-covered foam pads or cradles that can be tuned to fit your hull. Your boat dealer can probably steer you toward the rack system that best matches your boat and car. If your dealer either doesn't carry racks or have a recommendation, a windsurfing, surf, or bicycle shop will be a good place to start your search.

If you're looking at a variety of racks with different load-carrying capacities and construction, be sure to err on the side of caution. Although a good open-water boat may not be particularly heavy, it will offer considerable wind resistance at highway speeds. Also remember your boat will be wet and maybe sandy, so choose a rack with a tough, corrosion-resistant coating.

Install your new rack so the boat is well balanced and stable. In the case of most cars, this will mean with the greatest possible spread. Most open-water boats are built with the maximum strength in the cockpit area, so if your boat balances well and this suits your car, set the racks at either end of the cockpit.

Your boat's design—and the builder's recommendation—will dictate how you carry it on the racks. If it has the flat bottom of a Laser or a Warning, you'll probably carry it upright on pads—possibly the easiest way to carry a boat. It saves you the inconvenience of having to turn it over when loading and unloading. The more-rounded bottom of a Maas 24 or a Pocock Wherry would be better off nestled in cradles. Some boats, such as the original J-Shell, ride well upside down, resting on their splash boxes.

Most seats provided with open-water boats have a pair of keepers designed to hold them on the tracks while you're in the boat, or moving it about on the beach or dock. Don't rely on these keepers to hold the seat while the boat is traveling on your car. Take a minute to remove the seat before transporting the boat. Also make sure that anything loose in the boat, such as a cup-style bailer or water bottle, is removed before loading it on your car. If your boat has a skeg or fin, be sure it won't vibrate lose in transit.

When you strap your boat to the rack, again err on the side of caution. If there's any doubt in your mind that the boat is not tied down securely enough, don't chance it—add another rope or strap.

There is a do-and-don't list to follow when strapping down your boat. Do protect its gelcoat from abrasive straps and pads; if necessary add a piece of carpet between the strap and the deck. Don't strap it down so tightly that you deform the hull or deck. And do check the racks to be sure they haven't vibrated loose. This takes just seconds, but it can be as vital as strapping down the boat.

The average open-water boat will overhang most cars, and even most trucks, both front and rear. To avoid any legal problems resulting from this, check your state laws or consult your local auto club or a policeman about allowable overhangs. There are a lot of misconceptions about these regulations (even a lot of street cops don't really know the correct answers), so it's a good idea to get your information from a very reliable source. You'll also need to mark the rear of the boat while it is in transport. If a red flag is mandated, how big does it have to be? If a light is required, what is the minimum wattage?

Some might think using a trailer is easier than car-topping, especially for a heavier boat such as an Encounter or Appledore Pod, but this really isn't such a good idea. Trailers, especially small trailers, are not as well sprung as a car. A trailer's vibration and bouncing can quickly destroy a lightly built boat.

Although they are reasonably light, open-water boats—anything 16 to 24 feet long and 5 feet wide—can be awkward and intimidating to maneuver

Top: A Maas 24 on a car rack equipped with cradles. There should be a red flag on the stern. Bottom: Padded cradle and carpet help protect the fragile gelcoat.

alone. Some rowers find it advantageous either to buy or build a small cart to move their boat from the car or boathouse to the water. There is a variety of carts designed for sailing dinghies available today, and most will work well with rowing boats. If one of these doesn't meet your needs or budget, commercially available wheels and axles can be mated to a 2 x 4 framework, with carpeting added for padding. If your boat is either on the heavy or awkward side, a cart can make life much easier.

While making plans for moving your boat, give some consideration to the sculls; the blades are most susceptible to damage. A pair of padded covers can prevent chipping and splintering. You can either buy these from a specialty shop or have them made at a local sail loft or canvas shop. When hand-carrying your sculls, always keep the blades forward; they'll be less likely to knock against something.

▬ TUNING UP

If your dealer is a rower, you can expect him to help you set up the boat when you take delivery. If he doesn't know much more about it than you do, try the coach or rowing coordinator of the local rowing club. If there's no local club, you and a friend can do the setup yourselves. It may take a bit longer, but it will be a valuable learning experience.

No matter how you get it done, it is vital that someone tune the boat properly *before* you try to row it. If the boat is "fresh out of the box," chances are it's nowhere near being set up the way it should be. If the boat has been around the shop for a while it may have been rowed by a dozen people, but unless you're extremely lucky, it won't be set up for you. Fight the urge to take the boat out and row it. Unless the boat is properly set up for you, trying to row is going to be frustrating at best.

▬ OARLOCKS

The oarlocks must be set for height and, in some cases, pitch and spread. Set the height first.

Oarlock height refers to the distance between the horn (the highest point) of the seat and the bottom of the oarlock's inner surface. The easiest way to measure this is to lay a scull across gunwales. Slide the seat under the oar and measure from the horn up to the bottom of the oar, then go out to the oarlock and measure from the lower inside surface of the lock down to the bottom of the oar. The sum of these two measurements is the oarlock height. Your dealer or owner's manual should tell you the best way to adjust the height on your particular boat. In the past it was done by shimming the riggers where they attach to the hull, or by bending the sill, or plate, on which the oarlock rests. Most modern oarlocks have built-in height adjustment that uses spacers placed between the bottom of the lock and the sill. This simple adjustment not only allows for quick tuning, but lets you fine-tune for conditions by adding or removing spacers.

Since the handles of your sculls will overlap during both the pull-through,

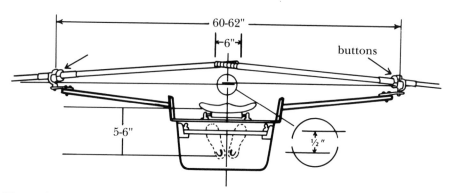

The cockpit, viewer facing forward.

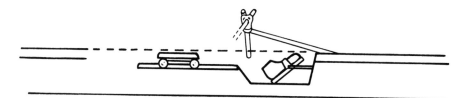

The cockpit, side view.

or drive, and recovery portions of your stroke, you'll be rowing with one hand passing over the other. In the United States, it is standard practice to row left over right. Setting your own boat up this way will allow you to move from boat to boat without having to adapt your style. To permit rowing left over right, you'll want your left hand (starboard side) oarlock a half-inch higher than the right hand (port side) lock. If you don't have enough clearance and are forced to compensate by lowering your right hand, the boat will list to port. If you compensate by rowing with your left hand unnaturally high, it will put a strain on your left shoulder and cut the arc of your left oar, causing the boat to steer to starboard. If there were even less clearance (oarlocks set at equal height) you would have to row with your hands level, one in front of the other. If you were to row left in front of right, your right oar's arc would shorten, causing you to steer to port. Some builders (Chris Maas, for example) build a height difference into their riggers, and you will need to know if this has been done before you start tuning. It's much easier to set up with this built-in adjustment because you won't have to consider the difference in height.

If you are a person of average size—say 5-feet, 9- or 10-inches tall, 160 to 170 pounds—the height of your left-hand oarlock should be 6 inches, and your right-hand lock 5 $\frac{1}{2}$ inches. If you are heavier than average, they should both be a little higher; conversely, if you are smaller than average, they should both be a little lower. You can check the height by sitting in the boat with the oar blades, not the shafts, just buried in the water. When you draw your hands toward you they should come to your body at the lower portion of the rib cage, just below the chest. This is the most efficient release position for using your muscles. If, when you begin to row, you find your hands hitting the tops of your thighs during the recovery portion of your stroke, raise the oarlocks by quarter-inch increments until you clear. Later, when you have more experience and are rowing in varied conditions, it will be important to understand how to tune the locks to the conditions.

The next adjustment to be made is the pitch of your oarlocks. Both oarlocks and oars may have pitch, either intentionally designed and built in or not. If the vertical surface of oarlock is perpendicular to the surface of the water (that is, is absolutely vertical), it is expressed as zero degrees of pitch. If the flat of the oar sleeve is perfectly aligned with the oar blade, it is also expressed as zero degrees of pitch. The total pitch we are concerned about is the sum of the inclines (fore or aft) from the vertical of the flat of the oar sleeve and the vertical surface of the oarlock.

Pitch is important, as it controls the angle of the blade at the catch when it enters the water. It also sets the angle through the drive of the stroke and at the release—but it's the catch that's most important. If the blade enters, or "takes" the water absolutely vertically— that is, with zero degrees of pitch—the blade will not bite the water. With no pitch, a blade will tend to knife in and dig deep, burying the shaft and forcing your hands unnaturally high. To prevent knifing in, you'll need to induce some positive pitch.

Unlike racing oars, open-water or recreational oars do not have pitch built into them intentionally. But no matter what oars you're using, you'll need to check them for pitch before adjusting your oarlocks. To do this, rest the sleeve on a level surface with the blade cupped upwards, then place a level across the blade. If it levels, the oar has zero degrees of pitch. If the oar does have some built-in pitch, keep this in mind when you set the pitch in your oarlocks. Also, if the oars have any pitch, mark them so you always use them on the same side of the boat, each in the lock that has been pitched to be compatible with that particular oar. The easiest way to mark an oar is with a strip of tape, either near the grip or the collar. Red for starboard, green for port are the traditional markings. Oars with no built-in pitch will be easier to work with; if you order sculls, be sure to specify they be built with no pitch.

In the past, setting pitch was an almost mystical art, something coaches and boatmen accomplished with special, frequently homemade, tools. In some cases it can still be a bit mysterious, and if you have non-adjustable oarlocks, setting the pitch is one way a dealer can really help you. Most dealers have pitch gauges, and the job is much easier if one is available. Whoever pitches your locks—your dealer, your rowing coach, or the guy on the beach who knows the most about rowing—should be asked to explain the process, because you'll want to be able to check and adjust the pitch yourself as your rowing improves. If your dealer looks at you blankly when you ask him about pitch, if there's no rowing club, and you've yet to meet the local guru, you'll have to buy a pitch gauge or use a triangle and a protractor to do the job. A pitch gauge is better.

In our discussion of setting pitch we will deal with a gated composite oarlock, such as the Latanzo. For years this lock was virtually the industry standard and is still very popular. If you've purchased a Martin Marine boat, or any other that came with an Oarmaster rig, the brass locks that come with it cannot be adjusted for pitch. On the other hand, they can be removed and replaced with locks that may be pitched.

To set the pitch, level the boat on a pair of sawhorses or cradles and turn the oarlocks to their proper rowing position—that is, with the body of the lock abaft the pin. First check for any existing pitch. If the tops of the oarlock faces angle toward the stern, they already have some positive pitch, and you will have to take that into account in your adjustments. If the tops of the oarlock angle toward the bow, the locks have negative pitch and must be removed before the proper positive pitch can be set.

There are several ways to adjust the pitch, and you will need to decide which method is best for you and compatible with your boat's construction. You can insert a tiny shim between the oarlock retaining nut and the sill; you can bend the stainless steel pin around which the oarlock pivots; or you can bend the metal riggers or sill. If you choose any of the bending techniques, be careful not to put in so much torque that you put an unnatural strain on either the boat or the component you're bending.

For many years, bending the pin has been the preferred method of setting pitch on this type of oarlock. Remove the oarlock, bend the pin, replace the lock, and take your measurement. Always measure pitch off the lock, since it's the lock, not the pin, that the oar contacts.

While it's time consuming and maybe a little intimidating to set your own pitch the first time out, the task should not be ignored. A word of caution— bending the pin may weaken it. Find out if your brand of pins has a history of breaking. If they do, don't weaken them by bending.

Fortunately, there is an alternative to bending and shimming. If you pay the extra money for adjustable oarlocks, setting and changing your pitch will be far simpler. Stampfli and Concept II both offer oarlocks with easily adjustable pitch. The Stampfli locks have interchangeable pre-pitched shims, which slide in and out of the oarlock face. The Concept II locks are adjusted by inserting a pair of bushings at the pin, changing the attitude of the lock in relation to the pin. In both cases check if your pins are out of plumb or if there is any pitch in your oars before you set the pitch.

The best way to see positive pitch is to place an oar in a lock as if you were rowing. If the upper edge of the oar blade angles toward the stern, you have positive pitch. If you're a beginner, six degrees of pitch will be a good starting point: It will allow you to bite the water at the catch without exaggerating problems caused by too much pitch. The more positive pitch you have, the less efficient your feathering (turning the blade surface parallel to the water during the recovery portion of the stroke) will be and the less clean your blade work. The more proficient you become, the more you can decrease the pitch. Eventually, you will take your pitch down to around three degrees, depending on your style and equipment. Less pitch will make your rowing smoother, but using it takes practice. Depending on how much you row, after your second month in the boat you might try reducing your pitch. If you find your oars knifing in, put some positive pitch back in and concentrate on your blade work for another month before taking it out.

There are fads in open-water rowing as in any other sport. Some very fine oarsmen are currently rowing with a lot of positive pitch and are winning races this way. They claim the positive pitch helps them "pick the boat up" at the catch and during the drive. Maybe it does, but there's an old saying: "You have to know the rules before you can break them." Try reducing pitch and see how you feel. If, later, you find you miss the greater pitch, go back.

The third adjustment you'll want to make, if possible, is oarlock spread, the center-to-center distance from the starboard to the port pin. On many open-water boats, this adjustment cannot be made, as there is only one locating hole in the sills for the pins. On other boats there are either two holes in each sill or a slot providing a modicum of movement. Assuming you are using either 296s or 298s, your spread should be 60 to 61 inches. The greater your spread, the lighter the load on the oars as you row. If you adjust your spread, it is very important that it be even on both sides of the boat. Therefore, you will have to measure not only the pin-to-pin distance, but from each pin to the centerline of the boat. If the distance from the starboard pin to the centerline is 30 3/4 inches, and from the port pin 30 1/4 inches, the discrepancy will throw off your arcs, make one arm work harder than the other, disrupt your balance, and make steering a straight course a matter of constant small corrective strokes.

On most oarlocks, you'll need to make one final adjustment. On the gate that closes across the top of the lock there are three nuts: a large locking nut with either a knurled surface or a plastic grip, and two smaller hex nuts. The

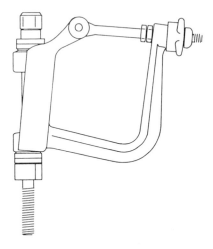

A gated oarlock. (*Courtesy Chris-
tian Maas*)

large nut locks the gate in place. The two smaller nuts set the width of the oarlock by acting as an inner stop against which the lock's after upright rests. The
stopping nuts may be set so near the gate's hinge that the oarlock is too tight,
preventing the oar sleeve from pivoting from the drive to feather position.
Place an oar in each lock and set the lock nuts so that the oar can roll freely,
not sloppily, from drive to feather and back again. Tighten the lock nuts
against each other with an open-end wrench.

■ THE SCULLS

Turn your attention now to the sculls themselves. In most cases the oars will
have arrived with the sleeves (the plastic sheaths that rotate inside the oarlock)
in place, but more than likely the buttons, or collars, will have come taped together, dangling from one of the sculls. Some buttons have two cheeks, some
just one. If yours have two, they should be installed with the larger facing the
oar blade. This surface will rest against the inboard surface of the oarlock. It is
vital that the buttons be located in exactly the same place on both oars. If they
are not, one oar will traverse a greater arc through the water, constantly
steering you in the direction opposite that side of the boat. The easiest way to
check button evenness is to stand the oars on their grips on a flat surface and
make sure the buttons touch. If they miss by an eighth of an inch, take the
time to realign them—it is that important.

The first time you set the buttons, locate them so the oar handles overlap by
six inches; this will place your left hand directly above your right as they cross
each other during the drive and recovery. You may want to change this setting
as you become more proficient and learn more about your boat, but it's a

good place to start. The less overlap you have, the farther from the boat the blades will be during the drive. This gives you a greater arc, which is good, up to a point.

When you adjust the buttons, do so in small increments, never more than a quarter-inch at a time. A quarter-inch per oar results in a half-inch difference in overlap, but more important, it causes a significant difference in the arc the blade travels through the water, and the load on the oars.

The law of diminishing returns is applicable to a large arc. Depending on your size and strength, the weight and efficiency of your boat, and the distances you row, it can be too draining to move your boat with an excessively large arc. If it feels like you're lifting weights each time you lift the oars, or if the boat feels extremely heavy in the water, move the buttons toward the blades. This will lighten the load by decreasing the arc. It will also result in more overlap, but in time you will get used to this.

No one can tell you exactly where to set the buttons, it's strictly a matter of personal style. Some people like to row with a slightly heavier load, usually coupled to a low, powerful stroke rate. Others prefer a lighter load and higher stroke rate.

■ FOOT-STRETCHER PLACEMENT

The last components requiring attention are the foot-stretchers. Their proper location will greatly enhance the quality, efficiency, and comfort of your sculling. Your body type dictates stretcher placement: If you're tall, the stretchers will be nearer the stern; if you're short, they will be closer to the bow. If your legs are longer or shorter than normal for your height, you will have to adjust the stretchers accordingly.

I can't overemphasize the importance of foot-stretcher placement. If they are too far aft, you will be cramped over the oars and get the handles caught up in your clothes or against your body. If they are too far forward, your catch will be short and your finish uncomfortably long, resulting in a short, weak stroke. With the stretchers too far forward you will also feel less secure in the boat and it will tire your hip joints.

When you first launch the boat (in shallow, calm water) check the foot-stretcher location. Checking before you get far from the beach will give you one less thing to worry about, and will make it easier to adjust the location.

When you put the seat in the boat, be sure the horn, the highest portion, is toward the stern. This means the cutout for your coccyx is toward the bow. To check the foot-stretcher placement, assume the layback position (see Chapter 5), with the blades still in the water, your arms pulled in. Your arms should be in a natural rowing position with the hands in front of the body, not pulled past the body to your sides. Be sure your shoulders are relaxed and your elbows down. Take your thumbs off the ends of the grips and point them at your body. The tips of your thumbs should just graze your skin. Don't lean back to get extra space, and don't adjust your body to the stretchers; adjust the stretchers to your body—that's what they're there for.

▬ BOARDING FROM THE BEACH

Launching off a beach in shallow water is easier than launching from a dock, so go off a beach if possible, at least your first time out. There are three ways to

Getting into the boat: Be sure to pull up on the rigger; that the blades are flat on the water; and to step into the center of the boat.

a gentle push with the dock-side leg and swing it aboard, directly into the stretcher. The push will take some practice. It should be strong enough send you far enough away from the dock so that your dock-side oar can take the water, but not so strong as to disrupt your balance. As soon as you've eased yourself down into the seat, put both hands on the oars and decide if you need to depress either or both handles. This will raise the blades slightly, keeping the water-side blade from digging in and the dock-side blade from scraping across the dock.

Getting back onto the dock is practically the reverse, but it requires some skilled boathandling while coming alongside the dock. You will want to come in slowly, and at a very shallow angle, being sure you don't damage the boat. Come in with the dock-side oar trailing, allow your rigger to pass over the dock, then swing the oar up and over the dock. Use your dock-side hand to press down on the dock-side rigger, holding the boat in position while your water-side hand holds the grips. Slide back to the release position and pull your water-side foot out of the stretcher and place it on the seat deck. If you don't have a lot of flexibility, lean your body toward the dock, forcing the dock-side rigger down, and use that hand to grab your ankle and pull your foot up onto the seat deck. Then, holding the dock-side rigger and the oar handles, stand up on your water-side foot and swing your other leg out of the stretchers and onto the dock.

If your dock is so high that your riggers won't clear without tipping the boat precariously, board at the end of the dock. With most boats, you'll want to swing the bow of the boat into the slip until the forward part of the rigger touches. Then, holding the boat (or a bungee cord around the dockside rigger) with one hand, slide the oars into their locks and close the dock-side gate. You probably won't be able to reach the water-side gate until you are in the boat. Holding the oar handles with your water-side hand and either the boat, the dock-side rigger, or the dock-side oar with the other, ease yourself down into the boat. You can either slide your feet directly to the stretchers and your butt onto the seat, or put a foot on the seat deck, then move your body into the boat the same way as described above. Don't forget to close the water-side gate.

Getting out is a simple matter. Unlock the water-side gate as you come into the dock slowly, bow first. Stabilize the boat by holding the oars with your water-side hand and hold the dock with your dock-side hand. Then use your legs and dock-side arm to boost yourself up onto the dock in a sitting position.

■ YOUR FIRST ROW

Once the boat is roughly tuned and you've decided the best way to board, it is time, at last, to introduce her to her natural element, the water. Wait for a calm day, and if it's at all possible, choose a small, protected cove, which will give you a more secure feeling than open water. Try to find a place with a minimum of boat traffic and obstacles such as rocks, buoys, and piers. It may be the nervousness of learning a new sport, or the novelty of facing away from the direction you are traveling, but most beginning rowers are over-anxious about hitting obstacles, and the fewer you have to contend with, the happier you'll be.

Even if you've chosen a day without a breath of wind and absolutely no chop, you'll want to launch as if conditions were less than favorable—it will prevent you from developing bad habits. If you're launching off a dock, you don't have much choice in how you orient the boat to the wind; however, if you are launching off a beach, you have a wider range of options.

When launching, you will want to get away from the beach as soon as possible, especially if there is an onshore wind and its attendant sloppy water. To get off quickly, put the boat in the water with the bow pointing away from shore, allowing you to row clear immediately. If you find yourself being blown back onto the beach, take a few quick strokes even before your feet are firmly in the stretchers. A second benefit to pointing the bow away from the beach is that it presents less surface area to the onshore wind and chop. If the wind is blowing offshore, still point the bow away from the beach; having the stern to the wind will give the same benefits. In a crosswind, angle your bow into the wind. Rowing boats don't offer a large surface area when compared with a sailboat or a powerboat, but neither do they have an underbody or weight to prevent sideslipping, so they blow around quite easily. The problem with starting out with the bow pointed offshore, is that you'll have to wade farther out to reach the cockpit, but that's a small price to pay when compared with getting blown back on the beach sideways.

Although you may have taken sculling lessons or rowed dealers' boats before you bought your own, the first launching of your new boat will be both exciting and a little intimidating. There will be no coach or dealer there to watch your every move and correct you or make suggestions. Taking a friend along, even one who knows nothing about rowing, is good in case you need a hand. If you can find someone who has had some experience rowing sliding seat, so much the better.

Open-water boats are not designed or built to be dragged on the beach: Their gelcoat is thin and easily rubbed away, their fins are vulnerable, and if you have a bailer, its rubber seal can be damaged by sand and pebbles. Put your boat directly into the water, then do your final rigging. When you put the oars in their locks, make sure the locks are on the after sides of the pins. This places the pressure plate, or face, of the lock against the pin, allowing it to take the strain of the stroke. If the oarlocks are reversed, you will be putting an unnatural strain on what should be the trailing upright. You could damage the lock, your stretcher placement will be all wrong, and the pitch on the blades will be reversed. The error will be more obvious if one oarlock is in the proper location and the other is wrong.

Having a friend along really helps when it comes to getting into the boat for the first time. Have your friend hold the stern when you board and while you get the sculls sorted out and your feet in the stretchers. As soon as you put your first foot aboard the boat, balance will become more important to you than it has been since the day you took the training wheels off your two-wheeler. Once you're comfortable on the seat, your feet are secure in the stretchers, the oars squared to the hull, and the blades flat on the water, have your friend release the stern so you can experiment with the feel of the boat.

Sit quietly for a moment and experience the sensation of being in your new boat on the water. Move your body gently from side to side and feel the oars stabilize you. After you have convinced yourself of the boat's stability in that position, move the oars up and down independently of each other and notice the movement of the boat. This little drill will illustrate that as long as you hold the oars square to the hull, blades cupped up with their backs resting on the water, you're very stable and secure. If you begin to feel unstable, go back to this position.

If you have to brush hair out of your eyes, scratch your nose, take a drink from your water bottle, or adjust your glasses, hold both oar handles with one hand, freeing the other for your task. If you must use both hands for some chore, such as putting on your socks, adjusting the foot stretchers or lacing up the clogs, the oars can still stabilize you. Simply slide aft on the tracks, cross the shafts over your lap and lean over them. This way they will be held captive between your legs and trunk, and you'll have your hands free.

Now is a good time to think about the proper grip on the oars. You don't have to hold them as if you were trying to choke the life out of them. Instead think of your hands as hooks, and hook the handles with your fingers; don't grasp the handles in the palms of your hands. Your thumbs should press gently against the ends of the grips. This accomplishes two things: It keeps your hands from slipping down the handles as you row, and it keeps the cheeks of the buttons in contact with the inboard face of the oarlocks. This slight pressure against the handle tip is another factor affecting your balance. Having the sculls firmly contacting the locks will make you feel more secure in the boat. Your wrists should be straight.

Don't row away from shore without first thinking about how you're going to get back. When you come in, you'll want to approach the beach at about a 45-degree angle. Once you're in shallow water, kick the stern around so that you are parallel to the beach. To do this, stabilize the boat with the oars, then give one or two short strokes with the shore-side oar. Later on, you will do this in one stroke while you're moving, but for the first time or two, caution is best. Once you are parallel to the beach, stabilize the boat and get out. Though your boat's finish will probably survive a few beachings it's better not to get into the habit of running it up on shore.

Before you start pulling on the oars, here's something to think about. Almost every rowing coach or instructor will tell you that their students' gender makes a major difference in how fast they learn to row. Before people experience rowing, they tend to perceive it as an "arms" sport. This myth has been around for years, and before the sliding seat, it was true. Today, however, the truth is that rowing is a "leg and back" sport, arms being only the third most important muscle group. Because of the misconception, men, who are used to doing everything with their arms, tend to try to overpower their boats. Most men must learn to think in terms of lifting heavy objects, an activity for which they would use the power in their legs. Men must also think about technique—technique before strength, technique before speed.

In the beginning, all oarsmen catch crabs—that is, they have trouble getting blades out of the water at the release. If you are rowing with more power than technique, a crab can actually pitch you out of the boat. This is a difficult and humbling way to learn that you have fed power into your stroke before you knew how to deal with it. Even if you don't throw yourself out of the boat, you will have myriad balance problems if you try to row too hard too soon.

Women are accustomed to compensating for their lack of upper body strength by doing tasks more efficiently with their legs and backs, and that's the secret to rowing well. Because they are not as strong, women tend to learn technique before men. For both sexes, the key to rowing well is technique, a concept that may be harder for men to grasp than women. If you're a man, try not to be macho; don't try to row like an Olympian the first day out. Take the time to learn technique. The rewards are worth it.

After you've learned about balance and repeated "technique, technique" a hundred times, have your friend take hold of your stern again. Go into the release position and check your foot stretcher location by making sure your thumbs just clear your body. If you're alone, keep the blades in the feathered position; and even though they will not be square to the hull, they will provide some balance. If you discover your stretchers are off by an inch, don't worry about it, just remember to correct them when you get out of the boat. If they're off by more than that, reposition them before you row. Also check the height of your oarlocks—in the release position, with the blades buried, see that your hands come to your body at the abdomen. After that, push your arms away from your body, lean forward, and depress the oar handles to make sure you have room to get the blades out of the water without smacking the tops of your thighs.

Once these checks have been made, it's time to start rowing.

▬ TECHNIQUE

While the rowing stroke is one continuous movement with no "start" or "stop," you do have to start somewhere. Starting from the catch position will be the most comfortable because it is somewhat stable. Don't worry about feathering the first time out; simply keep the blades squared and go through the sequence.

To get into the catch position, push your hands down, drawing the blades out of the water. Then push your hands away from your body so they extend straight out, parallel to the water. Pivoting at the hips, lean toward the stern, then use your legs to slide you aft, bending at the knees but keeping the same body angle. As you do this, run through the sequence in your head; it will give your brain something to work on. The sequence is legs, back, arms; then arms, back, legs. On the pull-through, or drive, the legs come down, the back swings through, and the arms bring the oars into your body; in the recovery, the arms come away, the back comes over, the legs come up. With this chant running through your mind, take the water with your blades by rotating your arms at the shoulders. Push your legs against the rigid lever of your back. Just as the legs straighten, the back should open up, and finally the arms pull in. Just before your hands reach your rib cage, depress the handles, lifting the blades from the water. Push your arms away from your body, lean forward, then come aft on the slide to the catch position. You will probably be quite jerky at first—if you do have a friend holding the stern, repeat the stroke several times before you venture off the beach. If you're alone, go ahead; chances are, you feel less stable than you are.

Before you get too far from shore, you should know how to turn the boat around. When you need to make a turn, go to the stable position, leaving the oar on the side toward which you intend to turn square to the boat and resting on the water's surface with the blade cupped up. Then take short strokes with the other oar. Don't worry about your back or legs, just do arm strokes. Most beginners seem hesitant when making turns. They take tiny little stabs at the water, then don't get the blade all the way out of the water when they're making their recovery. Hitting the water during the recovery, they counter any advance they made with their short turning stroke. Some coaches suggest small, precise strokes for turning. The operative word is "precise." Try it; if it works, great. My former coach believed that rowing does not reward the timorous. She believed in long turning strokes. Even a small person can get eighteen inches of arm travel without using legs or back. Reach out, put the oar in the water as close to the bow as you can, and pull steadily through. Then lift the oar blade well clear of the water for the recovery, set it firmly near the bow, and do it again. Three good strokes like that will turn most boats through more than 90 degrees. Try both long and short strokes and see which works best for you.

Once you're confident that you can stabilize the boat and turn it to avoid an obstacle or get back to the beach, it's time to practice your stroke. Unless you're going to hit something, don't worry about rowing in a straight line. That will come naturally as your skill improves. Don't make a series of correcting strokes, rowing with first one oar and then the other, to keep an imaginary course; just try to maintain a rhythm so you get the feeling of one stroke melding into the next.

Again, balance is going to be of utmost importance to you on this first outing, and you will find that nearly everything you do affects it. You will need to "keep your head in the boat," meaning you can't be looking around too much. The head should be kept stationary, looking dead aft, but not down, except when looking over your shoulder to see that your course is clear. Beginners tend to want to look around far too much; they check for obstructions in their course on every stroke and watch their oar blades in the water. In most cases you only need to check for obstacles every five to 10 strokes, and when you do, you'll find you can keep your balance better if you look during the pull-through, when the oars are in the water. As for watching your blades to check their depth, learn where your hands are when the blades are at the proper depth and look at your hands, not at the ends of the oars.

If you find the boat is listing to port, you probably have too much clearance between your hands at the crossover during the pull-through. Beginners often are worried about hitting the backs or knuckles of their right hand with their left. Actually the hands should be almost touching on the pull-through, and many rowers rest the heel of their left on the top of their right during the recovery. The closer they are to the same horizontal plane, the more stable the boat.

Synchronizing the oars as they enter and leave the water, and controlling the speed of the slide during your recovery also affect your balance. At the catch, the blades should drop as one; at the release, they should come out together. Throughout the entire stroke, the oars should be thought of as a single entity, not as individual components. Later, when you start feathering, it will be very important to your balance that the oars leave the water square, then feather. A clean release is not only crucial to balance, but also to your endurance and back. Blades leaving the water out of square tend to try to lift heavy shovelfuls of water, disrupting your balance, putting a strain on your back, and causing you to row in circles.

Some beginners feel out of balance when their oars are out of the water; therefore, during recovery, they rocket down the slide to get their oars back in the water as soon as possible. In fact, this uncontrolled speed coming down the slide only upsets the boat's balance. To maintain balance, the ratio of stroke time to recovery time must be greater than 1:1. The more efficient your boat, the larger ratio it will be able to use, but a 1:1.5 ratio might be a good place to start, and a 1:2 ratio is certainly not unheard of. This slower slide will also allow the boat to run out, or glide, working for you.

You can demonstrate the importance of a controlled slide for yourself. Get up some speed, then do a couple of strokes with an exaggeratedly fast recovery and feel the boat hobbyhorse. After the boat calms down, do a second pair of strokes with a very slow slide and feel how the boat smoothly runs out, turning your energy into distance covered.

With all this in mind, go on rowing. Don't try for speed or power, simply practice the sequence of the stroke. If you feel tippy, slow down. If you still feel unstable, nervous, or tired, go to the rest position until you regain equilibrium (see photo, page 5). It is nearly impossible to keep the flow of the stroke if you are out of balance, nervous, or tired, and not maintaining the sequence will only make you more nervous and out of balance. Try not to get frustrated—rowing is fun, rowing is relaxing; there's a first time for everyone. By your third time in the boat it will be hard for you to remember how nervous and uncoordinated you felt the first time.

If you begin to feel comfortable in the boat and you think your stroke's pretty decent, you can start feathering. Some coaches recommend a practice that can quickly become a bad habit: dragging your oar blades along the surface of the water, or tapping them on the surface during recovery. Many beginners do this in the mistaken belief that it aids their balance. In fact, it slows the boat, and if either oar catches some chop, it will substantially disrupt your balance. All coaches agree that this is a bad practice; the disagreement comes as to when it's best to break students of the habit. Some coaches feel, as with all bad habits, that it's easier not to start than to correct it later. They say get the oars out of the water at the release and keep them out until the catch. There are no halfway measures here. You can't lift the oars for part of the recovery and let them slide on the surface for the rest of it, and you can't let them tap the surface at intervals. If the oars touch the water at different times, the one that touches first will suck its side down, destabilizing the boat. This will probably cause you to overcompensate with your body or the other oar, and set up a side-to-side rocking motion. If you find yourself tapping the water when you start feathering your oars, push your hands down farther. If the practice persists, go back to no-feather rowing for 10 or 20 strokes, then try again.

Other coaches feel very strongly that spending a week or two with the blades dragging on the surface teaches the student to relax his shoulders (a hard thing to teach), and the blades can be lifted later. Either way you want to do it is fine, but remember, the ultimate goal is to get the blades off the water.

Give yourself enough time for your first outing to get a good feeling for the boat. Don't worry about how far you row, how straight your course is, how fast you are, or where you go—just get comfortable with the boat.

If, after you feel pretty good about your stroke, you still don't think your balance is what it should be, there are a couple of drills you can try to improve it. The first is simply no-feather rowing, a good drill to add to your repertoire. It forces you to keep the blades well clear of the water during recovery, cleaning up your blade work. This drill will be much easier if you have some speed before you start, so get the boat moving, then switch to no-feather. If the bottom edge of the blades catch on the surface of the water, depress your hands more on the next stroke. After 10 or 20 strokes go back to feathered rowing and see if you feel the difference.

The second drill is the pause drill, which will help you control the speed of your slide. The pause drill is simple and very effective. As the name implies, this drill simply requires you to pause in the cycle of your stroke. Once you have released, pushed your arms away from your body, and pivoted into the lean-forward position, you pause before starting the slide. Hold your position for a couple of seconds, then make a slow and controlled slide. Ten to 20 strokes in the pause drill should be enough to make a difference.

■ COMMON PROBLEMS

There are some common problems beginners tend to suffer. Some of these, like tapping the water during recovery, or feathering before the blade releases the water, can develop into bad habits. Others will prevent you from becoming an efficient oarsman. Still others can cause pain or injury if they are not corrected.

One of the first problems many coaches notice is that their students lift with their backs to take the water at the catch, instead of swiveling their arms at the shoulders. This is called "rowboat" or dory-style" rowing, with your arms traveling in an oval pattern rather than parallel to the surface of the water. This style of rowing can be bad for your back along with being inefficient. There are two ways to detect this, either by feeling it in your body or having a friend on the beach to watch for it. If you are new to rowing, having a spotter will be best.

A second problem is lack of hand discipline, such as not rolling the oars all the way up to the square position before the catch. This causes the oars to enter the water under-squared and "knife-in." If this is not corrected, it will encourage dory-style rowing. A more subtle form of dory-style rowing also produced by lack of hand discipline is known as "over-the-hill" rowing, in which the back goes through its proper swing but the arms take an oval route. Again, the feel of your stroke should warn you of this problem; so will the depth of the oar blades during the pull-through.

If you are lucky enough to have a spotter, tell him to watch the blades. He should be able to see a little mound of water over the blades as they travel through the water. If there is no mound, the blade is too deep.

Another very common problem is not keeping your back rigid at the catch and early part of the drive. Try to think of your back and arms as levers connecting your legs to the oars. For every inch your butt moves toward the bow, the handles of the oars should move an equal amount. If you let your back flex, you are sapping power from your stroke and can end up injuring your lower back by making it work harder later in the stroke.

As you progress in the sport, the length of your stroke will become increasingly important. Coaches and coxswains regularly implore their oarsmen to "Keep it long!" Often, beginners don't do much of a layback because it feels uncomfortable and unstable. You must go back to 12 or 15 degrees or you will lose the power at the completion of the pull-through, effectively cutting the stroke short. Conversely, some over-achievers go to extremes of layback. If you find yourself doing a sit-up after each release, you will be working your body too hard and not adding enough power to make the extra strain worth the exertion. The longer you row, the more comfortable you will feel in the proper layback position, and your body will tell you when you're exceeding that 15-degree angle. You can check your layback by rowing with your feet resting on top of the stretchers. If your layback is too extreme, you will feel like you're falling over backwards.

At the other end of the stroke—the catch—some try for too much reach. After you take the proper body angle, rocking forward out of the release, maintain it. Don't get to the catch and try to extend your reach, or lunge into a greater angle. You don't really gain anything by doing this, and the sudden shift of weight will sink the stern slightly, checking the run of the boat. Be aware of your forward lean from the start of the slide, and maintain it.

An uncontrolled slide is another fault coaches regularly observe in their beginning students. Along with feeling insecure during the recovery and hastening the slide to increase stability by getting the oars back in the water, some beginners see a quick slide as a way to increase speed. The converse is in fact true—a controlled slide increases speed. Slamming back into the stretchers, like lunging to gain extra reach at the catch, simply disrupts the boat, scrubbing off speed. The weight of your body rocketing aft sinks, or checks, the stern and radically slows the boat. This means you have to get it moving again with the next stroke. Allow the boat to work for you, to "run." The same 1:1.5 or 1:2 ratio of stroke to recovery that helps you maintain your balance also allows the boat to "run out" throughout the recovery. The more proficient you become, the more you will be able to feel what is right for you and your boat.

Taking the water at the catch seems to offer some problems to new rowers. Aside from the difficulty of getting the blades in the water at precisely the same time, there are some other difficulties. One is known as "skying the blades," which consists of lifting the blades just before the catch. This is caused by dipping the hands down just before you roll the blades up into the square position. Most new rowers say they do this in an attempt to keep the oars from tapping on the water before the catch. As long as you haven't lifted your hands during the recovery, you don't need to take this precaution; the blades will square up and drop directly into the water without tapping. Skying the blades upsets the balance of the boat by disrupting its flow; it's not natural for the oars to go up, then down. They should go straight back, then into the water, with you relaxing at the shoulder joint to place them. Here again, having a spotter on the beach will be helpful.

Another problem with taking the water that your spotter will be able to see better than you is splash. The most common problem is excessive back splash—that is, splash off the backs of the blades towards the bow. This is caused by taking the water too soon, while you're still in the recovery portion of the stroke. Doing this cuts the length of the stroke and puts the brakes on the boat. You want to take the water during the last one or two inches of recovery. The perfect sculler (does such a creature exist?) will have virtually no back splash, but in the real world we need to think in terms of how little back splash we can create. A small back splash, a two- to four-inch fan, is acceptable. More than that is not. If your spotter on the beach sees larges sprays of water coming forward off the blades, delay taking the water a little more at each catch until he indicates the splash is insignificant.

If there is no back splash, either you are the perfect sculler, and can stop reading right now, or there is front splash. While a modicum of back splash is acceptable, no front splash should be allowed. Front splash, water deflected off the blade faces toward the stern, is caused by taking the water after you've already started the pull-through portion of your stroke. The oar is actually striking the water after your legs have started their drive. This shortens the stroke and robs power from the beginning of the pull-through; it also jolts the boat and can stress your body. If you see this splash out of the corner of your eye, or your spotter on the beach calls your attention to it, simply take the water a little sooner, always keeping in mind the pitfalls of back splash. Be sure the blades are in the water before your legs start their drive.

■ BACKING AND TURNING

After you're comfortable rowing back and forth, have found an acceptable stroke, and have practiced turning the boat, there are two maneuvers that you should learn. Unless you've had a couple of lessons, you won't be attempting these your first time out. But as soon as you feel ready, learn both backing and the spin turn. They are handy skills to have in your repertoire.

Backing, as the word implies, refers to rowing the boat backwards. To accomplish this, start at the forward end of the slide in the rest position. Once you're stable and comfortable, roll the oars so the blades are cupped toward the bow. Without using the slide, draw the oar handles to your abdomen, lower the blades into the water and push away with your arms. Don't try to feather or take long strokes; square blades and short strokes are the trick to this maneuver. You may feel out of balance at first, but it will come in time.

The spin turn is a faster way to turn the boat through 45 to 360 degrees—quicker than rowing with a single oar. There are actually two ways to accomplish a spin turn. Which one you choose to use will depend to a great extent upon the stability of your boat and how comfortable you feel aboard her. The first and most stable method of making a spin turn requires that you go to the rest position in the middle of the slide. While the blade of one oar rests on the surface with its cupped face up, roll the other oar so that the cupped face is pointed toward the stern. Push the handle away from you, take the water and, using only your arm, draw the handle to your abdomen. Return the oar to the stable rest position, roll the other oar so that the blade face is pointed toward the bow, and make a stroke as if you were backing the boat. Repeat these alterating strokes until the boat is facing the proper direction.

The second method is slightly faster but considerably less stable; try it only if you feel very secure in the boat. Everything is done as in the first example, except you move the oars simultaneously—there is no oar at rest for balance.

After you've spent some time in the boat—enough to be comfortable but not enough to develop bad habits—it's time to work on refining your stroke.

- 5 -

The Perfect Rowing Stroke
and Monitoring
Your Progress

THERE is a Zen saying: "If perfection could be achieved, it wouldn't be worth having."

No honest sculler will claim to have the perfect rowing stroke. Olympic gold medalists don't have it, world champions don't have it, and neither do oarsmen who have been practicing for 45 years. Nevertheless, every sculler strives for it, and that's one of the beauties of rowing—you can always choose to improve.

If no one has this perfect stroke, why work toward it? You've finally gotten comfortable in the boat, you don't feel like you're going to be pitched out every other stroke, and you can get from point A to point B without too much trouble. Sure, you'll probably admit, a better stroke might make you faster, but you're not out to win a national championship, or become an Olympic sculler. What's wrong with continuing on the way you've been going?

It's human nature to want to improve at something you enjoy. Proficiency at any endeavor is gratifying. You'll enjoy your rowing more if you know that you're rowing better in August than you were in June, and that you will be better still in September. There is also the theory that fun on the water is directly related to your speed across it, and you gain speed as your stroke improves.

Human nature, ego, and the joy of increased speed aside, there are some very practical reasons for you to aspire to the perfect stroke. One of these is avoiding pain. You can hurt yourself if you row improperly. In fact, you can develop major lower back pain from either dory-style rowing or from using your back too soon in the drive. Even if you don't injure yourself, you will find that a less-than-proper stroke is not as efficient, meaning your workout will be harder on your body.

Before you can improve your stroke you must have the right mental set.

There is a common fallacy, especially among beginners, that the stroke has a "beginning" and a "finish." In fact, the stroke is one continuous, fluid motion that melds with the next stroke and the one after that. You "begin" when you take the water on your first catch, and you "finish" at your last release; between those two moments, everything should flow together.

▬ THE PERFECT STROKE

With the concept of "flow" firmly in mind, we will go through the sequence of a single stroke. The catch is the normal place to begin this kind of discussion for two reasons; it is a stable position and it starts the power portion of the stroke. At the catch, you are leaning forward, over your knees, with your ankles

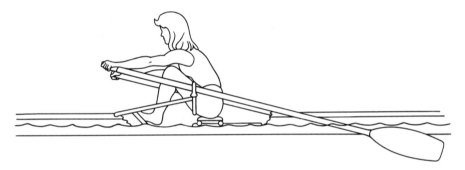

At the catch, the arms are straight and locked, the body bent forward, the knees compressed, and the heels raised.

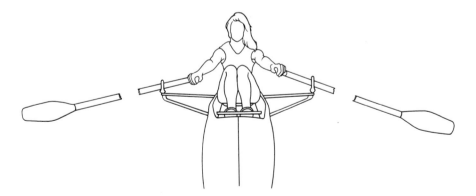

The catch as seen from the stern. The knees are together, and the thumbs are on the ends of the oar handles, where they supply a light pressure to keep the buttons in contact with the locks.

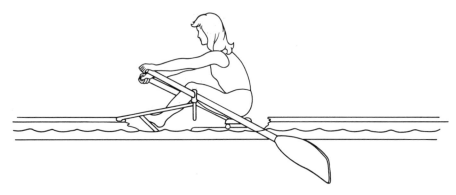

At the beginning of the drive, the legs supply all the power. The arms are still straight, acting as levers to deliver the power to the oars, and the back is still bent.

just a couple of degrees shy of the vertical and your oars are squared up, hovering just above the surface of the water. To take the water, or initiate the catch, pivot at your shoulder sockets, lifting your hands a couple of inches while keeping your arms straight. Don't lift your back at this point; you don't use your back to put the oars in the water. It's all a motion of hands and arms starting at your shoulders. Consciously flex your lats (the latissimus dorsi); if they are not flexed, your back will stretch, taking power from the drive of your legs. Your elbows are also locked and rigid; they may want to pull at the catch, but they're not strong enough. That's why the legs supply the power for the first part of the drive. As the oars take the water, your legs start to push. At this point, nothing else is happening; the oars have taken the water and the legs have begun their drive. The back is set against the legs, maintaining the same forward angle. The elbows are locked. The power of the legs is transferred through the rigid back and arms to the oars. For every inch the legs drive the seat toward the bow, the oar handles should move a corresponding inch. Anything less and you are allowing your body to flex.

When your legs are about halfway down, the back begins to open up. As it swings, your shoulders, like your hands, move on a horizontal plane; they do not lift vertically. Just after you start to swing, the arms begin to bend. Use your lats, not your biceps, to bend the arms. This gives more power and an entirely different feel, the elbows coming in near the sides of the body, then sweeping past. If you were to use your biceps, the arms would "chicken-wing," raising the elbows upward. At the moment the legs flatten out, the back should reach its layback position and the arms will finish their pull. All through the drive, the oar handles should move in a horizontal plane, not an arc. The blades should

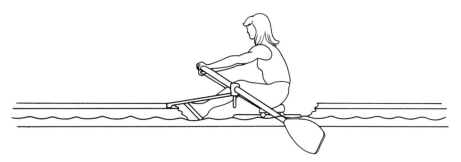

As the legs come down, the back begins to open up. The arms remain locked.

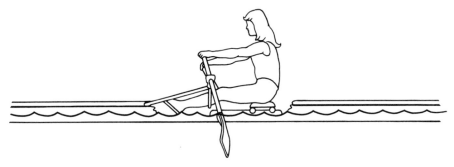

The legs are almost down, and the back is swinging. The arms are still straight.

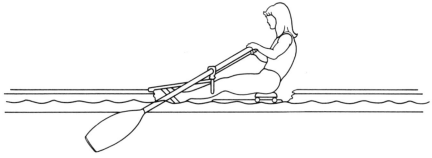

The arms pull last, finishing at the sternum as the body achieves its full backward lean.

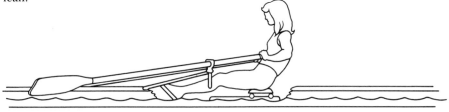

The hands drop straight to the lap, lifting the blades before they are feathered.

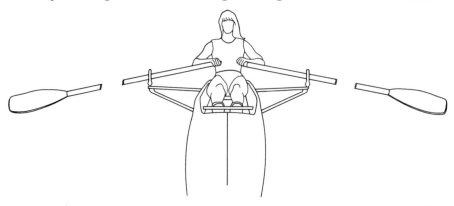

The release as seen from the stern. The hands have just finished at the base of the sternum and are dropping into the lap, releasing the blades. The elbows are kept low.

On the recovery, the arms are extended first. Then the body leans forward, and finally, the legs control the recovery down the slide.

be just covered; in fact, if you glance at them out of the corner of your eye (keep your head in the boat) you should be able to see what appears to be a mound of water traveling with them. If you don't see this moving mound, or "bubble," your blades are too deep. Rowing with your blades deep affects your balance, and is inefficient as it decreases your arc and therefore your leverage.

Your hands should finish the drive somewhere between your bellybutton and sternum. If they come into your lap you will "wash out," letting the blades emerge too early and cutting the length of your stroke. When your hands come into your body, push them straight down into your lap, making a square corner as you lift the blades. The blades must still be squared as they leave the water. If you feather, even a fraction of a second too early, the blades will meet a lot of resistance as they emerge, and you may catch a crab. When the lower edges of the blades are free, feather by using your fingers and thumbs to roll up your hands.

As soon as the blades are feathered, push your arms away from your body, getting their weight out of the bow quickly. When the arms are nearly straight, your body swings forward, pivoting at the hips, and takes the angle you'll use at the coming catch. As we saw in the last chapter, if you attempt to induce more forward lean just before you take the water at the catch, you'll check the stern, cutting short the boat's run. Only when your hands have passed over your knees and you've achieved all of your forward lean, do your legs begin to bend. You can't let your muscles lose control of the slide, or you'll rush it, checking the boat. Your hamstrings *must* control the slide, giving you the proper ratio of recovery to drive. As your legs bend, pulling your entire body out of the bow, begin to curl your fingers, squaring up the blades to take the water at the catch. The blades must be squared before you pivot your arms to take the water. If they are not, you will have to break the flow of the stroke to square up, or risk having the blades strike obliquely and "knife in."

The perfect stroke doesn't take long to read about, but you can spend a lifetime attempting to master it. While balancing the boat, thinking about your course and any obstacles on that course, there are hundreds of points to remember about each stroke, and since all the movements are interconnected, each affects the one that follows. If you become too compressed at the catch, if your ankles go past 90 degrees, there will be no power in the beginning of your drive. If your oars dig too deeply during the drive, they are not only inefficient, but they make the release more difficult. If you rush your recovery, you will both unbalance the boat and check her run; then you'll need to get her started again on the next stroke. Then there's the rigging—if you have too much pitch, or have the locks set too high, you'll wash out. Everything is connected, everything flows, from taking the water to release and from stroke to stroke. Remember to think of it that way—a continuous flowing motion aboard a well-tuned boat.

This flowing motion is the result of every muscle group in your body working in concert. Knowing which muscles are supposed to be working at which times will let you feel when the stroke is correct. The more you get used to this feeling, the sooner you'll notice the strange sensations that signal something amiss in your stroke. Therefore, it's important to understand the muscles that control your rowing—what they do, and when they make their contribution.

As you take the water, the anterior deltoids place the oars, and a fraction of a second later the lats, biceps, triceps, flexors, and all the little muscles in the hands flex to transfer the power from the legs through the back and arms to the oars. As the quadriceps drive the legs down, the triceps engage to assist the lats as the boat picks up speed, and the gastrocnemii in the calves also come into play. In the layback, the abdominals and the radials are working, and the pectorals and biceps push the oars away from the body while the abdominals remain flexed. Then the body swings forward, with the lumbar triangle supplying the motive force. As the body starts the recovery, the hamstrings control the very important speed of the slide.

After you've rowed long enough that the newness of the sport has worn off, and you've become accustomed to how you feel after an outing, listening to your body can tell you a lot. If your abdominals are considerably more tender than usual, you may be taking excessive layback at the release, forcing your stomach muscles to pull you up as they would in a sit-up. If the flexors of your forearms are tight and sore, you were probably holding the oars too tightly. Your muscles should feel relatively the same after each row.

Obviously, if your regular row is five miles and you do a 10-mile piece, you will be more tired and maybe sore, but all the soreness should be relative. If your body doesn't feel the same, figure out why. It could be that you just didn't stretch out as well as you normally do, or the morning was colder, or you slept differently the night before. On the other hand, you might have started gripping the oars tighter or doing 20-degree laybacks.

■ FINE-TUNING YOUR BOAT

As you become more proficient in your stroke, you will find you need to spend some extra time fine-tuning your boat: You will demand more from her, and the rough tuning you did when you first got her will no longer satisfy those increased demands. Also, your body will change as you row, and you'll have to alter the rigging to match.

If you have lost a significant amount of weight, you will notice that during the recovery the clearance between the tops of your thighs and the oar handles is excessive. To bring the boat back in line with your body, decrease the oarlock height. At the same time, you might look at the height difference between the port and starboard locks. That difference must be sufficient for correct left-over-right rowing, but you may have become familiar enough with the technique that you can tolerate an eighth of an inch less and still keep your hands clear. Anything you can take out is good because it will bring the oars closer to the same horizontal plane.

While you're working on the locks, you will want to decrease their pitch. You should have set it unnaturally high—six degrees of positive pitch—when you first tuned the boat, because the extra pitch helped you bite the water at the catch without knifing in. Now that your style is improving, take the pitch down to make it easier to keep the oars in the water. Don't drop the pitch immediately to three degrees, but take out a degree or two and you'll feel the difference.

After you adjust the rig, you may need to experiment with the button location on your sculls. If the load seems light, try moving the buttons inboard. Again, don't overdo it the first time—a quarter-inch is a major adjustment in this area. A generalization on this adjustment: Smaller people should have greater spread and lighter loads, while larger people can tolerate less spread and higher loads.

Once you're happy with the load on the oars, think about where you've been sitting and how you have oriented yourself to the riggers. As scullers become more comfortable in their boats they usually want to sit a little farther away from their oars to lengthen their stroke and allow their bodies a freer swing. Try setting your stretchers a little closer to the bow. In many open-water boats stretcher tuning is limited to coarse adjustments. The better boats allow you to tune in half-inch increments; in many they are adjusted in one-inch steps, and in some tuning is limited to two-inch bites. If your stretchers can't be moved to the desired position, don't be afraid to either drill new mounting holes or use shims or spacers to properly position your feet. Don't accept what you've been given if it isn't adequate.

An adjustment we didn't discuss when you were setting up the boat is height over heels—the distance between the bottom of the heel cups (or shoes) and the center of the seat. There are two reasons you might want to make a change at this point. First, if your calves have been hitting the ends of your seat tracks at the release, moving up the heels can correct this. Second, height over heels determines your position at the catch. The greater the distance between your heels and seat, the more forward lean you can achieve. This allows you more upper body swing, while the shorter distance you have requires more leg power. If you have a weak back, raising your heels can help protect it. Again, adjust in small increments.

■ REFINING YOUR TECHNIQUE

After you've retuned your boat to match the changes in your body and ability, you'll need to concentrate on yourself. All the problems you dealt with when you first began rowing sliding-seat can rear their heads again and again, each time more insidiously than the last. Your hands can begin "over-the-hill" rowing so gradually that you won't notice it until it becomes a major problem. You may start slowly decreasing your layback and lean forward until you are almost vertical throughout your stroke. Your blades may tap the surface on every fifth or sixth recovery, then on every fourth stroke and so on until you're sliding them across the surface on each recovery, scrubbing speed off the run and potentially upsetting your balance. Your blades can dig deeper and deeper with each mile you row, becoming progressively less efficient. You can sky the blades by dipping your hands just a quarter of an inch before you take the water. Unchecked, that habit can progress until finally you're terribly out of balance just before each catch and have no idea how you got that way. Then there's the speed of the slide, which can creep up until your ratio is 1:1 or even 1:0.75, unbalancing the boat, checking its run, and wearing you out.

As your stroke improves, other problems become important to deal with. If you were either "bucking the oars" or "bucketing" when you first started rowing, it wasn't so important—at that time your top priority was to get used to the rhythm of the stroke and that balance of the boat. Now that you're concentrating on the length and flow of your stroke, you cannot permit either of these style flaws. "Bucking the oars" refers to shortening the stroke by releasing before the hands have come all the way to the body. To get the proper length at this end of your stroke, go all the way into your layback, bringing the oars right up to your body before releasing. "Bucketing" also happens when your body is in the forward end of the tracks, but takes place at the start of the recovery. It consists of lunging forward with the body before the arms have fully straightened. This disrupts both the slide and the balance of the boat.

There is no way to rationalize your style faults. And don't get complacent or you'll never be rewarded with a better stroke.

A common problem scullers have when they begin improving is understanding that the number of strokes per minute cannot be equated to power or speed through the water. It's how you row each stroke, not how many strokes you row, that matters. Many beginners rationalize speeding their recovery as a way to take up the stroke rate, thinking they'll produce greater speed through the water. You can row 20 strokes per minute at full power with a good slow recovery, or 40 strokes per minute with almost no power and a rapid recovery. The first will be efficient and save your body, the second will be inefficient and sap your stamina. It's power and technique which produce results, not stroke rate. The East German Olympic women rowers trained for hours at full power while rowing 18 strokes per minute. Gordie Nash trained for and won the 1984 Catalina to Marina del Rey race, a 32-nautical-mile open-ocean endurance test, rowing 22 strokes per minute. He teamed with Kevin Strain and they won the men's doubles class in 1986, 1987 and 1988 rowing in the mid to high 20s. Shirwin Smith and Marie Hagelstein hold the women's doubles record for the same race—a record they set rowing in the mid 20s. A powerful stroke combined with a low stroke rate is more efficient, both for moving the boat through the water and conserving your strength.

If, during a race, you are nearing the finish line rowing bow to bow with your archrival, or if you're in the middle of a channel trapped between an oncoming ferry and a commercial fishing boat, you can gain needed speed by taking the stroke rate up, but you have to do it properly. Flailing away with the oars and rocketing up and down the slide won't make you go any faster. In fact, it will probably slow you down.

When you want to take the stroke rate up, it must be done first with the hands and arms, then the body and finally, the legs. At the release, push your arms away from your body faster and swing the body into the lean forward position more quickly (being careful not to "bucket"), but, as soon as you have your full forward lean, *control the slide.* If you don't, you will check the stern, more than counteracting any gains you were making by taking up the rate. As you take up the rate, you'll find the speed of your drive increases slightly. Therefore, the speed of your recovery can increase correspondingly—but it must always be controlled, and the proper ratio kept in mind.

If you want to prove to yourself just how important a controlled slide is to speed, endurance, and balance, find a pair of buoys or landmarks about a quarter of a mile apart in an area not affected by wind or current. First make a timed run of your course with your body flying up and down the slide, say with a stroke rate between 36 and 40 per minute. When you finish, check your time and make a mental note of how you feel and how the boat felt. After you've taken a breather, row back down the course, concentrating on power in the pull-through and a slow, controlled slide. Keep your rate down at about 20 to 22 strokes per minute. After your second run, compare your times and how you felt after each. Your time should be better, you should be less tired, and the row will have been more pleasurable.

There are some drills that will set you up, physically and mentally, for the proper stroke. When you first row away from the dock or beach, try about 50 strokes of no-leg rowing. Set your legs straight but don't lock your knees; they should have a little flex. Start rowing using only your arms, and swinging the body through its arc. This will warm up your back and abdomen and stretch the hamstrings. After 50 strokes, feed in about half the slide, still swinging the body through its full arc. This will work the legs into the stroke gradually. After 50 repetitions of the half slide, go to full slide.

If your oars have been tapping the water on the recovery, or if your release hasn't been as clean as it should, start a no-feather drill as soon as you've warmed up your legs and lengthened to a full stroke. Done as a regular drill, no-feather rowing is a little more involved than was discussed in Chapter 4. Start with some speed for stability, then square up the blades and set your wrists. Be prepared to carry your hands slightly lower through the recovery than you would if you were feathering, and be ready to feel the boat lurch. If the lower edge of a blade catches the water on the recovery, the boat will dip toward the side that hit. Don't stop, and don't cheat and half-feather at this point—relax and lift the oar higher. If you can't push it through and the boat stops, revert to feathered rowing to regain speed and balance, then force yourself to go back to no-feather. You should complete at least 10 consecutive strokes to make the no-feather drill worthwhile. In the beginning it will be terribly frustrating, but it can be done, and the results will justify your efforts.

Those three drills—no-leg rowing, half-slide rowing, and no-feather rowing—will start your row in the proper way, both physically and mentally. You'll be loose and warmed up; your mind will be on the boat, and you'll be ready for a good row. There is also a cool-down drill to follow. It's fine to come back to the beach sweaty, but you shouldn't come in gasping for breath with your heart pounding and jump out of the boat. About half- to a quarter-mile from the beach or dock, paddle down for a few strokes, then initiate a pause drill. The pause drill, discussed in Chapter 4, helps you control the speed of your slide while it cools you down.

■ STEERING

Be aware of your stroke each day, keeping it long, fluid, powerful and well-timed. As your stroke improves and becomes steadier, you will need to develop your steering skills—you don't want to stop, row with one oar to correct your course, then pick up the stroke again.

Before you can steer, you must first set your course. Pick a destination no more than a mile away, making sure the course is clear of buoys or any other obstructions, then point your bow toward it. With your boat lined up, find a landmark directly astern as a reference point. If you begin to drift off course, realign yourself by reaching out a little farther with one oar at the catch, and the extra power of that arc will turn you. Reference to a stern point doesn't mean you should never look over your shoulder. There might be something in the water you missed when you set your course, and there may be other boats, swimmers, or windsurfers sharing the water with you, so glance forward every 10 strokes or so. Remember to look forward while you're in the drive portion of the stroke, when the oars are providing stability. The reason you chose a course of a mile or less is that it gets progressively harder to keep a stern point over longer distances. If your ultimate destination is several miles away, and you don't have a compass, break it down into a series of shorter hops and it will be easier to stay on course.

■ MARKING YOUR PROGRESS

There are three good ways to monitor the improvement in your rowing in general and your stroke in particular. The first consists of simply watching your wake. When you were first learning to row, you were so slow there was no wake, so just the appearance of a wake shows improvement. When it first appeared, it probably wandered across the surface like a drunken snake, but that didn't matter because you were learning the rhythm and flow of the stroke. As you improved you learned to make minor corrections in the stroke almost subconsciously, and the proof of that is a long, straight wake flanked by matching "puddles," the boils left in the water by your release.

Watching the "puddles" will give you a very accurate indication of how efficient your stroke has become. Of course, if your stroke rate is inconsistent, the distance between these disturbances will vary; however, if your rate is consistent, the spacing will be even and obvious. The greater the distance between puddles, the more efficient your stroke. Obviously, the distance between puddles will differ from boat to boat. You can't expect a 73-pound 19-footer with a 23-inch waterline beam to have the same run as a 40-pound 24-footer with a 14-inch waterline beam. The distance will also vary with weather conditions; your run won't be as long in a headwind and chop as in glass-smooth water. Nevertheless, once you've observed your spacing in a variety of conditions, you'll have a good idea of where the puddles should be. If you're used to seeing your puddles boiling three feet off the stern as you strike the water at your next catch, and suddenly they are flanking the stern as you strike, you'll know you are rowing with an erratic stroke rate or rushing the recovery.

The third way to monitor your efficiency is by taking your heart rate. You may, for example, row a two-mile piece in 20 minutes and find that your heart rate at the end is 150 beats per minute. This becomes your base rate. Turn your attention to a particular problem that you need to work on, such as tapping your blades during recovery or sloppy blade work at the release, and concentrate on it until you have it under control, whether it takes a week or a month. If you don't have any particular problem, just spend a couple of weeks rowing, concentrating on keeping a steady stroke rate and keeping your stroke "long and strong." Then do your base distance again under similar conditions. If you cover your two miles in less than 20 minutes and your heart rate is still 150 at the finish, you have become more efficient.

▬ HANDLING ROUGH WEATHER

Many who buy rowing boats to complement (or become) their exercise regimen say they will never row in the ocean or across large lakes; all they want to do is row in protected harbors, bays, lakes, or rivers. Some of these people may never leave the confines of their little patch of flat water, and that's fine. On

Rowing in windy conditions on Narragansett Bay. The oarsman is using the sculls to keep a straight course more than to power the boat.

the other hand, as most new rowers improve their stroke, become more comfortable in their boats, and get in better shape, they will venture farther afield. You may not immediately row into the open ocean, but many bays, lakes, and harbors are big enough to kick up if the wind begins to blow, especially if it's blowing against the prevailing current or tide. If you start rowing long pieces and there's a possibility of conditions changing for the worse, be prepared.

Many rowers revel in rough going—they love getting out in sloppy water, getting wet, and driving their boats hard—but it takes some skill and a lot of practice. This is not meant to dissuade you from rowing in rough water, just as a few words of caution. The boat in which you have become comfortable rowing on flat water may feel entirely different in the rough stuff. Always remember you are rowing in a potentially hostile environment and take it easy. Get into rough water rowing slowly. Don't go from a flat, protected bay to a 20-knot day with breaking whitecaps. If you can, take a more experienced oarsman along with you on your first outings. Most important, be attentive to your instincts and don't let misplaced pride or machismo get you into trouble. If you feel a little apprehensive, that's probably fine—go for it. But if you get to the harbor mouth and you're looking at a lot of white water and you're really frightened, turn around and go back. Pick a time when things are a little calmer.

Rough water brings two major problems—lack of stability and difficulty getting the oars across the water during the recovery. To improve your stability, shorten the stroke. This doesn't mean using less of the slide; it means cutting both the forward lean at the catch and the layback at the release. These are the two least stable positions when rowing, and reducing the angle of each will go a long way toward making the boat more stable. This shortening of the stroke should only be used until you become comfortable in the conditions you're encountering. Once you're comfortable, lengthen the stroke again.

In extreme conditions you may have to both shorten your body swing and reduce the length of the slide. In these conditions, waves will cut your boat's run, and shortening your stroke will help make up for this. When you find the right stroke length, you'll feel your boat level out.

If you know you are going to be encountering rough, windy conditions, and if you chose adjustable oarlocks, you can raise them before you leave the dock or beach. Depending on your size and the conditions you expect to encounter, repositioning just one or two spacers will allow you to push your hands a lot farther down during recovery without smacking the tops of your thighs. If the water is really rough, the oar blades are going to slam into the chop no matter how far down you push your hands. Try reducing the amount of feathering. If you just roll the oars through 45 degrees, the blades will strike the chop at an angle. The boat will still rock, but when the rounded back of the blade is presented to the chop at an angle, the blade will tend to lift, minimizing the effect of the impact. It's normal to tighten up in rougher conditions; as much as possible, relax your arms to avoid cramps.

When you encounter a headwind, delay your roll-up (squaring the blades before they take the water at the catch). The longer you delay it, the less time the blades will be square to the wind and chop. Reducing the effect of the wind on the blade is a benefit, but the real advantage of delaying your roll-up until the last possible moment is that the chop won't strike the squared-up blade. A steep chop can actually smack the blade hard enough to rip the handle out of your hand, and just knowing there's a possibility of this happening will probably cause you to tighten your grip on the handles. Try to resist this very natural reaction—if you hold them too tightly for too long the result will be painful forearm cramps. Take care that the delayed roll-up does not become a habit you carry over into flat-water, light-wind conditions.

In downwind situations, you will probably find you're having a little trouble balancing the boat. On the other hand, you'll have more speed due to the wind and chop. You can shorten your stroke to stabilize the boat, but you'll want to stay as long as possible to take advantage of the extra speed. The speed of downwind rowing can be exhilarating, but it can also be dangerous, especially in open water. Until you're sure of yourself, keep a rein on your enthusiasm.

If it's quite rough and you find yourself surfing the wind waves, shorten your stroke, especially at the release. By reducing your layback, you will keep weight out of the bow, minimizing the chance of burying it and causing the boat to spin out. As the unweighted stern lifts, pulling the fin out of the water, the boat can spin and bury an oar. The combination of speed, spinning boat, and a buried oar can either jerk the oar out of your hand or pitch you out of the boat. If you start to take off on a wave that you think is too steep, slide your weight right aft to keep the bow up. If you start to broach, you can drag the edge of a blade, turning the boat toward the dragged blade, straightening you out.

If you're going out specifically to surf, you'll need to learn about placement, timing, and wave choice, and that all comes with time. But you have a couple of advantages a surfer doesn't have: First, you are much faster, so your timing and placement aren't as critical; you will be able to row into swells from a variety of locations. Second, you can shift your weight to help you get into a wave and trim once you're on it. If you feel like you've just missed a swell, take a last powerful stroke and throw yourself into an exaggerated layback—the extra weight in the bow may just make the difference between missing the swell and catching it. Once you're on the swell, get your weight out of the bow and reposition yourself nearer the center of the slide. Riding swells and chop is an advanced technique, one that is not for everyone, so don't try it until you're ready, and take another oarsman along for safety.

Remember to keep your stroke as long and strong as possible. If you run into a patch of rough water, shorten up if you need to, but when you're in the clear, lengthen out again. Frequently, rough patches will be quite temporary, caused by tide, current, or wind, and passing through them should not dictate your stroke for the rest of your row. For instance, harbor entrance channels are frequently areas of very confused water—conflicting wakes caused by boats going in and out, compressed tidal runs, reflective waves coming off breakwaters, and even ocean swells can make them veritable washing machines.

- 6 -
Accessories, Maintenance, and Clothing

A CLEAN, well-equipped, well-maintained boat performs better and encourages you to do the same. Your open-water rowing boat is a highly tuned assembly of components. Each element that goes into the boat must be chosen for compatibility with the others and maintained properly to operate efficiently. A lot of the responsibility for choosing the proper components falls to the builder, but as we discussed earlier, there are choices you will have to make and accessories you can add. While their maintenance is simple, it must be done or your rowing program will suffer.

Your boat's components can be divided into seven groups: the sculls and their sleeves and buttons; riggers and oarlocks; seat and tracks; foot stretchers; hull; fin; and any accessories you've added. Except for the accessories, everything else came with the boat when you bought it. We discussed maintenance of basic components in Chapter 3; here we'll review some of those maintenance tips, look at some other equipment and how to care for it, and talk about clothing that will make rowing more comfortable.

▬ SCULLS

Both wood and composite sculls need protection from the sun's ultraviolet rays. They should be stored inside, or covered. Wooden sculls will need to be varnished more frequently than their composite cousins, but you can't ignore the UV inhibitor on your carbon-fiber looms. The blades are susceptible to damage, and padded covers are a good idea. Plastic sleeves need some lubrication, but be sure to use a *small* amount of silicone or Teflon-based lubricant—don't slather them with Crisco or Vaseline.

▬ RIGGERS

There are three types of riggers on open-water boats. The first type is found on drop-in units such as Martin's Oarmaster and Graham's E-Z Rigger. Both of these are aluminum, though some earlier models were fiberglass. Currently, the most common are the standard triangulated riggers, which consist of two or three tubes joined together at the outboard end to support the sill, and attached to the hull at widely spaced locations for strength. These are usually constructed of stainless steel, anodized aluminum, or fiberglass cored with foam and carbon fiber. The latest innovation is the wing rigger, which came to open-water rowing from European shell racing. All the wings currently produced are composite. Their builders claim the wings allow them to produce lighter boats, as they don't have to build in as many structural connections required for triangulated rigging. They are also more aerodynamic and keep the boat dry, eliminating the splash of waves and chop against the forward rigger. No one type of rigger is inherently better than any other type; each design must be inspected for flex, twist, and ease of adjustment.

Riggers require very little maintenance. Marine-grade stainless steel will develop a thin surface film of rust if it is not kept clean, so give your stainless riggers a quick wipe-down every so often and they will stay bright for the life of the boat. Aluminum and glass riggers require the same attention. The bolts attaching the riggers to the hull should be checked for tightness once a month. They also need to be removed about once a year and packed with white grease. This will ensure that you can remove them easily if you need to.

A winged Maas 24. (Courtesy Maas Boats)

The height of Oarmaster riggers is adjusted by a pair of stainless steel bolts in the base of the rigger. When tightened, they act as stops that set the height of the oarlock. These bolts should be removed and greased periodically, or they will corrode in place.

Keep your oarlocks clean. Any sand or grit in the locks will wear on both the lock and the oar sleeve and button. If you use a good lubricant on your plastic sleeves, you won't need to add lubricant to your oarlocks. You should inspect the pins regularly. Remove the oarlocks from the pins, wipe down the pins, and inspect them for pitting and rusting. Take the pins off the boat occasionally, clean and inspect the threads, then pack them with white grease. If you find your pins are pitted or badly rusted, replace them. Remember—the lock has to be able to swivel freely on the pin, so when you put the oarlock back on, don't tighten the top retaining nut excessively. If you store your boat outside and don't have a cover for it, at least cover the oarlocks to keep them clean.

▬ SEAT AND TRACKS

The overwhelming majority of open-water boats available today have wooden or composite seats with four wheels that ride in a pair of extruded aluminum tracks. These seats look something like a Lone Ranger mask, the "eye-holes" being cut-outs for the ischium bones and the cutout for the "nose" designed to relieve the coccyx. When installing your seat, the cutout for the coccyx should face the bow.

The aluminum tracks must be kept clear of sand or grit, which will wear down the wheels and cut through the tracks' anodizing. An occasional wipe with a damp towel will keep them clean. Don't lubricate the wheels; they roll very well without it, and most lubricants eventually become gummy with anodization and grit and actually wear and slow the wheels. The seats have a double-action feature; they roll on the wheels for the length of the track, then slide on the axles, allowing a bit more fore-and-aft movement. The axles slide on narrow ribs molded into the seat's undercarriage. Sometimes these ribs need a *tiny* amount of the same light Teflon- or silicone-based lubricant you use on the oar sleeves. Occasionally wipe down the stainless steel axles, which may begin to develop a thin film of corrosion. If you have a wooden seat and store your boat outside, either remove the seat or cover it to protect the varnish from the elements.

It's a sad fact of rowing life that seats occasionally squeak. Often this problem is not one that can be solved with more and more lubrication. Through use, some seats become slightly out of square. There are plastic keepers on most axles designed to keep the seat on the track, and these occasionally shift.

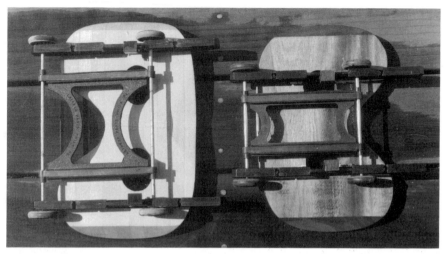

Seats come with different axle lengths. When ordering a new one, be sure you know this vital measurement.

If your seat squeaks and it is clean and lubricated, take it off the tracks and check to see if the keepers haven't shifted, throwing it out of square.

If you decide to change seats, or break one and need to order a new one, be sure the wheels and axle lengths are compatible with your tracks and their spread. There are several wheel sizes and at least three standard axle lengths available. Also, inspect the keepers for compatibility with your tracks. Most of them are supposed to be interchangeable, but theory and practice don't always match.

The Oarmaster seat is a little different. Instead of having wheels riding inside a cupped track, the Oarmaster has cupped wheels that roll on a narrow track, a configuration reminiscent of railroad wheels and tracks. The Oarmaster tracks must be kept clean. Some rowers use a very small amount of light lubricant, but this can be messy, and most forgo lubrication without apparent harm. The seats do not have a double action, so there are no axle supports requiring lubrication. Like any other wooden seat, the Oarmaster should not be exposed to direct sunlight and the elements when not in use.

Since you only contact the boat in three places, your hands on the scull's grips, your feet in the stretchers and your butt on the seat, you might as well make yourself as comfortable as possible. The hard wooden and composite seats in open-water boats are somewhat like the hard seat of a good racing bicycle. At first it is quite uncomfortable, but after awhile most people adapt. Some, though, never seem to find the seats comfortable, and there are several kinds of seat pads available to add a layer of cushioning. If you just can't get used to the seat, try a commercially available pad, or make one from foam rubber, closed-cell foam, or neoprene. Remember, if you use a seat pad that raises you in the boat, you will need to readjust your rigging. One hint: If you buy a pad that doesn't allow water to flow through, cut a couple of small holes to line up with the cutouts in the seat. That way you won't be sitting in a puddle.

▬ FOOT STRETCHERS

Foot stretchers tend to vary more from boat to boat than any other single piece of equipment, and can be the least comfortable of the three contact points. One trick to being as comfortable as possible is keeping the stretchers clean and free of salt build-up.

If you have leather clogs, rinse them regularly with fresh water and keep a leather preservative such as saddle soap or Armorall on them to keep them soft and prevent their drying out. Velcro straps can get quite stiff and abrasive as they become salt-encrusted. They should be removed from the boat regularly and soaked in fresh water to remove the salt. The metal or plastic heel cups that come with clogs and Velcro straps usually have small drain holes to allow sand and water to wash out. Many rowers find these holes inadequate and drill them out for better drainage. This is fine if you have plastic heel cups, but enlarging the holes in metal cups will violate the protective coating and allow them to rust. If you installed track shoes, they should also be rinsed off after a row in salt water.

Since the stretchers are in the lowest part of the boat, they tend to get the wettest. No matter how well built they are, they'll require a little extra care. Even if you're the only one using the boat, you won't want them to rust and freeze into a single position. Take them apart occasionally and keep the nuts and bolts properly lubricated.

Frequently the only wood on an open-water boat is located at the stretchers. If this wood is teak or shedua, it will probably be oiled when the boat arrives. Re-oiling the wood will take almost no time and will keep it bright. If the wood is mahogany or spruce, it was probably varnished at the factory. This means that once a year or so you will need to sand it lightly and apply a fresh coat of good marine varnish to protect it. Even if there is no other wood on the boat, the soles of your leather clogs are often wood, and these need the same care as any other wood.

If you store your boat outside and don't have a cover for it, toss a towel or something over the cockpit area to keep it clean.

▬ FINS

Fins and fin boxes don't need much preventive maintenance, but they do require a little thought. Some fins fit loosely in their boxes. If yours wobbles, you run the risk of losing it while you're transporting the boat, or rowing. The easiest way to secure it is marine-grade silicone. Squeeze a bit of silicone into the box, insert the fin, and carefully wipe off the excess. Use a strip of tape to hold it in place while the silicone cures.

The biggest problem with fins is that rowers forget they have them when they're moving their boats around. Fins can break with careless handling. Set the boat so the fin hangs over the edge of the dock, or block up the boat so that the fin is not supporting the boat. Setting down the boat hard on the fin can either break the fin or punch out the fin box. The former is annoying, the latter involves a rather expensive repair. Take care not to bang car or storage racks with the fin.

▬ ACCESSORIES

Everything we've discussed to this point has either come with the boat or is absolutely necessary for rowing. There's another group of components, one that varies greatly: custom additions. Before adding anything to your boat, consider it very carefully. Think about the maintenance it may require or the special handling it might mandate. Also, if your boat is an open-water shell, keep in mind that your cockpit space is limited. You won't want to add anything that will take up too much space or inhibit your movement as you slide through the rowing stroke. Be sure you need what you're contemplating, and remember, you'll have to expend the energy to row that extra weight around.

If you made the wise decision to order a suction-style bailer, it will require a little extra care in beach launching and retrieving. Be sure it is closed and locked both going into and out of the water. Don't drag your boat on the sand. You may want to use Armorall, or a similar product, on the bailer's seal, and at some point you might have to replace the seal itself.

If you go high-tech and install a Strokecoach, knotmeter, or other electronics, remember that electronic devices and water are natural adversaries. Any electronic aid, no matter how well it's designed to survive in a marine environment, will require a regular program of preventive maintenance, even if it's just cleaning contacts and replacing batteries.

I've never met a rower who bought a rearview mirror and liked it. Most seem to get used a few times and discarded. One serious problem with hanging something under the sill—as most mirrors are—is the difficulty it presents

Left: Looking at the boat's bottom, a bailer in its closed position. Right: Bailer in its open position.

in rough water. In choppy water it's not uncommon to have the oarlock submerged at times. Hanging a mirror under it will only provide more drag and more contact with the water.

Before you add something even as commonplace as a water bottle holder or a compass, consider how you get in and out of the boat and all your movements associated with the stroke. You don't want to cut or drill holes in the boat, mount a piece of hardware, and then find that your hands hit it at the catch, or your foot hits it getting into the boat. Also think about the ergonomics of using whatever you add. If you mount a water bottle holder so far aft that you have to take your feet out of the clogs and slide the seat all the way aft so you can stretch to reach it, is it really helpful? The same is true of a compass, Strokecoach, or knotmeter that's located so you can't read it. Also, ask yourself if something you plan to mount above the lip of the cockpit or protruding from the deck will affect the way you transport or store your boat.

There are a few accessories you can get that don't actually fit on the boat. One of the handiest of these is a pair of slings. Usually constructed of wood or PVC tubing and nylon webbing, slings provide a temporary place to keep your boat between car or boathouse and the water. A pair of sturdy, lightweight slings makes a convenient place to rig your boat, or wash it down without setting it on the ground. Most rowers build their own slings, but several companies offer slings, some beautifully crafted from hardwoods.

▬ THE HULL

Finally, there is the hull itself, which will be fiberglass, Kevlar, or of cold-molded WEST System construction. For our purposes, WEST System and

Kevlar hulls require the same kind of day-to-day care as "maintenance-free" fiberglass. Anyone who has ever owned a fiberglass boat knows it is not truly maintenance-free, and open-water rowing boats are no exception to this rule.

If you row in salt water, rinse the boat with fresh water after each row. If it's allowed to dry on the boat, salt promotes corrosion and forms a crusty film attracting dirt and grime. This film accelerates the deterioration of the gelcoat or, in the case of a WEST System boat, the varnish.

If you can't store the boat inside, cover as much of it as you can, and at least protect the cockpit and oarlocks. If the boat is stored outside through the rainy season, or in snow, store it upside down. If this isn't practical, leave the bailer open. Even if you can store it inside be sure to leave the inspection port(s) open. This will allow air to circulate through the hull, preventing condensation and drying out the results of any small leaks. If the boat is stored outside where this is not practical, remove the drain plug. This will provide some drying ventilation for the interior, but more importantly, it will break the hull's seal, allowing air movement. If you don't do this, some real problems are possible. In hot sun, the air inside your boat will expand, and if it's trapped, it can literally burst the hull. Even if this heat expansion doesn't crack the hull/deck seam, the constant stress caused by the expansion-contraction cycle will weaken the hull.

Depending on how often you use the boat and how it's stored, clean the hull, deck, and cockpit interior regularly with a non-abrasive powder, liquid cleanser, or special fiberglass cleaner. Once a surface is clean, a good buffing with a light-duty fiberglass car wax will bring back the luster it had when it was new. The wax will also add a thin layer of protection, which is very important if the boat isn't covered. One thought on waxing, however: If you wax the hull below the waterline it will slow the boat marginally through the water.

Since the boat's hull slides through oil and gas slicks on the water and occasionally grinds on beaches and docks, it requires something extra in the way of maintenance. Any dings must be repaired soon after they happen. If a ding is ignored, it will enlarge and suck up water, making the boat weaker and heavier. Once a ding is repaired with either fiberglass cloth and resin, chopped glass or foam and resin, or resin alone—depending upon its severity—it needs to be sanded down to restore the hull's fairness. Even if you have a professional make the repair (a good idea), you should do the final sanding yourself. Only the person who rows the boat will put in the time necessary to achieve perfect fairness. The sanding should be done in the same way a sailor would prepare the bottom of his racing boat. Use either a large sanding block or a fairing strip (a thin piece of wood or a chunk of foam flexible enough to conform to the configuration of the hull but firm enough to keep the sandpaper in constant contact with the boat). Start with sandpaper in the 220-grit range and work your way down to wet-and-dry 600 grit to finish the job.

Proper care and storage of your boat will slow the aging process, but eventually any gelcoat finish will start to fade. You can have your boat refinished with polyurethane paints, which will make her look like new, but surface preparation is demanding and these paints are tricky to use, so be sure you have the work done by a professional experienced in boat painting. If you've chosen a WEST System boat, the resins used in its construction are vulnerable to ultraviolet rays. It is vital to keep a good coat of UV-inhibiting varnish on your boat at all times. If you store the boat inside, or if it is well covered, you will probably have to do a light sanding and varnish only once a year. If she is left out in the direct sun and unprotected from the elements, more frequent refinishing will be necessary. If you damage and repair the boat, varnish the repaired area as soon as possible.

Maintenance of modern open-water rowing boats is not the time-consuming regimen it was with traditional boats. Most of today's boats require only a couple of minutes of care for every hour of use and a little more attention periodically. No special skills or great dedication is required—just a little time. The results in boat performance, longevity, pride, and retained value are more than worth the minimal effort.

■ ROWING CLOTHES

Like the components, the clothing you wear while rowing must be properly selected and cared for to allow you to function at your peak. If your clothes are too heavy or too binding they will inhibit you; if they are too loose, they can snag your hands or the oar handles. If you wear too much, you will be unnecessarily hot; too little and you will be cold.

In the past, few companies made clothing specifically for oarsmen. Things are getting better, but choosing clothes still requires some careful selection. Some "rowing clothes" available today are more fashion than function. Your rowing clothes should be both functional and comfortable while providing adequate protection from the weather, either cold or hot.

There are a lot of clothes you just can't wear while rowing. Slash and kangaroo pockets on jackets and sweatshirts—unless they can be zipped closed—can trap your thumbs when you push your hands away from your body at the start of the recovery. Some rowers solve this problem by wearing their sweatshirts inside out or backwards, but this tends to play havoc with the hood. If you want, you can row in cut-off jeans, corduroy walking shorts, or your old jogging shorts, but these are not the best choice. Jeans and cords take forever to dry if they get splashed and the seams can become a major irritant when you're sliding back and forth on a hard seat. While rugby and jogging shorts dry quickly, they have the same problem with their seams. Jogging shorts, and most swim suits, are also rather short and ride up when you sit down. They don't provide sun protection for your upper thighs.

Your upper body, which is more susceptible to heat loss, is also more exposed while rowing. Your head and trunk are up in the wind and spray. If you become cold, your muscles will tighten and you'll lose a lot of the swing in your stroke.

Find sweatshirts without pockets, or remove them, or add snaps or Velcro. Authentic rugby shirts are a great alternative to the sweatshirt, although they have no hood, which is not necessarily all bad. Some oarsmen prefer bicycling jerseys because they like the pockets sewn into the back. A good oiled sailing sweater is warm, but it's bulky for the protection it provides. It can be itchy, and may take a very long time to dry.

A good rowing jacket should be neither too loose nor too tight. A lot of rowers find the best jackets in camping and mountain-climbing stores. My best rowing jacket is actually a vest made by Patagonia. It has a flat nylon shell and a high-tech pile the company calls "Synchilla." It's tough, lightweight, and water-resistant. When it does get wet, it dries quickly. The large armholes do not restrict movement and the two slash pockets can be closed with heavy plastic zippers. The vest was not designed for extreme conditions, but it is loose enough that you can layer under it with a T-shirt and rugby jersey for added warmth. The only feature it doesn't have that I would like is a tail flap to protect the small of my back as I go down for the catch.

As with sweatshirts and jackets, the pockets of shorts can cause problems for your hands. Baggy nylon shorts are good—if they don't chafe or bind—but be sure they don't have wide pockets that balloon out to catch your thumbs. There are many companies selling what they call "rowing shorts." A pair of true rowing shorts should have a padded seat, high rise, and be long enough to cover at least most of your hamstrings. A common rule of thumb in rowing, as in other "leg-sports," is that the knees should be covered if the temperature is below 65 degrees, but this is a matter of personal discretion. Lycra tights, long the fashion in racing shells, are becoming popular in open-water rowing. They have the advantage of being warm and form-fitting but not binding. Even though they come in a rainbow of colors and patterns, select a dark color—either black or dark blue—because they will quickly become stained. Indelible black marks will appear on the backs of your calves where they contact the ends of the tracks when you're in the layback position. The traditional warm clothing of choice has always been sweatpants, also non-binding, but quite a bit looser and sloppier. If you row in sweats, remember the stains off the tracks are there to stay on your new Pierre Cardin or Halston sweatsuit. Some rowers are using the new neoprene shorts, which they say are good when it's cold and wet. They also provide a bit of padding.

If you row in an extremely cold climate, look into a pair of long underwear. Most expedition clothiers make some, and the new stuff is as far removed from the old, red wool longjohns as a Maas 24 is from a flat-bottomed work skiff. The new fabrics are lighter, more comfortable, and thermally efficient. There are several different types on the market, so look at more than one before you buy.

Some clothes are fine for a daily workout, but inappropriate for longer rows. For instance, the Lycra tights you wear for your early morning row can become uncomfortably hot on a long row, and they're impossible to get off in a boat.

For many oarsmen the key to dressing is layering. This technique is well known to those who live in the Northeast, where the weather can change dramatically in the space of an hour. It's not as well understood by those of us who live in parts of the country where the weather tends to be more predictable and stable. On the morning of the Around-Goat-Island Race in Newport, R.I., one year, the weather went from a sunny 70 degrees to wind, thunder and lightning, clouds, rain and hail, and back to sunshine—all before lunch. The local rowers didn't seem to have much problem with this, but the rest of us spent most of our morning trying to figure out what to wear.

The idea behind layering is to select several layers of light clothing appropriate for different weather conditions, and to add or subtract these as the weather changes. On a cold morning, you might put on a pair of tights and a top made of polypropylene, wool, Capilene, Thermax, or silk. These materials will hug your body and wick away sweat, which would chill you. For this reason, you won't want to wear cotton T-shirts next to your skin when it's cold. On top of your inner layer, add sweatpants and a rugby jersey and, finally, a vest and hat as an outer layer. As you and the day become warmer, start peeling clothes off. If it gets colder, or an afternoon breeze picks up, you slip the jacket or jersey back on. Make sure that you have room in the boat to store what you're not wearing, and that you can change easily in the confines of your boat. If you have to lie down on your living room floor to wriggle into a pair of tights, they aren't appropriate for a long row where you want to change them.

■ SOCKS, GLOVES, AND HATS

Some oarsman swear by socks, gloves and hats, others swear at them. If you think they'd make you more comfortable, try them and make up your own mind.

Starting at the feet, thick, warm socks are important in many climates. Whether you have clogs, Velcro straps and heel cups, or track shoes attached to your stretchers, a pair of good sweat socks will protect your feet from chafing and blisters. If you are going to wear socks for cold weather, go to a camping or mountain-climbing store. Modern climbing and sports socks are made from fiber blends that wick moisture away from your skin, provide more warmth for their weight and bulk, prevent blisters, and dry quickly when they get soaked. Remember, the farther up the calf they go, the warmer they will be. If you board the boat from the beach, tuck them in your waistband, then put them on in the boat. Wear a fresh pair of socks for each outing, especially if you row in salt water, which will stiffen the socks as they dry and attract moisture next time you wear them.

People new to rowing always ask about gloves—a subject about which no rower is ambivalent. Those who wear gloves say they keep their hands warmer, protect their skin, and provide a better grip. My former coach hated gloves. She claimed scullers should not wear gloves because they desensitized your hands to the "feel" of the oar in the water. Very few flat-water rowers wear gloves except in the coldest temperatures. On the other hand, quite a few serious open-water rowers have started wearing gloves. At first they tended to use traditional fingerless sailing gloves, the kind with a leather palm and mesh back. They became stiff after immersion in salt water and had to be rinsed and occasionally treated with a leather preservative. The mesh back provided no protection from the sun, so you had to apply sunscreen before you put on the gloves. Not made for rowing, these gloves didn't have a long life expectancy on the oars. Now, most wearers of gloves have switched to Thunderwear, which makes a rowing glove with a neoprene back and a leather-like palm called "Thunderhide." They are well made, last one or two seasons and seem impervious to the elements. If you want to try gloves, get a good pair and give them a long enough tryout to find out if you really like them or not.

Hats are a necessity. On cold mornings, a good hat helps you retain vast amounts of body heat; on hot days, it can save you from baking your brain. For the cold, I recommend a good knit cap rather than a sweatshirt or jacket hood. A hood can block your vision when you look over your shoulder; the hat turns with you. Woolen watch caps were the standard for years; they were warm but itchy. Now expedition clothiers, such as Patagonia, are making watch caps out of new high-tech fibers that are just as warm and don't itch. An added benefit is their array of bright colors. A brilliant red or yellow cap has to make you a little more visible on a cold gray day than the old navy-blue caps.

If you are looking for protection from the sun rather than for warmth, there are several options. A sun visor shields your face and keeps sweat out of your eyes, but does nothing to protect the top of your head, your ears, or the back of your neck. Mesh-back baseball caps provide good ventilation but don't protect you any better than visors. A full-fabric baseball cap protects the entire head, but it can get hot and still doesn't protect the tops of the ears or the back of the neck. Wide-brimmed canvas or woven straw hats offer the best combination of protection and ventilation. In a hot climate, or if you are sensitive to the sun, a hat of this type is essential to your rowing wardrobe. Look for a hat with good ventilation and a chin strap to save it from being blown off in a sudden gust of wind.

▬ SUNGLASSES

If you are going to wear sunglasses, spend the extra money for a really good pair. The new unbreakable frames and lenses pay for themselves the first time you sit on them. A keeper that lets you hang the glasses around your neck is a sensible precaution against losing your investment overboard. Some of the tighter keepers can also prevent the glasses from slipping down your nose when you sweat.

There are some very real health and safety reasons you should wear good sunglasses when you're on the water. Just as the sun can damage your skin, it can injure your eyes. Think of sunglasses as "sunscreen for the eyes." Good sunglasses should cut less than 20 percent of the visible light, otherwise it will be just plain hard to see. While allowing 80 percent or more of the visible light through, they should stop between 95 and 100 percent of the potentially damaging ultraviolet, infrared, and blue rays.

Current studies offer the most damning evidence against ultraviolet rays. Though less than seven percent of the sun's rays are ultraviolet, they seem to be the most harmful. Rowers are particularly susceptible to the ill effects of these rays, because water reflects nearly 85 percent of the UV rays striking it, as opposed to land, which reflects only around five percent. Studies point strongly toward UV rays as a major cause of cataracts, and, as exposure to the sun damages your skin on a cumulative basis, evidence shows the same is true with your eyes—each exposure to UV rays adds to the damage done by previous absorption.

A little less is known about the effects of infrared rays on the eye. While normal exposure may not cause permanent damage, it does cause the eyes to become hot and dry. This can result in eye fatigue and general discomfort. Some studies suggest that, as with UV rays, infrared damage may be cumulative.

Blue light is the latest of the three invisible lights to come under scrutiny. While there is no proof that blue light is physically harmful, it can be dangerous in other ways. The glare created by blue light can cause eye strain and, especially on the water, it can hide potential hazards. Brilliant glare off the water can conceal shallows, floating debris, and even a small boat.

Search for a quality lens. Either glass or plastic should be of "optical quality" and have a precision curve so that it doesn't distort. Hold the glasses up to an overhead light so that it reflects in the lens. If the reflection is evenly curved, then it's an optical quality lens. In color range you should look into the neutral gray or light brown tones, staying away from red- and yellow-tinted lenses. When you look at UV protection, you'll find that, unlike sunscreen SPF numbers, there is no standard numerical rating system with sunglasses. Look for glasses that cut 98 to 100 percent of these rays. Polarizing will help cut glare, which is both an important safety and eye strain consideration.

Several years ago I was rowing in Mexico and was about to take a shortcut between the land and an outcropping of offshore rocks. The shortcut would have saved me more than a mile on a hot afternoon when a mile seemed like a long ways. The sun was bright, and the water was as shiny and opaque as a sheet of beaten silver. I was wearing a pair of Hobie sunglasses with polarized lenses, which allowed me to see through the glare. I discovered the calm surface of my shortcut hid a bottom that was foul with boulders, some only inches from the surface.

Clothing and good dark glasses can go a long way in protecting you, but you will still need a good sunscreen. Many of us who started rowing in the 1960s, or before, have learned the hard way that sun damage can be very painful and costly. Study the different sunscreens available—you will want one that is waterproof, and you will want a high enough sun protection factor (SPF) to do some real good. Start with at least a 15 SPF, but if you are sun-sensitive, or have a history of carcinomas or melanomas, go with a higher rating.

▬ RAIN GEAR

In many areas of the country, if it rains you just don't go rowing. In other areas, if you let a little rain keep you off the water you lose a lot of chances to practice your sport. Rowers must choose their rain gear carefully. There's a wide selection of good gear on the market, some of it for bicyclists, some for offshore sailors, and some for mountain climbers. There is none made specifically for rowers. Good rain gear that suits the oarsman's purpose is not easy to find. The fixed-thwart rower definitely has the advantage in this department. Most rainwear is either too stiff and heavy to give the sliding-seat rower the freedom he needs, or too loose to stay free of the seat's wheels. A fixed-thwart oarsman can row in a poncho or heavy foul-weather gear. The sliding-seat rower must balance dryness against bulk and flexibility. As with jackets and sweatshirts, beware of slash pockets, drawstrings and loose tail flaps.

In heavy fog or light drizzle you can probably get away with lightweight, flexible mountain-climbing or ski gear that will keep you dry, yet still breathe. If you expect a downpour, you'll have to wear heavier gear. Be sure you can row in it before you buy it. A good bike shop will have a selection of touring gear that might just work for you. Some biking and sailing gear comes with strips of reflective material sewn on, and this can only be a help in limited-visibility situations. Avoid hoods on rain gear; they limit your visibility at the time you can least afford it. Instead, wrap a towel around your neck to prevent water seeping in, and wear a good rain hat.

Like your boat, your rowing wardrobe will require light maintenance. While rowing, you will get splashed, and if you row in salt water, your clothes will become encrusted with salt, which will draw moisture out of the air. When this happens, your clothing will become damp, cold, and uncomfortable. If you row in fresh water, your sweat will have the same effect, and it will become particularly uncomfortable under your arms and your seat. It doesn't take much time or effort to care for your clothes, but you will appreciate the difference when you row, and you will see the difference in your performance.

- 7 -
Basic Safety

WHENEVER you set foot aboard a boat, any boat, safety should be your first thought. You will be venturing into an alien, sometimes hostile environment. Aboard even the best open-water rowing boat, you will be in a relatively small and fragile craft. Your two most effective safety aids cannot be mandated by the Coast Guard, harbor patrol, or any other government authority: experience and common sense.

Experience includes knowing yourself and your boat, having a thorough understanding of local conditions, and preparation. Learning your own limitations and those of your boat takes time and requires constant reassessment. Your limitations change as you grow and become more proficient, and what you perceive as your boat's limitations will also change as you improve and accumulate more time in the boat. If you harbor any doubt about your ability to make a passage safely, don't attempt it. It's always best to err on the side of caution.

Before you take up sculling, safety and common sense require that you know how to swim. A rower who is secure in his swimming will be more comfortable around the water, more relaxed in his boat, and eventually will become a better oarsman. Get a physical checkup before you begin rowing. Most of us tend to put off routine checkups, so taking up sculling is a good excuse to see your physician.

■ WEATHER

When you first start rowing, you'll need to study water and weather conditions. As time passes and your experience grows, you will judge conditions instinctively, almost subconsciously. As an oarsman, you will have to consider more than whether it's hot or cold, choppy or flat. You'll have to take into account both air and water temperature, wind direction and strength, and any significant changes you might expect while you're on the water. Also think about current, and if there is tide, when it will change. When you make your decision to row or not to row, make it not only on the conditions as they exist, but with an eye to expected changes.

Consider normal wind patterns in your weather assessment: Does the wind regularly switch from offshore to onshore at a given time of day, or does it tend to shift in a certain direction as the day wears on and temperatures change? Does the wind fill in for most of the afternoon, then glass-off at sunset? If the wind changes, does it affect other conditions? For instance, will the chop change with the wind? Tide and wind also interrelate. If the wind and tide are running in the same direction, the surface is likely to be quite smooth, but if either changes, a short, vicious chop may develop. Obstacles can also appear and disappear with the tide; if the tide goes out, can usually submerged rocks or sandbars become threats?

Air and water temperatures will dictate how far from shore you will want to venture. If either is low, you will want to be conservative, for the danger of hypothermia in the event of a capsize would be great. In extreme conditions, 150 yards offshore may be too far.

Fog is a slightly different matter. Potentially dangerous, it requires that you evaluate conditions and make an educated guess. Knowing local weather patterns helps, but don't rely blindly on this "knowledge." The fact that the fog has burned off at 10 o'clock every morning during the past week does not guarantee it will burn off at 10 o'clock on the day you plan a long row.

In all but the thickest pea soup, you will be able to see where you're going, but don't stray too far from familiar landmarks. An onboard compass and a thorough knowledge of your rowing grounds are essential in fog. The real danger in fog comes from larger craft sharing the water with you. The skippers of larger boats, both power and sail, rely heavily on their radars when fog closes in. This is fine for them; they can read blips on their screens from the relative warmth of their cockpit or pilothouse. It's not so fine for us scullers. Sitting low on the water, constructed almost exclusively of fiberglass and wood, rowing boats produce almost no blip on radar screens. These tiny signals are nearly impossible to distinguish from the sea return caused by waves and chop. In the fog, you must row defensively—you can't rely on other boats seeing you.

Fog suppresses and distorts sound. In a thick fog a single sound can seem to come at you from all directions at once. This impairs the reliability of your hearing, one of only two senses you have for detecting other boats. Obviously your other sense, vision, is also limited by fog. While you may be able to see well enough to guide your boat at five or six knots, remember that the powerboater traveling four or five times that speed while staring intently at his radar screen can't see you at all. If you think you hear another boat, stop and make sure you know where he is and where he's going before you proceed.

If weather conditions are adverse but not prohibitive, lay your course wisely. For example, many oarsmen prefer to row into a headwind or against the current, tide, or chop on their way out, then turn and get the benefit of the push on the way back in. If the weather is predicted to worsen as the day goes on, assume the weatherman is right and act accordingly. You can always deal with weather that is better than expected. Thunderstorms in particular are a threat to your safety on the water. If there is even a hint that one is approaching, don't go out.

With weather and water conditions in mind, look at your boat. If your oarlocks are adjustable for height, tune them for the expected conditions. If you have different fin configurations, choose the one that best suits that day's water. Make sure everything is in good working order and don't procrastinate on your maintenance. If a component is looser or tighter than it should be, or squeaks when it shouldn't, it won't get any better out on the water. Balancing an open-water shell a half mile from shore while you try to work on your seat or oarlocks is not a good way to relax.

■ SAFETY EQUIPMENT

After you've made sure your boat is in good order, turn your attention to your equipment. You *must* carry a personal flotation device (PFD), not just because the Coast Guard says you have to, but because it's the single most important piece of safety gear available. Since you need one, get the highest rating there is—a Type I. All Type I, II, and III vests are designed to keep you afloat with your face out of the water but Type I PFDs do this best. If there's any chance that you will be rowing into the evening hours or in fog, tie a whistle and either a hand-held strobe or flashlight to your PFD. The sound of a whistle travels much farther than your voice, and is easier to hear over the sound of a motor. The light will help searchers locate you in the dark.

If you are rowing an open-water shell with limited cockpit space, a PFD can be lashed or taped to the deck aft of the cockpit. Many racers, concerned about the bulk of a full-size PFD, are carrying PFDs that are inflated by CO_2 cartridges. While they are compact for easy storage, they are very expensive and have yet to be approved by the Coast Guard. Be sure to remove the chemical that causes the PFD to inflate when it gets wet, so that it doesn't fill if you ship some water. Also be sure to secure it well to the boat.

If you are rowing a traditional design, storage is no problem, but the loca-

Mark Steffy racing, with a light and a PFD on his boat's after deck.

tion frequently is. Since a PFD is not a regularly used item, it often finds its way to the bottom of the boat and under other gear. Find a convenient, easy-to-reach place for your life preserver and keep it there. One oarsman from Washington state who rows a fixed-thwart dory ties his PFD under the seat, using very light line that he can easily snap with his hands. It's out of the way and always handy. Aboard my old Peapod, I kept the PFD under shock cords on the stern flotation compartment. It was easy to reach and kept me from loading too much gear in the stern.

Bailers are vital to both your comfort and safety. If you opted for a self-bailer when you bought your boat, great! If you're rowing one of the newer open-water shells you could probably bail with your cupped hands because the cockpits of these boats are very small, but stopping to bail is no way to spend your time on the water. In a traditional design, or a recreational shell that doesn't have a sealed cockpit, keep a conventional bailer aboard. Whatever you choose—large cup, cut-down water jug, or bucket—be sure you tie it to the boat. If you're swamped, you're going to want the bailer close at hand, not bobbing on the surface 15 feet away. There are also hand-held pumps that can void a lot of water in a very few minutes.

Before sunrise or after sunset, the law requires you be able to show a bright light, which normally means a flashlight. There are some great waterproof flashlights available today. Many are smaller, lighter, and far more powerful than older models. Look for one that you can store comfortably within easy reach and, if possible, get one that has a loop so you can attach a lanyard. If you regularly row after dark you might consider attaching a permanent or semi-permanent light, and there are some very good battery-powered units available at marine hardware stores and chandleries. If you install one of these lights be sure to mount it so that you are not looking into it, as it will destroy your night vision. If it has a 360-degree lens, use duct tape to obscure the sector that would be shining in your eyes. Even if you do add a deck-mounted light, don't neglect to carry a flashlight. Low on the water, a deck light can easily be missed by the skipper of a larger boat, but the directional beam of a flashlight can be aimed straight in his face.

A Walkman-style stereo has no place on a rowing boat. Your ears are nearly as important as your eyes in detecting another boat. After all, your eyes only have an angle of view of about 45 degrees, while your ears can hear 360 degrees. Unless you are *sure* you are alone on the water, don't wear headphones.

There is a wide variety of emergency gear available. Any good marine hardware store or chandlery will have a section devoted to safety equipment—strobes, whistles, flares, smoke bombs, air horns, flashlights, and more. Find out what your boat is legally required to carry and consider that gear to be the bare minimum. If you row an hour a day in a river or harbor, you probably don't need much, but as your rowing program becomes more ambitious, remember to cover all your bases, both day and night, sight and sound. Make sure that what you buy is Coast Guard-approved, know any expiration dates, and check all gear regularly to see that it is in proper working order.

Your boat may be scrupulously prepared and you may have ideal weather conditions, but the most important safety factor—you—still needs consideration. How do you honestly feel? Has it been more than a week since you were last on the water? Are you stiff or sore? If you don't feel 100 percent, take it easy. The time to assess your physical condition and abilities is before you go out. When setting distance goals, be a little conservative. If you are rowing with a more experienced sculler who wants to venture farther across open water than you are comfortable with, say so. Don't allow pride to lead you into a potentially dangerous situation. If you start your row and conditions deteriorate, don't be afraid to cut your trip short. Gordie Nash made two unsuccessful attempts before he completed the rough circumnavigation of the Farallon Islands off San Francisco. "You learn more from the ones you don't make," he said after his successful third trip.

■ FLOAT PLANS

If you row alone, file a "float plan." The longer your row, the more important a float plan becomes. If your daily row takes you around your local harbor, it is probably enough just to let someone know what you're doing and where you're going. When you start crossing miles of open water, your float plan becomes more important. Before you leave, tell someone—not someone you met at the beach while you were getting ready to shove off, but a responsible person who cares whether you live or die—what your plans are. Provide as much information as possible: where you plan to go, possible stopping points along the way, a description of your boat, and anything else you can think of. Supply this person with the telephone number of the Coast Guard or harbor patrol, then tell him or her when and how you will get in touch with them after your row. If you don't make contact at the appointed time, your responsible person should notify the authorities that you are overdue. It will be your responsibility to remember to contact them as soon as you return from your row. If you've asked someone to wait to hear from you, the least you can do is call promptly.

■ CAPSIZING

Should your boat capsize, your first priority will be getting back aboard. A traditional design is not likely to turn turtle, but will probably settle upright after pitching you out. She may, however, list to one side, depending on the amount of water she has taken. Her design will dictate your reentry procedure, but as a general rule you will not want to get back aboard by going over one side or the other. With no one to counterbalance your weight, the boat would probably reward such an effort by turning turtle. The best method for reboarding is usually over the stern, which is normally lower and frequently wider than the bow. Grab the stern with both hands, pull yourself up with your arms while you kick like crazy and you should have no problem slithering back aboard. Once you're in the boat, stabilize it and congratulate yourself for having had the foresight to tie a bailer to the boat.

If the boat does turtle, the drill will be a little more involved. You'll have to right it the same way a catamaran sailor rights his capsized craft—with your body weight. Maneuver the hull so that it's lying abeam to the wind, then swim to the leeward side. Use a knee or foot to press down on the leeward rigger or gunwale. This will force the windward side to rise. Grab the windward rail or rigger as it rises and hang your weight from that side. She should flip over, spilling a lot of water in the process. As she comes upright, be careful you don't get hit by one of the sculls. Once she's floating rightside up, you can go ahead and board as described above.

An open-water shell is more likely to turn turtle than a traditional design, but she will also be easier to right. Follow the same drill: position her beam-to, press down on the leeward rigger, and use your weight on the windward rigger to pull her over. Again, remember the sculls and don't get hit.

Getting back aboard may prove to be more difficult, as most open-water shells have less initial stability and far less room for maneuvering in the cockpit than traditional designs. You will probably want to come aboard over the bow. This will put you in the boat facing the right direction and you will avoid having to work your way around the riggers, which are usually braced aft, not forward. The reboarding procedure will be easier if the bow is pointing either dead downwind or into the eye of the wind; either will minimize the boat's rolling motion. Work your way up near the bow and pull yourself up so that you are straddling the boat. This should be relatively easy, most boats' fine entries provide very little flotation and the bow may actually sink under your weight. Once on the bow, use your legs in the water as if you were on a surfboard or windsurfer, they will stabilize you. When you're up and stable, grab the gunwales with your hands and pull yourself aft. As your weight moves aft, the bow will rise and the boat will become somewhat less stable, but having your legs in the water will help. When you reach the cockpit, straighten out the sculls and get them in the stable position before you try to bring your legs aboard. Once the boat is stabilized by the sculls, move onto the seat, put your feet in the stretchers, and either bail or open your bailer.

At her Open Water Rowing school, Shirwin Smith has developed an alternative way to reboard a turtled shell. She has graciously allowed me to include it here:

> Swim up to the rigger of the upside-down shell. This places you roughly near the middle of the boat. Push down on the rigger next to you; the shell will begin to roll upright. Smaller people, especially those rowing heavier, wider shells, may need to kneel or stand on the rigger. As the boat turns onto its side, reach up and pull back on the upper edge of the deck to help bring the boat all the way over. As the shell rolls over, most of the water will spill out of the cockpit, making it easier to turn upright.
>
> Once the shell is upright, move up next to the rigger, facing the middle of the cockpit. Take the oar on your side of the shell and position it perpendicular to the boat with the blade feathered. Hold onto the handle of that oar—you'll be pressing it against the seat deck—then grab the opposite edge of the deck and pull yourself partway across the shell on your stomach. The oar you're holding will brace the boat while you do this. A kick of the legs helps to propel you across the cockpit. From that position, about halfway across the cockpit, even the shortest sculler can reach the other oar. Position it perpendicular to the shell with the blade feathered, and hold both handles together with one hand.
>
> With both oars in your hand, the shell can be easily braced while you bring yourself the rest of the way into the boat, no matter how rough the

Shirwin Smith demonstrates the proper method for reboarding a turtled boat. (Continued on page 102.)

water is. Another kick of the legs and a pull with the free hand will bring your body across the cockpit. The oar blades will alternately lift high off the water while you're doing this, but just one oar blade on the water at any time is enough to keep the shell from rolling over again.

Once your upper body is completely across the cockpit, roll over and sit up, still holding onto the oar handles with one hand. Once you're sitting up, lean back toward the bow to give yourself a little extra room, and swing your legs over the rigger and into the cockpit. The taller you are, the more you'll need to lean back. While you're bringing your legs aboard, one hand is holding the oar handles and the other is on the deck, bracing you as you lean back. To get up onto the seat, continue to brace with one hand on the deck and put one foot down between the stern end of the tracks. Between the hand and foot you can lift yourself onto the seat. If the seat has fallen out of the shell, sit on the tracks and row with an arms-only stroke until you are next to the seat (it should be floating, but you might want to test its buoyancy in shallow water to be sure!). Pick up the seat and put it back on the stern end of the tracks with your feet on the deck on either side of the stretcher.

Once you're on the seat, get your feet back into the foot stretchers, open the self-bailer and row. You should be able to do all this in a minute or even less, in all kinds of water conditions.

Try both drills and see which works best for you and your boat. Practicing a capsize drill in calm, shallow water will make you more comfortable aboard your boat. Knowing you can get back aboard will ease your mind when you are offshore, and the knowledge will help you make better decisions whenever and wherever you row.

If you ordered shoes with your boat instead of clogs or straps, be sure you don't lace them too tightly. Otherwise, in a capsize, you might find yourself hanging upside down like a bat in a cave. The bat, however, has two advantages: It can breathe while it hangs there and can fly from its inverted position.

If something happens and you end up in the water, unable to reboard, *stay with your boat!* Anyone who has done any search-and-rescue work will tell you that a boat, even a small one, is far easier to find than a person. The boat will also provide some extra flotation and may allow you to stay partially out of the water. If you can pull just the top half of your body out onto the overturned hull, you'll be better off than you were in the water.

■ AVOIDING COLLISIONS

The greatest danger rowers face is being run down by larger vessels, and just about every other boat out there is a larger vessel. Even though your open-water boat may be quite long, her mass is small, and she offers very little protection. A good analogy would be a bicycle on a busy highway. In a collision, no matter who's fault it is, you lose.

Being narrow and low in the water, rowing boats are hard to see. Even small swells can easily obscure a rower. If you are in the path of the sun or moon, you don't have enough mass to show up against the light. As we said in our discussion of fog, even if the larger vessel is using radar, it probably won't detect you.

You must see other vessels first and anticipate their movements. Get in the habit of looking over your shoulder every 10 strokes or so. Since your boat is almost silent, you have the advantage of being able to hear other boats as well as see them. You can hear powerboats from a great distance, and even a sailboat makes quite a bit of noise. The sails in the wind, the hull moving through the water, and sometimes clattering winches all serve to warn you.

If a collision between a rowing boat and another vessel is to be avoided, in most cases it's the rower who will have to take the evasive action. You can't count on being seen by the operator of any other vessel. If the rare one does spot you, he probably won't understand the effect his wake will have on your boat and will speed up to cross your bow.

From three or four feet above sea level (eye height in an open-water boat) the oarsman's vision is severely limited. It's even more limited if there's a heavy ground swell running. The easiest ships to avoid are large commercial craft. You can see the upper works or running lights of a freighter, tanker, or cruise liner from several miles away. Watch the approaching ship to get a good idea of her heading and speed, then head somewhere else. Keep an eye on her in case she alters course. Whatever you do, don't try to race her. If she's cutting across your course, don't try to beat her unless you *know without a doubt* that the way is clear and safe and that it is better to go forward than backward. If there is *any* question in your mind, don't try it. Take a break, take a hit on your water bottle, and watch her go by. Remember, just because she missed you, you're not home free. At speed, some commercial ships can kick up a wave-like wake. Be sure you have allowed yourself plenty of room, and be ready to take the wake bow- or stern-on, whichever is best for your boat.

After commercial ships, the next easiest boats to avoid are sailboats. They're easy to see because of their tall masts, and they're usually slow. As a sailor, I would like to believe the average sailor keeps a better watch than his powerboating cousin, but experience doesn't prove this to be the case. One trick to avoiding sailboats is understanding their tacking and jibing angles. I once heard a rower complain that, no matter what he did to avoid it, "this damned sailboat kept zigzagging and heading right at me." In fact, the sailboat was simply short-tacking out the harbor's narrow entrance channel. Be aware of a sailboat's limitations, and you'll find it easier to avoid.

You can frequently see, or at least hear, large powerboats quite a way off, though they are often moving at such high speed as to nullify the advantage of seeing them early. As far as powerboats are concerned, the smaller they are, the more dangerous they are. My idea of a personal hell would be having to row forever through a pack of small aluminum powerboats driven by overweight, beer-swilling men in camouflage jackets trailing fishing lines. Small powerboats ride low in the water. Frequently the only way you know they're near you is by the sound of their motors. If there's a ground swell running, you'll have to wait until you are up on a crest to look around for them, and pray they're not hidden from you in a trough.

When avoiding any kind of boat, if at all possible, do not row across its bow. Doing this, you force the other skipper to react to what he *thinks* your intentions are. No matter who has the right of way, be prepared to yield.

If you work at expanding your knowledge of water and weather conditions, learn to accurately judge your abilities and the situations that could affect your safety, and take the time needed to prepare yourself and your boat, you won't have to spend much of your on-the-water time thinking about safety. You can't foresee every situation, but knowledge and thorough preparation can see you through almost anything.

- 8 -

Health, Fitness, and Rowing

THERE are two kinds of exercise: anaerobic and aerobic. For too many years, most people who worked out did so with anaerobic exercises, because few understood the benefits of aerobics. Anaerobic exercises are "start-stop" exercises such as golf, tennis, handball, baseball, and football. They do not place continuous demands on the heart and lungs; instead, they require high output intermittently, allowing the body intervals of rest. Aerobic exercise, on the other hand, places continuous demands on the body throughout the workout. Sports such as jogging, swimming, cross-country skiing, and rowing all are aerobic.

■ THE PERFECT EXERCISE

In addition to being an aerobic exercise, rowing offers benefits that most other sports do not. You can start rowing long before you can legally drive, and you can continue to enjoy it well into your eighties. Rowing does not have a high injury rate, either from contact (such as in football) or from punishing the joints (as in jogging). Sliding-seat rowing is a complete exercise, working the entire body, so you don't need to complement your rowing program with any other exercises. Sculling burns approximately twice the calories as jogging in a given period of time, and it puts you on the water, which many feel is the main attraction of the sport. Instead of dodging traffic and breathing exhaust fumes, you glide over the surface of a lake, river, bay, or the ocean, enjoying the immeasurable psychological benefits of the activity while working every major muscle group in your body.

Frederick C. Hagerman, Chairman of the Department of Zoology and Microbiology at Ohio University, wrote an article entitled "Rowing for Your

Health," published in *Rowing USA*, the magazine of the United States Rowing Association, from which he has allowed me to quote:

> Intensity (of exercise) need not be exceedingly high in order for the healthy individual to benefit from rowing; exercising at 65 to 75 percent of maximal work output is sufficient to elicit a training response that can be regulated by utilizing a target heart rate. Maximal heart rate can be estimated by the simple formula of 220 - age; a target heart rate for the desired percent of maximum can be calculated using the following formula: percent of maximum desired x (maximum heart rate - resting heart rate) + resting heart rate. For example, if a 30-year-old person with a resting heart rate of 70 beats per minute wants to work at 70 percent of his maximum heart rate, then 220 - 30 = 190, and .70 (190 - 70) + 70 = 154, the target heart rate. Thus, a heart rate of 154 should be maintained for the duration of the exercise if the desired training stimulus is to be achieved.

To realize the maximum benefit from rowing, you will need to do steady-state, long-distance workouts on a regular basis. According to Hagerman, "The duration and frequency of exercise are probably the two most important factors for improving physical fitness. The beginning exerciser should strive to exercise at least 15 minutes, working up to 30 to 45 minutes after 8 to 10 weeks of regular aerobic exercise. It is best to exercise at least four days per week, with the exercise bouts spread evenly over a seven-day period. If this schedule can be increased to five or six days per week, results are even better. It must be remembered that duration and regularity are very important, and that rate of work or intensity should be kept well below maximal levels. In this way, a person can maintain adequate physical fitness and, at the same time, keep fatigue and injuries to a minimum."

Discussing the physiological benefits of rowing, Hagerman continues:

> The ability to take in, deliver, and use oxygen is probably the best measure of physical fitness. Rowing (sweep) and sculling on a regular basis seem to be among the most potent stimuli for increasing oxygen consumption. Oxygen transport is largely dependent on the cardiac output, or the heart's ability to deliver blood, and is defined as the product heart rate (number of beats per minute) times stroke volume (amount of blood ejected by heart with each beat). Numerically, cardiac output at rest is approximately 5 liters per minute and can be increased by elite oarsmen to nine times this value during maximal rowing efforts.
>
> An individual beginning a regular sculling program might expect the

resting heart rate to decrease significantly after a period of four to six weeks. This is because the heart muscle is accommodating gradually to the increased work load, and, as a result, stroke volume increases. Since the conditioned heart can now deliver a larger volume of blood with each beat, it can become less rate-dependent and thus more efficient. It is not uncommon for the resting heart rate to drop from an average of 75 beats per minute to 55 beats per minute after some weeks of regular aerobic exercise. At the same time, stroke volume is increasing. Because the resting heart rate usually declines over time, it is important to monitor this rate regularly and readjust the target training heart rate upward accordingly to maintain the training stimulus.

We know that a workout program, no matter how well thought out and how rigorously adhered to, is only as good as the fuel we give our bodies. Exercise and nutrition must complement each other. Consult a nutritionist or read one of the many books on the subject. Since books on nutrition, health, and sports performance appear regularly, check with your local library or bookstore for the latest title. Before making the decision to change your diet radically, check with your doctor.

▬ THE RIGHT WORKOUT FOR YOU

Whatever motivates you to row—the need for a fitness program, the love of racing, the challenges of long-distance passages, or the desire to simply get out on the water—you'll want to take full advantage of your time in the boat. You will gain far more from a planned workout than from just going out and rowing. Even if you have no interest in racing and the phrase "fitness program" is repugnant to you, you and your rowing will benefit from a planned schedule.

Before getting in the boat, do some stretching (including at least the two stretches discussed later in this chapter). Once you're in the boat, warm up gradually. Don't jump in the boat and leave the beach or dock at full pressure—let your body get ready before you start pulling hard. Whether you're rowing sliding-seat or fixed-thwart, row for 10 to 15 minutes at quarter- and then half-pressure. If you choose to start with one of the technique drills of no-leg or no-feather rowing, that's great, but don't consider it part of your warm-up time. Your warm-up should consist of full-stroke rowing—five to seven minutes at quarter-pressure, and an equal time at half-pressure. Once you're warmed up, there are several ways to improve your rowing, but they all have two factors in common: heart rate and duration.

You won't want to do exactly the same workout each day. There are two reasons for this. First, you'll "plateau out" and stop gaining at the same rate.

Second, you'll get bored in the long run and lose interest. After all, how many times can you row the same course and maintain enthusiasm?

There are various routines you can use to keep up your interest while achieving maximum fitness. You can do a long-distance row (say, 12 miles) once a week and two or three hour-long rows the other times you go out. If a long row doesn't appeal to you, you can do different drills during your regular hour-long rows, or row to different locations.

Rather than simply rowing from point A to point B and back, or doing laps around a given course, you can row pyramids. Pyramids can be based either on time or number of strokes. In both forms, pyramiding is a useful technique—it keeps the mind occupied while it builds the body. To do "time" pyramids, warm up, do one minute at three-quarter-pressure strokes, then one minute at quarter-pressure, then two minutes at three-quarter-pressure and two minutes at quarter-pressure, progressing up to four or five minutes. Then work your way back down the same pyramid. Going up to five minutes and back in this way will result in a sustained workout of 50 minutes after warm-up. To do "stroke" pyramids, start with 10 strokes at three-quarter pressure, then 10 at quarter-pressure, move up to 20 at three-quarter-pressure and 20 at quarter-pressure, and so on up and down the pyramid. These pyramids will have the effect of a steady-state, long-distance workout because the light-work periods they include are not long enough for a full recovery.

If speed is your goal, interval work will be better for you than pyramids. Intervals involve getting your heart rate back down under 100 beats per minute before the next high-pressure piece. For instance, if you do a minute at three-quarter-pressure or higher, you'll need 3 to 3 $1/2$ minutes of slow, easy paddling to get your rate down before the next pressure piece. The better your condition, the sooner your heart rate will drop, but a 1:3 pressure-to-rest ratio is a good place to start. As with pyramids or any other technique, a conscientious warm-up period is essential for interval training.

Some open-water rowers, iconoclasts by nature, shun any kind of structured workout. They're on the water to row, not count strokes or take pulse rates. Some of these rowers train by balancing speed against endurance for an hour at a time. They go out and row for an hour, making note of the distance covered. The next time out, they try to go farther in the same period. This kind of workout works best for those who are inclined toward long-distance racing.

■ STAYING IN SHAPE

If you were a runner and you did nothing all week—no running, no exercises, no stretching—you wouldn't expect to go out on Sunday and run 10 miles and get anything from it. You would also expect to pay for it later. Rowing is no different. If you can get out on the water only one day a week, you are going to be miserable afterwards unless you do something to stay in shape the rest of the time. You may enjoy rowing so much that you are on the water five or six times a week, but you could still find exercise beneficial and stretching important. If you want to race competitively, you will need to augment your rowing program—your competition does. If your climate doesn't permit year-round rowing, you'll need some form of exercise program during the winter so you won't suffer when you start rowing in the spring. All the exercises discussed here are as valuable to the once-a-week rower as they are to the competitive sculler.

It seems that there is a gym or fitness club on nearly every corner, offering stationary cycles, weights, jogging tracks, swimming pools, and a wide variety of exercise machines. As an oarsman, you understand the need for flexibility along with a strong back, legs, and arms—and a powerful cardiovascular system. If you go to a club and explain to an instructor why you're there, he or she should be able to design a workout for your needs. If not, change instructors or clubs.

If you don't have a club near you, or you don't like the idea of working out surrounded by mirrors and people in designer tights, you can devise your own exercise regimen. Any stretching you do as part of your exercise program will help your rowing, but stretches borrowed from running and gymnastics can be particularly helpful. Whatever else you do (or don't do), there are two stretches that should be considered mandatory. The first of these will stretch your hamstrings, which are vital to getting the proper lean-forward during the recovery. To do this stretch, stand with your feet together, then bend at the waist, letting your arms drop and keeping your legs straight. Don't "bounce" to get your hands closer to the floor, just hang. The longer you hold this, the better, but don't force it—straighten up before you feel any pain.

The second stretch will work your back, important to both your lean-forward at the catch and, to a lesser extent, your layback at the release. Lie on your back and swing your legs over your head so that your knees flank your head. When you first do this exercise you may have to support your hips with your hands. As with the first stretch, don't force it, just let your body stretch into position. Remember, these are stretches, *not* exercises. Forget the old "no pain, no gain" philosophy; do these slowly and carefully, and let your body work itself.

There are some sports that you can practice in the off-season to keep in shape for rowing. If you can only row once a week, they will help bridge the

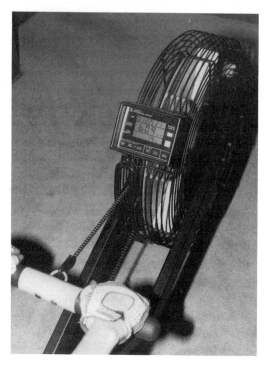

Using a Concept II Ergometer: The readout shows the rower is hitting 21 strokes per minute, has been rowing for 1 minute 22 seconds, and has burned 14 calories—a rate of 609 calories per hour.

gap between outings, and if you are training for competition, they will increase your stamina and strength. As long as your shins and knees are in good shape, running can be beneficial. As an aerobic exercise, running will build up your capacity for long-distance rowing. Jumping rope falls into this same category, with the cold-weather advantage that it can be practiced indoors. Cycling is also good—many racing scullers cross-train on bikes. If you live in a cold climate, indoor cycling on a trainer or stationary bike is a great winter exercise, but as soon as you can, get outside and ride; it will help your timing and balance. Swimming is also a good, compatible exercise, but you may find it more difficult to get your heart rate up.

Perhaps running three to five miles a day doesn't appeal to you, you don't want to spend the money on a bicycle, and swimming isn't possible or desirable. There is another exercise for you—running stairs. This is a great workout, takes little time, and can be done nearly anywhere. A few minutes spent running stairs provides as much benefit for your legs and cardiovascular system as a longer time spent running on the flat.

Finally there is the ergometer, the machine rowers love to hate. I don't know any rowers who really enjoy regularly working out on an erg, but sometimes it's a necessary evil.

If you live in a cold climate, an erg maybe the only thing standing between you and slothfulness. Please note, here we're talking about true ergometers, not so-called "rowing machines." There are dozens of rowing machines on the market, some available for as little as $70. I'm sure some are quite good, but I don't know of any that reproduce the true rowing stroke as well as the ergometers. The two best known are the units by Coffey and Concept II. Serious exercise machines designed for hard use, both these units sell for over $600. That's more than the cost of a new set of composite sculls *and* a Strokecoach. Before you even begin to think about owning an erg, find one in a gym or rowing club and try it out. Don't just sit on it for five minutes—put in some time over the course of a couple of weeks. You won't want to spend hundreds of dollars on one of these machines only to discover you hate it and never use it.

Both the Coffey and Concept II machines have electronic readouts to monitor your workout. They can be preprogrammed for a variety of different workouts. One of the biggest advantages the ergometer offers is the stroke count on the electronic readout. Once you've rowed long enough to ascertain exactly the right stroke rate for you and your boat to cover distance most efficiently, you can duplicate it in your workouts. In a very short time, you can train yourself to row an hour at a time without varying your stroke rate by more than one stroke per minute with a consistent energy output. Of course the machines, good as they are, can't take into account chop, current or wind, but it's a great way to teach yourself the proper rhythm and feel of rowing. "Suggestions for Further Reading," includes a book on the use of these machines with recommendations on a variety of different workouts.

The 22-Minute Drill

If you don't want to (or can't) run, jump rope, cycle, swim, or use an ergometer, there is something else you can do—The 22-Minute Drill. This drill works wonders for rowers at any level. Beginning and intermediate scullers can use it to get in or stay in shape, and it's a valuable tool for the experienced endurance rower. The drill can be done at home with minimal equipment (a bar and some weights) or at a health club with free weights. As the name implies, it is not a time-consuming workout, so it can fit easily into anyone's schedule. The drill works your respiratory system and increases your overall strength. The use of free weights, as opposed to weightlifting machines, has the added advantage of improving coordination, balance, and timing. Free weights also work opposing muscle groups, keeping them strong to prevent injury. Like rowing, when you start the drill, you should feel some muscle soreness. If you feel any other pain, stop immediately.

The 22-Minute Drill consists of seven exercises. After working your way up to the full drill, each exercise is repeated 10 times per cycle, and the entire cycle is repeated six times, all within 22 minutes. In order, the exercises are: power clean, bent-over rows, snatch, squats, dead lifts, military press, and curls. When you start, you will need to be conservative about the weight you load on the bar. Start light. A man of average size should start at under 40 pounds, but if you have no weightlifting experience, or it feels too heavy, go down to under 30. In the beginning, the amount of weight on the bar isn't as important as completing the drill. It will be better for you to do the entire drill with 20 pounds of weight on the bar than to quit after 10 minutes with 40 pounds. In the beginning, repeat the cycle only 3 times, because, as with sculling, the full 22-Minute Drill is something you have to work up to. No matter how long you've been on the program, do the 22-Minute Drill no more than 3 times a week at regular intervals.

After you do some stretching to limber up, check the clock and start the drill with the power clean. Start with the bar at your ankles, not touching the ground, knees bent, buttocks tucked under, and head up. Push up with your legs, then with your back, and your arms will carry the bar to your chin. Then slowly lower the bar back to your ankles. This exercise is directly related to rowing, and works your legs, back, and arms.

After 10 repetitions of the power clean, move to bent-over rows. With your legs straight but not locked, lean over so that your back is nearly parallel to the ground. Keeping your legs and back straight, bring the bar to your sternum 10 times. Bent over-rows work your lats (latissimus dorsi) and your lower back.

The third exercise, the snatch, starts with the bar on the ground. This is the only time the bar should touch the ground during a cycle. Bend your legs, pick up the bar, then thrust with your legs and straighten your back; your arms will finally put the bar over your head. Along with working your legs, back and arms, the snatch will improve your coordination and balance more than any other exercise in the drill.

After 10 repetitions of the snatch, move to the squats. Place the bar behind your head, resting it on your shoulders. With your back straight and head up, bend your knees to about, but not past, 90 degrees, then straighten your legs. Squats are like doing deep-knee bends, but with weights on your shoulders. Squats work the quadriceps, hamstrings, and gluteus maximus.

Dead lifts come next. With the bar in front of you and your legs straight, bend at the waist and let the bar hang from your arms. When the bar is just off the floor, straighten up, using only your back. This will work your lower back.

After 10 dead lifts comes the military press. Start with the bar at your shoulders, wrists bent, and push up. Bring the bar down below your chin, then push up again. The military press works your pectorals and biceps.

To complete the cycle, do 10 curls. You can either keep the same grip (palms toward your body) you've been using throughout the drill and do "French curls," or reverse the grip for more common curls. Whichever grip you choose, start with the bar at your waist and lift it to your chest, bending your arms at the elbows and keeping them right against the sides of your body. French curls will work the triceps and forearm muscles, while the regular curls work your biceps. These exercises represent the full drill and, at the beginning you should be able to complete three cycles in 22 minutes. If you can't, try reducing the weight, and don't worry if it takes a little longer than 22 minutes.

After you've worked your way up to six full cycles, start paying attention to the time. If you can run through the drill in less than 22 minutes, it's time to increase the weight. Add weight in small increments—no more than 5 pounds at a time—so you don't strain yourself. The 22-Minute Drill is hard work, but doing it regularly will make you a better rower.

Rowing's rewards are not limited to the physical benefits of the exercise. For several months I have been rowing three or four days a week with a woman relatively new to the sport. She started rowing for the fitness, and while she has experienced positive changes in her body, she says the biggest benefit is the peace and order her morning row brings to her life. This very real feeling is shared by most rowers.

- 9 -

Where Can Open-Water Rowing Take You?

IF PROPERLY chosen and cared for, your first boat can last a lifetime. The same craft you bought as a beginner will still provide hours of enjoyable, healthful exercise 30 years later. Of course there will be advancements in the sport, but if you're happy with your boat there's no reason to go out and buy a "better" boat. On the other hand, we all change with time, and what we want from our chosen sport may also change.

Many people take up rowing as a path to fitness, only to find that the means becomes an end in itself. The thrill of rowing—blending one long, powerful stroke with each successive one—combined with the beauty of one's surroundings and the mental and emotional peace rowing brings, supersedes the benefits of exercise. The more you row, the more you want to row, and the more you demand and receive from your rowing.

After some time at the oars, you may decide you wish to explore aspects of the sport that did not interest you, or that you weren't aware of, when you first started sculling. For instance, when many choose their boats, they can't even imagine rowing in unprotected waters, but when they get their first taste of it they wonder why they waited so long to try it. After becoming comfortable in their boat, many rowers want to try their hands at racing, and some are intrigued by the challenges of long-distance cruising. This desire to grow in the sport often means buying a "better" boat, which usually translates as "faster" or "bigger."

If you decide you need a "better" boat, go back and review all the reasons that caused you to choose your first boat. Many of them, especially the logistical considerations, will probably still be valid, and should be kept in mind along with your new goals. Many of the boats you checked out the first time will deserve a second look, and there will be new craft to examine and row. Your first boat will have been an invaluable learning experience, and should make selecting your second one much easier. You'll also find that your second boat does not involve as great a financial burden as the first. Kept in good condition, open-water rowing boats do not depreciate greatly; selling your first boat should go a long way towards paying for your second.

What follows is an introduction to the joys of expanding your rowing experience. The second half of the book will go into more detail on many of these and other subjects.

▬ RACING

If you decide to try your hand at racing, you may not have to change boats—at least not at first. Many traditional rowing clubs, where they have raced true racing shells exclusively, are yielding to pressure and have finally begun staging heats for open-water boats, which they insist on calling "recreational" boats. Frequently they offer starts for one-design classes, if there are enough boats of single design to warrant it. One-design racing is gaining in popularity, it gives rowers a chance to see how they compare to others rowing identical boats. These races are often handicapped by age, allotting a few seconds per year to the older rowers. At the 1989 Masters' Nationals in Oakland, California, one-design heats were offered for Maas Aeros and 85 rowers took part.

If there are not enough boats of a single design, open classes are offered. Open-class divisions are usually determined by the length (and sometimes weight) of the boats entered. Often one design or another will be favored by the luck of the draw, but this is not terribly important to the novice racer. In the beginning you are there to gain experience, not to win races. Races staged by traditional clubs are usually run over the same course used by their racing shells, so they are short (1,000, 1,500 or 2,000 meters), straight-line affairs on flat water. As an introduction to formal racing, this type of event can be a great learning experience. Racing in several events over a period of time will show you how your boat-handling skills, speed and strength have progressed.

Any kind of racing will require that you develop new skills while refining the ones you already possess. You'll also need to learn about race organization, order of start, restricted zones, and a variety of other details. This is most important if you plan to become involved in the very structured, formal world of traditional sculling races. Before your first race it would be wise to meet with the sponsoring club's rowing coordinator, coach, starter, or race committee chairman to learn how the race is organized before you go out on the water.

Whether you're lining up in lanes to do a 1,000-meter sprint, or jockeying for position behind a long line at the start of a 10-mile open-ocean race, your starting technique will be the same. The significance of the start in a short sprint is obvious—there's very little time to make up for a bad start, but your start will be just as important in a long open-water race. In an open-water race, where competitors aren't segregated into lanes, a good start allows you to break into the front rank, giving you clear water rather than having to row through your competitors.

At the start, take four to six quick strokes with just your arms. Although they are considerably weaker than the legs, the arms are much faster. These "arms only" strokes serve to break the boat's inertia and get her moving. Once the boat begins to respond, lengthen the stroke, going first to half-slide, then to three-quarter, and finally to a full slide, making your stroke long and strong. As soon as you've lengthened to a full stroke, pour on 20 full-power strokes (a power 20) before settling down to a lower but still powerful stroke rate. Don't let the adrenal rush of the start get the better of you, burning you out before you're halfway down the course. For most open-water boats, a rate of 22 strokes per minute is a good figure to start with, but experience will teach you what is best for you and your boat. Just remember, power and smoothness through the stroke is more important than racing up and down the slide.

Steering in a race is one of the skills you will need to develop, and a little different than the kind of steering you might do during your daily row. Unless you're rounding a mark at 90 degrees or more, you can't break stroke to pull hard on one oar. Instead, learn to steer by increasing the arc of one oar. On a straight course you will just be staying in your lane, and this kind of steering will be almost automatic. If you're rowing a long, open course with marks and protruding headlands, it will be more involved. If you're leaving a mark of the course to starboard, you will need to lengthen the stroke of your port oar. These will be gradual turns that require some forethought, not spin-turns that stop the boat. Extend the reach of your right hand for a couple of strokes, and feel the bow begin to turn. Depending on the radius of the turn, and your boat's turning ability, you may want to even up on the stroke for two more pulls, then reach out with your right hand again. It will take practice to learn to hit your apex, but it will come. Your turns will be wide, but you won't scrub off speed and you will keep a good, even stroke rate throughout. Some coaches will tell you not to increase the arc of the outside oar, but to decrease the arc of the inside oar. Try both and see which works best for you.

As you near the finish you'll need to evaluate your competition, but always make sure you row your own race. Don't let a competitor draw you into a sprint to the finish if you're not ready. Don't let someone else dictate your strategy—he could be starting his sprint too early and fade at the finish, dragging you down with him. Let experience and your body teach you when you want to make the kick for the finish.

If you think traditional shell racing is your goal, racing an open-water boat in flat-water races is a good way to find out without investing a lot of money in a fragile shell. Spending time at regattas will also allow you to see what different clubs have to offer. Most clubs have coaches, seminars, and club-owned trainers and shells for the use of their members. Many even have trailers, and will deliver boats to the regatta site for you. As a member, you will be able to avail yourself of these coaching services and soon be racing a trainer, all at minimal cost.

▬ TRAINERS

A trainer is the logical intermediate step between an entry-level open-water boat and a true racing shell. Trainers are longer, lighter, and narrower boats, and therefore considerably faster. The trade-off is that they are also less stable. Trainers share many performance characteristics with the new breed of advanced open-water singles, such as the Maas and Trimline 24s, though they don't have the open-water capability. The first time you sit in a trainer, you will probably feel as if you had never rowed sliding-seat before. A trainer will force you to refine the skills you learned in your first boat. Clean blade work, a controlled slide, and smooth, constant application of power will become very important all over again.

Just boarding a trainer demands a level of skill that most entry-level open-water boats do not require. Most trainers are built heavily enough so you won't put your foot through the bottom if you step in the wrong place, the same cannot be said of racing shells. The wrong step in a shell can be very expensive, and the experience you gain in a trainer will save you not only a lot of money, but also a great deal of inconvenience and embarrassment.

Getting aboard a trainer or a racing shell is much like boarding an open-water boat using one of the methods discussed in Chapter 4, but it requires more finesse and balance. Before attempting it, review these methods. In your open-water boat, your technique has probably become a bit sloppy. As you've become familiar with the boat you've learned to rely on its stability rather than perfect form. You will find boarding a trainer from the beach far easier than boarding from a dock.

Start by making sure both oarlocks are closed and locked, then push the seat forward to the release position. After you have squared the sculls to the hull and are sure the blades are flat on the water, keep a firmer grip on the oars than you may have become used to doing. The hand gripping the shore-side rigger should be prepared to give a little more lift than it would with your open-water boat. Step directly onto the seat deck with your water-side foot

Four trainers await the waters of San Diego's Mission Bay.

while you balance the boat with the sculls and lift the shore-side rigger. Shift your weight to the foot on the seat deck, lift the other foot, and swing it directly into the stretchers. Pretend you are boarding a shell and *do not* step into the bottom of the boat. With your foot in the stretchers, ease down onto the seat, then slip the other foot to the stretchers. Though it is possible to board most trainers in shallow water by straddling them, sitting down, and pulling your legs in, this method is not recommended. A trainer is designed to prepare you for a racing shell, and racing shells should not be boarded by straddling. The cockpit of a racing shell is surrounded by a splash (or wash) box, which is very lightly constructed. Straddling a shell and swinging your legs aboard can easily damage the box.

You board a trainer from a dock the same as you would an open-water boat, but with the same precautions you observe when boarding from the beach. The first time you get into a trainer, from a beach or a dock, have someone spot for you, standing by to grab the boat or a rigger for extra balance.

It will probably take three or four outings in a trainer before you feel as comfortable in it as you do in your open-water boat. If you've decided you want to race a shell, this time will be invaluable. Most traditional clubs regularly race trainers in their regattas, and you will learn a great deal rowing several heats in these events. Without the intermediate step of a trainer, the transition from entry-level open-water boat to racing shell would be difficult at best.

■ THE RACING SHELL

Many still think the racing shell is the pinnacle to strive for in racing a rowing boat. Racing a shell successfully requires both skill and finesse. In a shell, you refine your skills even more than a trainer, although at first you may feel you're taking two steps backward instead of one step forward. All the unease you felt the first time you sat in your open-water boat or a trainer will return. Each flaw in your stroke or balance will be magnified. Even though you may never have dumped either an open-water boat or a trainer, don't be surprised

The narrow cockpit of a racing shell.

if you find yourself swimming the first or second time you take out a shell. It happens a lot—it's nothing to be ashamed of. In fact one very fine oarsman confided in me that when he first started rowing a shell, he thought it was a biathalon—row a while, swim a while, row a while.

If you do take a spill, you must either get back into the boat or get yourself and the boat back to shore. For the good of the boat, the latter is preferable. If you can *safely* swim and tow the boat to shore, or grab the stern of another sculler's shell and be pulled back to the beach, do it. As soon as you reach shore, empty the water out of the shell and reboard. Analyze the reasons for the spill, but don't dwell on the accident or lose your confidence.

If you are alone, far from shore, or the water is dangerously cold, you'll have to get back aboard or at least pull yourself out of the water. First, right the boat; this will be easier than righting an open-water boat since shells are narrower and lighter. Simply grab an oarlock and lift. When you've got it up as high as you can, reach down and grab the splash box or stretchers and push the boat over the rest of the way. As the boat rolls over, a lot of water will spill out of the cockpit. Once the boat is floating rightside up, straighten the sculls and square them to the boat with the blades flat on the water. Locate yourself forward of the riggers, facing aft. If you are boarding from the starboard side, grip the oar handles with your left hand to stabilize the boat. Place your right hand on the seat deck, push down hard and kick hard. As your body lifts, swing a leg over the boat so that you are straddling her. Without letting go of the oars, fix yourself in the seat and swing your legs over the splash box and into the stretchers. Boarding the boat in this manner may crack or break the splash box or rip the soft plastic deck, but this can be repaired. Your safety comes first: When you're in danger it's no time to worry about the boat. Don't worry about the small amount of water that will be left in the boat; just row back to shore and safety.

It is very unlikely that you would not be able to reboard your turtled boat in the manner just described, but if you can't, the boat can still provide positive flotation and keep you out of the cold water. You can clamber out of the water with the boat turtled or upright. If she is upright, use the riggers to pull yourself up and across the cockpit. If she is turtled, you can straddle her the way you would a surfboard or windsurfer, with your legs in the water for balance. The object is to keep as much of your body as possible out of the water—hypothermia is your worst enemy in cold water. Being on top of the boat will keep you warmer while making you more visible. And remember, never leave your boat. None of this is intended to scare you away from racing shells. They are difficult to master, but if you want to row flat-water, they are well worth it.

If you've enjoyed rowing a club-owned shell in a few races, it may be in your best interest to buy your own boat. Like all high-performance racing equipment, be it car, motorcycle, or sailboat, a shell reacts to the subtlest changes in tuning, and minor alterations of oarlock pitch or height will make a major difference in how the boat feels. As your skill improves, you will become more sensitive to each such change, and before rowing the club's shell you will have to invest considerable time retuning it to suit your body and style. It can be a very frustrating way to begin your day, working on a boat while beautiful flat water goes to waste. There is also the problem of fitting your schedule around those of other members' when you are rowing a shared boat.

If you decide you must have a shell, be prepared to pay heavily for the privilege of joining rowing's elite. Racing shells cost upwards of $3,000, and your new acquisition will also require more careful handling and specialized maintenance than an open-water boat. On the other hand, rowing offers no purer thrill than pulling hard across mirror-smooth water in a well-found racing shell.

▬ OPEN-WATER RACING

If you've done a few heats down the lanes in your open-water boat and decided that straight-line sprint racing isn't for you, there are other areas to investigate. Some builders, dealers, and rowing schools stage regattas—many with one-design classes—and rowing seminars. These are usually less formal events than traditional rowing club regattas. Typically, the races are run off the beach from point to point or around a convenient landmark or buoy. They are longer than the traditional sprints and are run in less-protected waters.

These regattas and seminars attract scullers whose skill levels and back-

rner of Nash's chart; the
water are great boats to
gn classes racing within
re rewarding.

less demanding, skills
rger role, and you will
and learning to pace
ody in a 1,000-meter
ng left for the kick.
regattas already have
Rowing Race around
allenge; in the High
gatta, in the Pacific
scullers from more
amarathon of row-
e crown. Between
open-water rower
l.

ou, but you did
uise the course,
y from a race.
of stroking past
o. This is ideal
ground swells,
ough enough
om to carry a

ree factors—
boat. Long-
he time. On
nd, spend a
ach to San
ed to Baja
shore and
cruise the
d passage
Waterway

y hard-core racers at these
an at traditional rowing club
camaraderie, fun, and learn-

g, a new form of rowing club is
t by traditional clubs. This new
oes not always offer the facilities
do have boathouses, club-owned
nly a small hard-core membership
cruises. After a race on Lake Tahoe,
open-water rowers are not "a group,
s is one of the factors that make each
g. What these clubs may lack in tradi-
e up for in enthusiasm.
new genre of rowing club stages longer
ter boats and the men and women who
egattas include one-design classes within
wing you to "run what you brung."
vater clubs, anywhere from three to more
y of conditions, but almost all are staged on
long and short courses offered, and a cruis-
A sculler new to racing can choose the short
vaters in company with others, while the hard-
se. Most of these events include a post-race pic-
erienced rowers a chance to mix with the old
ers are usually proud to show off their boats and
After the race the beach becomes an impromptu
ted can often find themselves rowing two or three
noon.
branch of the sport is where you want to compete,
re doing well and look into your own "better" boat.

Don't just look at the boats in the lower right-hand co
Trimline 24 and Maas 24. The fastest 24-footers on the
row, but they are demanding. Look also at the one-des
fleets in your area. You may find this type of racing mo

Open-water racing requires different, though no
than flat-water racing. Tactics and boathandling play a l
need to learn some rudimentary navigation. Stamina
yourself are also vital—it's one thing to drain your b
sprint, it's another to row 10 miles and still have someth

While open-water racing is relatively new, many of the
become classics. In Newport, R.I. there is the Small Boat
Goat Island; at Cape Ann, Mass., there is the Blackburn Ch
Sierras competitors row the Lake Tahoe North Shore Re
Northwest the Great Cross Sound Rowing Race attracts
than 1,000 miles away, and in Southern California, the ult
ing, the Catalina to Marina del Rey race is the jewel in th
Santa Cruz and San Francisco, there is a full calendar—an
could race nearly every weekend from early spring to late fa

▬ OPEN-WATER CRUISING

If you've tried a couple of races and decided they're not for
enjoy the atmosphere, you might try joining with those who cr
or become involved with a cruise that is planned separate
Cruising is more like going for a long row with friends; Instead
small inlets and coves, you can take the time to explore as you g
for your open-water boat; it was designed to take choppy water,
and waves reflected off rocks. It's maneuverable, and probably
to be beached so you can get out and explore. You'll have ro
lunch and some different clothes in the cockpit.

The length of your proposed journeys will be determined by th
your ability, your level of preparation, and the suitability of your
distance rowing cruises are more than feasible; they take place all t
the West Coast, people regularly row the 30 miles to Catalina Isla
day or two, and row back. The 60-mile journey from Newport Be
Diego is also popular. Each year more and more rowers are attrac
California's Sea of Cortez, where they can row past the desert
deserted islands. In the Pacific Northwest, rowers take vacations to
San Juan Islands, and each summer at least one rower takes the inlar
to Alaska. In the South, the Gulf of Mexico and Florida's Inland

Women's singles competition at Lake Tahoe.

grounds vary widely. While you will meet many hard-core racers at these events, the competition is generally less intense than at traditional rowing club regattas. The focus at these events is usually on camaraderie, fun, and learning, rather than strictly on competition.

With the rising interest in open-water rowing, a new form of rowing club is emerging to fill the needs of scullers not met by traditional clubs. This new breed of rowing club is usually smaller and does not always offer the facilities of the more-established clubs. While some do have boathouses, club-owned boats, coaches, and seminars, many have only a small hard-core membership that has come together to stage races and cruises. After a race on Lake Tahoe, competitor Don Wetterstrom noted that open-water rowers are not "a group, but more a hoard of individuals," and this is one of the factors that make each open-water race unique and interesting. What these clubs may lack in tradition and facilities, they more than make up for in enthusiasm.

Rather than traditional sprints, the new genre of rowing club stages longer races designed to challenge open-water boats and the men and women who row them. Though some of these regattas include one-design classes within the fleet, they are open events, allowing you to "run what you brung."

The longer races of the open-water clubs, anywhere from three to more than 30 miles, are held in a variety of conditions, but almost all are staged on open water. Often there are both long and short courses offered, and a cruising class is frequently an option. A sculler new to racing can choose the short course or cruise over the same waters in company with others, while the hard-core racers go for the long course. Most of these events include a post-race picnic, which gives the less experienced rowers a chance to mix with the old guard. The experienced scullers are usually proud to show off their boats and let other people row them. After the race the beach becomes an impromptu boat show and those interested can often find themselves rowing two or three different boats in the afternoon.

If you've decided this branch of the sport is where you want to compete, evaluate the boats that are doing well and look into your own "better" boat.

Don't just look at the boats in the lower right-hand corner of Nash's chart; the Trimline 24 and Maas 24. The fastest 24-footers on the water are great boats to row, but they are demanding. Look also at the one-design classes racing within fleets in your area. You may find this type of racing more rewarding.

Open-water racing requires different, though no less demanding, skills than flat-water racing. Tactics and boathandling play a larger role, and you will need to learn some rudimentary navigation. Stamina and learning to pace yourself are also vital—it's one thing to drain your body in a 1,000-meter sprint, it's another to row 10 miles and still have something left for the kick.

While open-water racing is relatively new, many of the regattas already have become classics. In Newport, R.I. there is the Small Boat Rowing Race around Goat Island; at Cape Ann, Mass., there is the Blackburn Challenge; in the High Sierras competitors row the Lake Tahoe North Shore Regatta, in the Pacific Northwest the Great Cross Sound Rowing Race attracts scullers from more than 1,000 miles away, and in Southern California, the ultramarathon of rowing, the Catalina to Marina del Rey race is the jewel in the crown. Between Santa Cruz and San Francisco, there is a full calendar—an open-water rower could race nearly every weekend from early spring to late fall.

▬ OPEN-WATER CRUISING

If you've tried a couple of races and decided they're not for you, but you did enjoy the atmosphere, you might try joining with those who cruise the course, or become involved with a cruise that is planned separately from a race. Cruising is more like going for a long row with friends; Instead of stroking past small inlets and coves, you can take the time to explore as you go. This is ideal for your open-water boat; it was designed to take choppy water, ground swells, and waves reflected off rocks. It's maneuverable, and probably tough enough to be beached so you can get out and explore. You'll have room to carry a lunch and some different clothes in the cockpit.

The length of your proposed journeys will be determined by three factors—your ability, your level of preparation, and the suitability of your boat. Long-distance rowing cruises are more than feasible; they take place all the time. On the West Coast, people regularly row the 30 miles to Catalina Island, spend a day or two, and row back. The 60-mile journey from Newport Beach to San Diego is also popular. Each year more and more rowers are attracted to Baja California's Sea of Cortez, where they can row past the desert shore and deserted islands. In the Pacific Northwest, rowers take vacations to cruise the San Juan Islands, and each summer at least one rower takes the inland passage to Alaska. In the South, the Gulf of Mexico and Florida's Inland Waterway have become rowers' territory. Farther north on the Atlantic coast, the Chesapeake Bay and the Delaware and Potomac rivers attract touring scullers. The Connecticut shore of Long Island Sound is a cruiser's paradise, with innumerable coves and rivers to explore. In late spring and summer, rowers take to the open ocean to explore the coasts of Massachusetts and Maine. In England you can rent a traditional boat to row from hotel to hotel on the Thames; and in Germany, Wanderrudern (literally "wander rowing") is attracting enthusiasts.

Just as racing requires new skills, so does cruising. Instead of power and speed, cruising requires planning, logistics, and endurance. The three factors of your success—your ability, your preparation, and the suitability of your boat—rank nearly equal in importance. If you have the ability and are well prepared, your boat is probably the least important element of the three. That is not to say you should attempt to row from Vancouver to Alaska in a leaky Sabot with a pair of six-foot oars. Your boat must be sound and chosen with the worst conditions you expect to encounter in mind, but it doesn't have to be the newest and fastest.

As a cruiser, your idea of a "better" boat may be very different from a racer's. Cruisers need load-carrying capacity and seaworthiness more than they need raw speed. Traditionally they have favored shorter, sturdier, beamier boats with the lines of the early workboats: dories, peapods and Whitehalls. Built from modern materials, and fitted with either sliding seats or fixed thwarts, these copies of traditional craft are great cruisers. With their greater interior volume they can easily accommodate a cruiser's food, water, and camping gear. Though not nearly as fast as a modern open-water rowing shell, a good traditional replica is far more seaworthy. While the open-water racer may be looking at the Maas Aero, Trimline 24, or Maas 24 as his "better" boat, the cruiser will work his way back to the left and farther up Nash's chart to find the Appledore Pod and New York Whitehall. This doesn't mean the cruiser won't be able to do the occasional race—most open-water races have a class for traditional designs. It also doesn't mean the racer will not be able to take a cruise if he wants to. One summer Chris Maas and his friend Greg Shell strapped waterproof bags to the decks of their Maas Aeros and cruised the Pacific Coast of Canada.

You don't need to race a shell over a 2,000-meter course, race an open-water shell across 30 miles of open ocean, or cruise 200 miles to grow as a sculler. Every time you take your boat out, you can improve. You can get the most out of each workout by making each catch, stroke, release, and recovery as perfect as you possibly can. Feeling yourself becoming a better boathandler and more efficient sculler is a better indicator of progress than buying a "better" boat.

- 10 -
Open-Water Rowing:
Breaking In

I N THE late 1980s there were articles in several boating magazines about long-distance trips under oars. *Small Boat Journal* ran a three-part piece by John Garber on his 150-mile row along the Maine Coast. *Northwesting* published a three-part feature by Chris Cunningham on his journey down the Ohio and Mississippi rivers from Pittsburgh to Florida in a home-built rowing boat. People wrote of rowing from Washington State to Alaska and in the Catalina to Marina del Rey race. Endurance rowing moved into the mainstream, and *Outside* magazine featured a cover picture of Ned Gillette and the boat he planned to row to Antarctica. Books appeared about transatlantic and transpacific rowing adventures.

In the 1990s, interest is still growing. Rowing shows up with increasing regularity in general interest and sports magazines. But what does all this recognition mean to the average rower? Perhaps the biggest advantage is that the rower undertaking a long journey under oars is not automatically dismissed as a nut!

One of the beauties of rowing is that it is an intensely personal sport. A hundred different people can row a hundred different types of boats for a hundred different reasons and none of them is wrong. You can row what you want for your own reasons, and your own goals.

Endurance rowing is the least structured facet of the sport; it means something different to each practitioner. To the person who uses his rowing boat for exercise and regularly does a lap or two around the harbor, endurance rowing could be a nine- or 10-mile row in the open ocean. To someone accustomed to rowing nine or 10 miles, an endurance row could be 15 or 20 miles to another harbor or launching area. The second half of this book seeks to encourage you to expand your rowing horizon, to demand and get more from your boat and yourself. Whether the goals you pursue take you 10 miles down the bay, the length of the Intracoastal Waterway, or across an ocean is of secondary importance. The satisfaction and growth come from accepting the challenge. Remember Gordie Nash's comment after he finally succeeded in rowing the rough 60-mile trip from San Francisco to the Farallon Islands and back: "You learn more from the times you don't make it." Set your own goals, and succeed or not, the effort will reward itself.

▬ HOW I GOT STARTED

Zen-master Shunryu Suzuki once said, "The destination is important, but it is the journey that is the ultimate reward." He could have been talking about rowing. My own first long-distance row was a comedy of errors and—if reaching your goal is how a cruise is to be judged—a failure. On the other hand, that journey taught me more than any rowing adventure I have enjoyed in the nearly 30 years since. I was 17 at the time, with all the self-assurance and immortality that youth imparts. I had been spending long hours rowing a fiberglass Schock dory from the rocky cove beneath my grandmother's Laguna Beach home.

The dory, which lived upside down on a wooden rack built onto a rock, was a nearly perfect boat for going in and out through the surf. Fifteen-and-a-half feet long with a four-foot beam, she was designed with the lines of a Gloucester dory. At 120 pounds, she was (for the time) reasonably light, and her flared

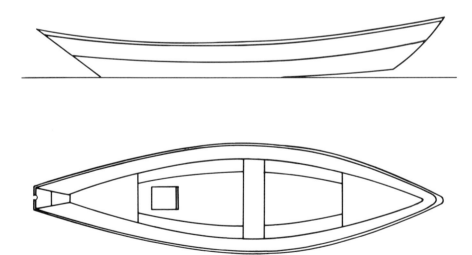

A Schock dory, the boat the author used for his first long-distance row.

sides kept her very dry even while going through the surf. She had a fixed mahogany thwart, and molded-in bow and stern compartments provided positive flotation. Power was supplied by a pair of 7-foot, straight-bladed spruce oars turning in a pair of Wilcox-Crittenden open horns.

My daily rowing could not be considered training; it was fun. There were short rows out to the offshore rocks, longer ones to other coves to visit friends, an occasional 16-mile round trip to Newport Harbor, and sometimes just a day spent in the boat rowing for the sheer pleasure of it. I had owned the boat for about two years, and probably put 2,000 miles on it before my first real adventure. I had learned a lot and of course I thought I knew all there was to know.

I was intrigued after a friend's 100-mile row and decided to attempt a row from Laguna Beach to San Diego, about 60 miles down the coast. The decision to go down, rather than up the coast was probably subconsciously based on familiarity with the prevailing northwesterly winds. In retrospect, I doubt that I gave any conscious thought to the winds—I certainly didn't give anything else about the trip much thought. I arranged for a friend to hang near her telephone so she could drive down and pick me up when I called, gathered a modicum of gear and provisions, and was off.

I had the good sense to leave at dawn, while the wind and sea were calm. In the early 1960s, Oceanside was the only harbor between Laguna Beach and the twin harbors of Mission Bay and San Diego. In fact, much of the coastline between Laguna Beach and San Diego was made up of surfing beaches, many controlled by the inhospitable Marine Corps. Conveniently located 30 miles south of my jumping off point, Oceanside promised to be a perfect spot to spend the single night planned for the voyage.

Provisioning consisted of going through the garage and grabbing gear, then raiding my grandmother's refrigerator. My small bailer would have been totally inadequate had I really needed it, and I don't remember a life preserver being aboard. I do know that I had an ample supply of chocolate chip cookies. One's priorities change as one ages.

I didn't make Oceanside that first day. I had brought a surfboard, strapped athwartships across the stern, and stopped off at Lower Churches (one of the surf spots where land access was denied by the Marines) to ride some waves. By the time I got back on task I had lost several hours of rowing time. Darkness found me about seven miles north of my day's goal. I didn't want to row into a strange harbor at night to look for a place to sleep; neither did I like the idea of landing on an unknown beach on a Marine base in the dark. There was only one other option: I spent the night in the boat. This was when I first realized how pitifully ill-prepared I was.

From Churches south I had been paralleling the outside edge of dense kelp beds. Understanding there was a very real chance of being run down in the night by a passing boat (there were no lights on the dory), I slowly rowed deep into the kelp. The theory was that speeding power boats would avoid the kelp, and, by extension, me. Of course there was no anchor, so to hold my position, I tied a short bow line to a heavy kelp stalk. As soon as I'd made the dory fast I became aware of the pounding of surf on the beach 150 yards away. I was tied to a piece of kelp by a line that would probably chafe through the seaweed. I was between an unknown beach with breaking surf and the open sea where there was the danger of being run down by a larger vessel. I had no light, no way to heat food or water, and inadequate clothing. The only bright spot was that I was reasonably sure the sun would come up the next morning.

There was no room to stretch out in the dory, and I doubt that sleep would have come anyway. I was constantly worried that the line would cut the kelp and I would be washed ashore in the breaking surf, to be accosted by gun-toting Marines who would treat me as a trespasser.

To many, Southern California is thought of as a land of perpetual warmth. I understand that a temperature of 49 or 50 degrees is not life-threatening, but when it's accompanied by heavy, wet fog, and you're spending the night in a small boat, wearing still-wet swimming trunks, a T-shirt, and light jacket, eating a soggy sandwich and chocolate chip cookies, it is less than pleasant. It was a long night.

The sun did come up and the voyage continued. If I had been wise, I would have pulled into Oceanside and called for a pickup. I rowed on while I was still feeling fresh and strong, reveling in the smooth water and the warmth of the morning sun. Besides, my pride was at stake—I had told people I was going all the way to San Diego. The northwesterly filled in early that day, giving me an extra push, and doubling my commitment to make the complete trip. If I had wanted to turn and go back to Oceanside I would have been rowing into ever increasing seas and wind.

By the time I was ten miles south of Oceanside, the chop was three to four feet and breaking, and the wind was blowing over 15 knots. Striking the starboard stern quarter of the dory, the wind and waves drove me off course, forcing me to correct constantly. The occasional wave also broke over the open stern and I had to keep the boat from broaching while I worked my tiny bailer.

Nineteen miles South of Oceanside I was wet, tired, and wishing I had never left Laguna Beach. Then I recognized the red tile roof of the La Jolla Beach and Tennis Club. I had 11 miles to go to reach the entrance of San Diego Harbor, then another four or five to get to my pickup point.

With two strong pulls on my starboard oar I gave up the journey. The beach at La Jolla is shallow and waves break well out to sea, but they are not powerful and I had rowed through them several times before. I impatiently waited through a set, then rowed hard after a smaller wave. The wave broke, sucking me along with it, and I rowed quickly through the white water, watching the next wave build behind me. It broke 20 yards behind the dory, and by the time its white water caught up with me, it had lost much of its punch, giving a gentle push towards the beach. Once ashore I called my friend to come collect me and slept on the warm sand until she arrived.

Every time I start on a row of any length I think of that first long trip and all the things I didn't have, such as a spare oar, first-aid equipment, life preserver, adequate bailer (and a spare), compass, lights, proper clothing, anchor—the list seems almost endless. The most important lesson I learned from that trip was that lesson of preparation.

■ THE STEPPING-STONE APPROACH

Thoughtful, knowledgeable preparation can not only make the difference between comfort and misery, but between success and failure, and, in the extreme case, life and death. Sylvia Cook, in the book *Oars Across the Pacific*, written with John Fairfax, says, "I learned that more than half the success of an operation of this nature is due to careful and extensive planning and preparation." You don't have to be rowing from San Francisco to Australia, or even Laguna Beach to San Diego, to enjoy the rewards of preparation.

One of the great joys of long-distance rowing is that planning and getting ready can be as exciting and rewarding as actually doing the trip. Responsibility for success on the water can be divided equally between the preparation of the oarsman and his craft. It doesn't do you any good to be in peak physical condition if your boat and provisions aren't ready, and the best-prepared boat and gear will not make up for weak arms, legs or back. Preparation of equipment parallels training, and they are both gradual learning experiences.

One of the most important considerations for a neophyte endurance rower is a realistic goal. If all your rowing time has been spent on a sheltered lake or within the confines of a harbor, it isn't realistic to plan a long open-water voyage or race as your first endurance row. There's nothing wrong with setting a long-distance passage as your ultimate goal, but it should be prefaced by more attainable interim goals. I call this the stepping-stone approach to distance-rowing.

If an oarsman wanted to get into open-water racing, a good long-term goal would be The Great Catalina to Marina del Rey Rowing and Paddling Derby. This open-ocean challenge should not be attempted by anyone who hasn't adequately trained. Even the experienced rower will want to work up to the Catalina race by setting a series of interim goals. There have been many different approaches to the Catalina race, but those with the longest periods of training and prepara-tion always seem to do best. A beginning racer, no matter how great his rowing experience, would want to start with some of the shorter open-ocean races, advancing in distance as his skill and knowledge increase. Each race would be a stepping-stone toward Catalina.

The same is true of cruising under oars. A five-day cruise through Puget Sound's beautiful San Juan Islands is a wonderful long-term goal, but not the best choice for a first long-distance row. A good intermediate goal might be a day-long coastal row or an overnight excursion to a nearby island. This could be followed by a longer, two-night trip. Each interim goal is rewarding in itself, and brings you one step closer to the long-term challenge.

As you learn more about your boat, you might decide to modify it. Modifications will undoubtedly lead to thoughts of the next boat, and everything you learn will help you make the decision when it comes time to buy a new one.

Some changes you make in tuning, clothing, and gear will undoubtedly be mistakes, but you will learn from them. As you train you will gradually evolve into a distance rower.

By using the stepping-stone approach to endurance rowing you will slowly increase your ability while learning about your boat and the water. You will gradually learn about yourself, not just as an oarsman but as a person. This knowledge will dictate what gear you want to take with you and what gear you can leave behind. Philosophically I'm a minimalist—I believe in taking only the bare necessities. I don't believe in giving a free ride to gear that doesn't earn its way aboard the boat. The longer you row, the more you'll see that; long-distance rowing doesn't teach you what you need, it teaches you what you don't need.

The joys and challenges of endurance rowing start with the decision to experience more from rowing. Each stroke of each training session will bring you closer to your ultimate goal. Planning sessions around the fireplace in winter will build enthusiasm and allow you the vicarious thrill of rowing. It may turn out that your "ultimate goal" will just be a stepping stone to a newer, more challenging goal.

- 11 -
The Boat

Virtually any rowing boat, with the exception of the true racing shell and the lowliest punt, can be used for endurance rowing. Many will require either major or minor modification, allowing them to carry gear or to make them safer in open-water, or both, and some will be more efficient than others. Chris Cunningham made his trip down the Ohio and Mississippi Rivers in a home-built Sneakbox, a rowing-sailing design that evolved from Barnegat Bay fowling boats of the last century. John Garber cruised the coast of Maine in *Gypsy Girl*, a plywood rowing-sailing skiff. Steve Gropp rowed around Vancouver Island in a 16-foot modified Banks dory. Art Hoban has cruised the Sea of Cortez in a 16-foot WEST System Kite Wherry of his own design and construction.

Dale Lawrence rows the coasts of the Carolinas, following the Inland Waterway in his plank-on-frame 17-foot Whitehall. Chris Maas and Greg Shell did a three-day cruise in the Pacific Northwest aboard open-water shells, an Aero and a Vancouver 21. Gordie Nash has rowed thousands of open-water miles in a variety of traditional designs and open-water shells. I have cruised several hundred miles in a modified 16-foot Appledore Pod. These are all different boats, but they did the job for their rowers. The design of the boat is not as important as the desire and preparation of the oarsman.

The perfect boat, like the perfect rowing stroke, probably doesn't exist. No matter what boat an oarsman rows, he'll be constantly thinking about modifications—or about his next boat. However, if you know what you want in a boat, you can come closer to perfection today than at any time in the past. The secret in selecting the best boat for you, or modifying the one you have, comes not so much from knowing everything there is to know about boats, but truly understanding yourself and what you expect from your boat. This understanding can only be gained by experience at the oars. If your desire is to emulate

Kavienga shortly after completion. The added rib shows clearly here, as does the compass mounted on the stretchers.

John Garber and row 150 miles of the Maine coastline, your TrimLine 24 advanced open-water shell will eventually have to be replaced by a more traditional design. If your goal is to win the Catalina to Marina del Rey race, your trusty old Banks dory will have to give way to an advanced open-water shell.

Do you want to race? Attend some races and decide if you're interested in one-design or an open-class. Shirwin Smith is working with the U.S. Rowing Association (USRA), attempting to break open-water singles into three categories based primarily on boat length. Category I would comprise boats with a maximum length of 19 feet and a minimum weight of 40 pounds. It includes boats such as Martin's Alden Ocean Shell, Small Craft's Lightning and

Typical of the new breed of high-performance open-water boats, the J-Shell has limited space in the cockpit for modifications.

Typhoon, Little River's Sprint, and Graham's Olympian and Trimline. Category II, with a 22-foot maximum and 38-pound minimum weight, would include Maas' Aero and Vancouver 21, Pocock's Offshore Racer, Small Craft's 266 Ocean Racer and the Rec Racer by Durham. Category III, 25 feet, 2 inches and 38 pounds minimum weight, would include the Maas 24, Graham's Trimline 24, Portage Bay's 24-footer, Coffey's Exercise Single, and Little River's ProAm 25. Doubles will also be divided into classes, probably two, with the break occurring at about 23 feet. Remember, at this writing these classes are still being structured, and may change.

At the same time classes are being formed, the USRA is advancing one-design racing. If you want to race one-design, check out some races in your area and see just which boats have one-design classes. If you would rather race in a category, look at the people racing the different boats and decide who you want to compete against.

Do you want to cruise? If the answer is "yes," do you want to do day-long coastal passages or overnighters? After you've answered these questions honestly, go back to Gordie Nash's chart in Chapter 2. Racing or cruising, you will be spending so much time in the boat that it would be a mistake to sacrifice efficiency for any reason: the new boat will have to be both light and stiff.

Light is a relative term. A racing shell is light, 30 pounds or less, but not an appropriate boat for open-water conditions. The top open-water shells, the TrimLine 24 and Maas 24, weigh in very close to 40 pounds, and this is light when compared with some other open-water singles weighing more than 70 pounds. The Pacific 30 and Dragonfly doubles weigh 80 pounds, light compared with a 120-pound double. Traditional designs, too, can be lightly built. Art Hoban's 16-foot WEST System Kite Wherry weighs 75 pounds, just over half the weight of a 15 ½-foot fiberglass Schock dory.

A lighter boat is better than a heavier one—but you can't sacrifice strength and stiffness on the altar of lightness. If a boat is not stiff, it reduces the power of your stroke by flexing and compressing rather than driving through the water, and it will not carry way as well during recovery. If you're going to be covering long distances, you want a boat that works for you, not against you.

Historically, serious open-water racers have gone to the lower right corner of Nash's chart, selecting their boats from the advanced open-water category. The California Wherry, Mass Aero and 24, and the TrimLine 24 were racers' boats. Endurance rowers interested in cruising have chosen boats from the upper left quadrant of the chart—dories, Whitehalls, and peapods, traditional and transitional designs long known for their seaworthiness and carrying capacity. Serious rowers of either persuasion have tended to ignore the middle of the chart. The boats there are too slow for the racers and don't have the gear-carrying capacity the cruisers demanded; they are boats for beginners or people not as interested in performance.

For a long time the opposite ends of the chart were thought to be exclusive. An oarsman either raced or cruised, and chose the "proper" boat for what he wanted to do. Now there is extensive crossover. Some racers have become intrigued by the challenges of cruising and have pressed their racing boats into service for two- or three-day cruises. More and more dedicated cruisers have moved to faster, more modern boats.

There are several reasons for this: The newer boats have improved, both in design and construction, and more younger oarsmen are becoming involved in the sport. Younger people tend to be less influenced by tradition than their elders. There is also a time factor in our busy world. Not everyone who wants to can take two or three weeks to go for a cruise. Shorter cruises with less gear can be made in open-water shells, which can cover significantly more territory in a given time than the slower traditional designs.

If you've decided what you want from rowing, studied Nash's chart and decided your boat isn't "right" for what you intend, it doesn't mean you have to run out and buy a new boat, or wait until you do to get involved in long-distance rowing. No matter what kind of a boat you row, you can start getting into endurance rowing the next time you go out. Add a little distance to your regular course. If you normally do three miles, do four, if a standard row is six miles, go seven.

For this type of rowing, most of the advanced open-water boats are perfect as they come from the shop—seaworthy, unsinkable boats that will take on any reasonable conditions. Most traditional boats—dories, peapods, and Whitehalls—are also naturals, though some may need extra flotation, such as foam or air bags.

Rowers of open-water shells without sealed cockpits, such as the Alden, Martin Trainer, and some Grahams should carry a bailer or bilge pump and probably install some extra flotation before venturing too far afield. This is not to imply that the flotation built into these boats is inadequate—it's just that every cubic inch taken up by flotation is one that won't be filled with water in case of a swamping.

There's a tendency among those who row traditional designs to feel they don't need the benefits of high technology, but I firmly disagree. If you're going to spend long hours in a boat—any boat—it should be as strong, light, efficient, and comfortable as possible. Even if you don't have a sliding seat and outboard oarlocks in your boat, you can still make improvements.

One very basic piece of gear many fixed-seat rowing boats don't have is a good, sturdy place to brace your feet. A simple, comfortable footrest that gives good leverage will help immensely. You won't need to mount clogs or shoes, but heel cups and single Velcro straps give more positive location. They also give more secure footing while rowing through heavy chop or surf.

We discussed scull and oarlock options in Chapter 3. If you're contemplating long-distance rows in a fixed-thwart boat, you might also want to think about increasing the efficiency of your oars' arc. Racing lifeguard dories regularly add wooden spacers between the oarlock socket and the gunwale, moving the socket outboard over an inch. Since each inch you move the socket outboard can increase the proper oar length by up to three inches, you can see that minor adjustments can allow longer oars to produce a wider arc. A word of caution: This modification can be the weakest part of your boat if it's not done right. On the lifeguard dory, where the gunwale is oak, up to a three-foot piece of similar wood is used to spread the load. The new oak is tapered at the ends to blend into the original gunwale, then glued and through-bolted into place. Each boat is different, but the most successful use as many as eight $5/8$-inch bolts. The sockets themselves are then through-bolted to the outboard side of the new gunwale. Variations on this modification can be used on many traditional boats.

You can bolt one or two items to an open-water shell, change the fin, but the boat remains pretty much the same as when it arrived from the dealer. Traditional designs offer much greater latitude in modification, allowing the oarsman to customize his boat to fit his own requirements.

One big question is whether to add decking, a dodger, or splash guards. In Southern California, where conditions are usually mild, I've rowed thousands of miles in open traditional designs with no serious problems, though I finally added a dodger to my latest boat. The oarsman has to know what is right for him and his boat in the conditions where he will generally row.

One of the benefits of adding gear to a traditional design, as opposed to a open-water shell, is room. A 16-foot peapod design will hold far more than a 25-foot Pro Am. There is a downside to this: rowers, even experienced rowers, tend to keep adding gear and equipment to these boats, and weight is just as important a factor in a traditional cruising design as it is in an open-water shell. Don't fall into the trap of filling up your boat with unnecessary gear: Remember, you have to move it with each stroke of the oars. I don't believe any boat—either a shell or a traditional design—should be loaded to its maximum. There should always be a safety margin. Remember that you are part of the payload. If your boat has a suggested maximum payload of 250 pounds and you weigh 235, this severely limits what you will be carrying. There are some very good open-water shells specifically designed for the lighter rower. If you weigh near the upper limit of your boat's rated payload, consider that when you think about strapping a watertight bag full of camping gear to the deck.

Never before have there been so many different designs available. This will allow you to get what you want, but there will also be a lot of tempting boats offered that do not fulfill your needs.

If you don't live near an active rowing center, traditional boats may be somewhat harder for you to find and evaluate. There are shops that specialize in replicas of traditional designs that will be happy to help you, but you really need to know what you want. There are vast differences between peapods, Whitehalls, and dories; even within the same type there are major differences. For instance, Banks dories, Beachcomber dories, and St. Pierre dories are all dories, but they are greatly different boats. There are some designs on the market today freely using names of well-known traditional designs, but which bear little or no relation to their namesakes. These aren't necessarily bad boats, but to me the traditional name suggests certain qualities and abilities that these modern pretenders may not share.

Whether you plan to buy an open-water shell or a traditional design, as an endurance rower you'll have to look at construction and safety features more carefully than the average boatbuyer. Inspect hulls and decks—and their joints. Carefully examine stretchers, seats or thwarts, and riggers or oarlock sockets. Look past the paint, varnish, or gelcoat—a shiny hull can look beautiful, but can hide a lot. Open inspection ports; look and feel inside. Above all, ask questions.

Most advanced open-water shells are very safe boats. Their small cockpits are sealed; they hold very little water and can be rowed while awash. While not bulletproof, all the top boats are strongly built. From design to design, their seaworthiness and speed vary slightly, but they are all close. Not all the boats charted as "advanced open-water" fit into the category of open-water shells. There are two boats whose performance has placed them in the advanced category that don't fit several of these criteria. One is the original Pocock Wherry. Designed and built as a training boat for racing scullers, it's an open boat that is less stable than the others in this category. A Pocock would require some extensive modification before being fit for serious offshore work. One, with a light plastic deck and extra flotation, did compete in several open-water races in California. To meet the demand for this type of boat Pocock now builds a decked wherry.

The other boat that does not fit the shell criteria is the California Wherry. More boat than shell, she is actually a modern copy of a racing boat from the early 1900s. The Wherry is partially decked but does not have a sealed cockpit. It's an incredibly seaworthy design, and an Elvstrom-style bailer makes her a perfect endurance rowing boat as long as you don't have to sleep aboard.

For the cruiser, sleeping aboard can be a very important consideration. Obviously, none of the open-water shells offer this feature, so you'll have to look to the traditional designs. Most of us need a space at least six and a half feet long by three feet wide to sleep comfortably, and this is quite a bit of clear deck space in a rowing boat. In most cases you'll be able to get this amount of space only if you can remove the rowing station or lift out the thwart.

An owner's happiness with his boat is the result of experience and careful study. Many oarsmen have spent a lifetime searching for the perfect boat, even as their knowledge and experience have grown, changing the parameters of the search. To the dedicated oarsman, the search itself is a source of excitement, reward, and fun.

- 12 -

Preparing Your Boat

HERE are some case studies of oarsmen who have modified or built boats with clear-cut endurance rowing goals in mind. Each boat presented has been designed or modified to meet the special needs of experienced oarsmen. Much of what they have done can be adapted for use by other endurance rowers. A warning though—look at *why* they did what they did. See if it really meets your needs before you copy.

Gina Billings regularly rows a Maas Aero on extended day-cruises along the Southern California coast. She rarely brings the boat into a beach, so she laid it out to be comfortable and efficient for a long day afloat. She painstakingly selected the right equipment, and her choices would be a good beginning for anyone, whether racing or cruising, in an open-water shell.

Billings replaced the leather clogs with track shoes for comfort and a more secure feeling. (See Chapter 3 for the procedure.) She drilled a pair of holes in the stern bulkhead of the cockpit and mounted a bicycle water-bottle cage behind her shoes. The cage is made of a plastic designed to withstand the elements, and it weighs only grams. The cage eliminates the problem of the water bottle rolling around in the boat, getting in the way, rolling out of reach, or being lost if swamped.

When she ordered the boat from Maas, Billings specified a bailer and compass, two important options for any endurance rower.

The compass, like the Elvström bailer, is another item borrowed from sailing: Maas removes the grips from hand-bearing compasses and mounts them on the centerline in the after end of the cockpit. There are several other good sailing compasses that can be located on the deck abaft the cockpit.

Billings replaced the standard oarlocks with a pair of Stampfli oarlocks from Switzerland. Like most high-tech locks, they are expensive, but worth it. She can not only change the pitch simply by removing a shim and replacing it

137

with another, she can change height just as easily. This allows her to tune the boat for the conditions she expects to encounter each time she launches. She also has a pair of fins—the standard fin that came with the Aero and a larger, rough-water fin Maas offers as an option. The larger fin hampers turning ability, but enhances tracking in wind and waves, especially when taken on the bow or stern quarter.

The only piece of gear Billings has on her boat that is not essential to the endurance rower is a Nielsen-Kellerman Strokecoach, which provides a stroke rate readout and has a time-from-start function. It weighs less than a pound and is mounted out of the way beside the compass. She claims it keeps her at a good steady rate and is a valuable training aid. (See photo on page 35.)

Billings carries her personal gear, an extra water bottle, and snacks in a water repellent fanny pack. While she rows, the pack rides low on her back, out of the way. When she wants to reach either of the two zippered compartments, she swivels it around so it rests on her lap. Leaving the beach early in the morning, she usually tucks a waterproof flashlight under the laces of one of her shoes.

When Mark Steffy rowed the Catalina race in 1986, he set up his Aero in a very similar manner—Stampfli oarlocks, rough-water fin, bailer, bulkhead-mounted compass, shoes, and a large water jug strapped to the after side of the stretchers. Event regulations require a navigation light, so he mounted one with a suction cup aft of the cockpit. He taped over the forward part of the lens so that he wasn't staring into the light for the entire trip. He also drilled a pair of holes in the hull/deck joint lip, one on either side of the boat. He ran a

Gordie Nash's ARS with "water wings."

shock cord across the deck and slipped his life preserver under it. Before the race Chris Maas built Steffy a handsome low splash guard that was fixed to the hull at the forward edge of the cockpit. The result of these modifications and additions was a boat capable of making long open-water passages quickly and safely.

In 1989, after rowing doubles and triples for several seasons, Shirwin Smith switched to a single. She chose one of the new Maas 24s and drew on her experience as a racer and coach to equip it with Concept II adjustable oarlocks, track shoes, bailer, compass, and an open-water fin. She also added a Strokecoach and a Signet knotmeter. For her own comfort she uses a half-inch neoprene seat pad, and pads the inside of one shoe to compensate for a slightly shorter leg. She also carries plenty of water. (See photo on page 161.)

The three rowers differed when it came to selecting sculls. Billings opted for 298-centimeter composite Maas oars because she prefers their knurled grips. Steffy used 300-centimeter Concept IIs in the 1986 Catalina Race. Smith chose 296-centimeter Concept II Ultralights. They all find the sculls perfect for their uses and styles of rowing.

If your endurance rowing goals are racing oriented, or if you're interested in making fast day trips in open water, study what Gordie Nash has done with some of his boats. Nash is the most visible of all open-water racers, having won races and set elapsed time records for courses on both coasts. Up until the 1986 racing season Nash rowed production-based boats. As he rowed and learned, he modified these boats, improving their efficiency—and their performance.

Along with his enviable racing record and the boats he has built, Nash is known for his "instrument panel." Over the years he has developed a group of instruments that surround his stretchers, monitoring both his own and his boat's performance. Arrayed at Nash's feet are a digital compass, digital knotmeter, Strokecoach, and a real-time watch. In a glance he can determine his course, speed, stroke rate, and how long he has been out. Along with these instruments, all Nash's boats have been equipped with suction-style bailers and quite a few water bottles.

In 1983 Nash modified an Alden Double by stretching it to 23 feet 4 inches and set a doubles records in the Catalina Race. In 1984 he dropped another Oarmaster in the same boat and gave it to the women's team of Shirwin Smith, Hillary Dembroff, and Karen "KC" Carlson for the race. In 1985 Nash rowed a 22-foot, 6-inch Small Craft ARS Mark II in most of California's open-water races, and went east to row one in that year's very rough Around Goat Island Race in Newport, R.I. This boat was a heavy 85 pounds, suitable for extremely rough conditions, and remembered for its black carbon fiber "wing." Shaped like a blunted "V," the wing attached to the deck aft of the cockpit and the arms swept forward to hold the oarlocks.

By the time he was ready to do the 1985 Catalina race, Nash's ARS had undergone some interesting modifications. Small blocks of balsa were carefully shaped, then bonded to both the bow and stern. They improved the hull's hydrodynamic efficiency by providing a finer entry and cleaner release. After attachment to the hull, the balsa blocks were painted over, and only careful scrutiny would reveal these modifications had been made. More obvious were Nash's "water wings." Nash first used these clear sheets of 4-mil plastic in 1980 on a Martin Trainer, which he rowed to first in class in Catalina. The plastic is duct-taped to the deck and extended out to the sill of the rigger, providing an effective splash shield.

Another boat in that year's race featured some extensive modifications by Gordie Nash. Once again he turned a double into a triple for a team of women. This time it was a Small Craft double, and the team consisted of Shirwin Smith and Hillary Dembroff, who had rowed the year before in the stretched Alden, and their new teammate Dolly Stockman. The standard 24-foot Small Craft hull was used, but Nash built a new deck, stretching the cockpit to allow for a crew of three. The trio finished only seconds behind a larger triple rowed by three men.

In the rough 1985 Catalina race Nash came second to Danish Olympic rower Per Hertig in another extensively modified open-water shell. Hertig rowed a boat specially put together for the race by Laser. Tad Springer, designer of the Laser shells, took one of its 24-foot double hulls, rigged it as a single, and decked it over with thin plastic sheeting to keep water out and weight to a minimum. The combination of the Olympian and long waterline proved unbeatable. The exercise showed just what could be done with an open-water shell when it's modified to meet a specific challenge.

If Gordie Nash hadn't already had plans for a new boat, placing second in 1985 would have surely sent him to the drafting board to design one. As it was, he had already spent several months refining the design of a double that he hoped would break the elapsed time record. In the past, good open-water shells with offshore capabilities had been pressed into service for distance racing, but Nash's Pacific 30 was the first open-water shell designed with long-distance open-water racing in mind. He wanted a fast boat that had stability and seaworthiness enough to be safe in a 14- to 16-knot crosswind.

Despite all Nash's experience rowing and building boats, the Pacific 30 did not just happen overnight. He knew what he wanted the boat to do, but he needed to figure out how. He spent hours rowing a Small Craft double, and decided the boat had the stability he required—so he factored that into his

Modified Latanzo rigging
used on the Pacific 30.

calculations. Then he drew out the waterline, making the boat narrower as it got longer, but keeping the stability factor constant. He brought naval architect Bob Smith of Mill Valley, California, into the project and supplied him with the criteria for the cockpit layout and hull shape, waterline length, stability, speed, and seaworthiness. One of these criteria was that the cockpit be small. With a sailing background, Nash knew the benefits of centralized weight, and he wanted the rowers as close together as possible. Bob Smith drew the boat, Nash modified the design, then Smith made revisions. The plans went back and forth five times before Nash and Smith were happy. After the plans were set down, and while the hull molds were being built, they decided to lower the freeboard. Nash claims that final, last-minute decision "made the boat."

The prototype Pacific 30 had a removable stern section to make it legal for cartopping. The weight was centralized; in fact the rowers sat closer together than they do in a racing double. Built from standard gelcoat and cloth, the boat weighed 120 pounds—it looked strong, seaworthy, and *fast*.

The prototype Pacific 30 debuted at California's Bay to Bay Race, a 20-mile race from Mission Bay to San Diego Harbor, with the distance evenly divided between open and protected waters. Nash and Kevin Strain won the event against some serious doubles competition, including old rival Per Hertig and his partner. Two months later they took the boat to the thin air of Lake Tahoe in the Sierras, and won the North Shore Rowing Regatta. At Tahoe they beat other doubles, including a racing double, on smooth water. One would have thought the boat an unqualified success, but not Nash—he had some more ideas before Catalina.

The prototype Pacific 30 and the boat Nash and Strain rowed in the

Catalina race were similar in that, in Nash's words, "They displaced water, two people sat in them and they had four oars." The second Pacific 30 was built of carbon fiber and not gelcoated, though the deck was sprayed with linear polyurethane. Nash and Strain went through the entire design, shaving weight. No structural com-promises were made; better materials were used. The ability to take apart the boat by removing the stern was eliminated, saving 15 pounds in bulkheads and fastenings. The weight of the second boat, rigged with customized Latanzo outriggers, and all electronics installed, was under 85 pounds. Nash and Strain won the 1986 Catalina Race, setting a new record. They rowed the same boat to victory in 1987 and 1988. Sisterships of the boat won other classes those years, and Steve Hathaway and Craig Leeds rowed another Pacific 30 to victory in 1989. The design has been an unqualified success.

Not many rowers can afford the time or money, or have the knowledge, experience, or desire to design and build a race-winning rowing boat. On the other hand, there's a lot of trickle-down technology from a project such as this. Nash took all the numbers from the Pacific 30, shrank them, and turned out the Pacific 24, a single version of the boat. His building techniques surely will be adapted by others to produce lighter, stronger boats. Few of us may ever row Pacific 30s from Catalina to Marina del Rey, but many of us will benefit from the fact that Nash built the boat.

TRADITIONAL designs offer more latitude for the oarsman who wants to tinker with his boat. My own Appledore Pod is a good example. Several years ago I wanted a cruising boat, but discovered nothing available that met my requirements. I had owned a number of boats by that time and had some definite ideas about what I wanted and did not want in a cruising boat. She had to be a relatively fast and efficient fiberglass boat, capable of doing serious offshore work. She had to be able to carry gear enough for a week and allow me to sleep aboard—which meant a traditional design. The speed and efficiency requirements meant the boat would have to be equipped with a sliding seat and riggers, and be stiff. She would also have to be strongly built and seaworthy.

The boat that came closest was Martin Marine's Appledore Pod, but I had some problems with the design. I wasn't happy with the twin box-like stringers that ran the length of the hull, making the deck space unusable. After rowing many hundreds of miles with an Oarmaster, I wanted a rowing rig that was lighter and more efficient. The 16-foot fiberglass hull, a faithful reproduction of a traditional New England design, was ideal for my needs—all I had to do was change the interior.

We spent some time with the bare hull and came up with a few relatively simple modifications that would make her fit my requirements. Since the Appledore was designed to be used with the Oarmaster,which doesn't transmit rowing strains to the hull, the hull had to be strengthened. We glassed and bolted a pair of plywood ribs to the hull near the rowing station. Flotation chambers, slightly larger than those in the stock boat, were glassed in fore and aft; the two foam-filled stringers runing the length of the hull became the foundation for a $^3/_8$-inch teak marine ply deck. A 9 $^1/_4$-inch square hole was cut in the deck aft of the ribs so the stretchers of a lightweight rowing station could drop in. The rowing station, a skeletal wooden framework supporting a Latanzo seat and tracks, was anchored in place by captive dowels that slipped into holes drilled in the deck. The rowing station could be lifted out and a hatch placed in the stretcher hole to provide a clear deck for sleeping.

The removable, hard, anodized aluminum riggers are L-shaped. The foot of each L slips into an aluminum bracket through-bolted to the hull near the ribs. A pair of $^1/_4$-inch stainless steel bolts anchor each rigger in place. The pin-to-pin dimension on the finished boat is 62 inches. With my feet down against the bottom of the hull and my butt just 4 $^1/_2$ inches above the deck, *Kavienga's* center of gravity is far lower than it would have been with the Oarmaster-equipped boat. The weight of the deck, riggers, and rowing unit are less than that of the discarded Oarmaster. The oarlocks are Latanzo gated locks and the original oars were 9-foot, nine-inch wooden Piantedosi sculls. I cracked the back of a Piantedosi when I hit a buoy and replaced the wooden oars with lighter, stiffer Concept II composite sculls. The first addition I made to the "finished" *Kavienga* was to bolt a compass to the rear of the stretcher board.

The biggest problem I had with *Kavienga* was with the raised plywood deck, which allowed water to collect under it. If I took my feet out of the stretchers and slid all the way aft on the tracks I could use a small scoop to lift water out of the hole in the deck. This was uncomfortable and inefficient. For some time I used a hand-held bilge pump. This was far more efficient than the scoop, but required that I stop rowing, gather up the pump, get it set up, then pump. A faster and easier method was needed.

My first plan was to remove the deck, fill the area under it with blown foam, hog out a place for my stretchers, then glass over the foam. I would mount a suction-style bailer in the foot well. The foam would give added flotation, and the bailer would be in the lowest part of the boat where the water would collect. Any water the bailer couldn't handle would be where I could get at it with a scoop or a bucket. There were some problems with this solution: It would mean that in rough conditions the deck would be constantly awash. Any gear on the deck would get wet, and I, sitting just 4 $^1/_2$ inches above the deck, could be sloshing through a lot of water while I rowed.

The pump and one of the storage hammocks installed aboard *Kavienga*.

I finally decided to leave the wooden deck as it was and mount a permanent bilge pump. The pump would always be set up where I could reach it comfortably with one hand while still holding the sculls with the other. I through-bolted a small Munster Simms pump to the deck just forward and slightly to port of the rowing rig. I drilled a hole in the center of the deck, and led the pick-up hose through the deck to rest in the center of the boat, and led the exhaust hose to a through-hull fitting high on the port side. The leads may not be as fair as the manufacturer would like, but the little unit pumps a lot of water very quickly.

The other problem the raised deck gave me was that anything loose in the boat promptly rolled under it, to be lost until the next time I brought the boat to a beach. I solved this problem in two ways. First I through-bolted some guides on the top of both the flotation compartments and ran shock cord through them so gear could be lashed down. (The area is reserved for light gear to keep weight out of the ends.) Then I bought a pair of 6-foot-long nylon mesh hammocks, the type used in cruising yachts to store gear and provisions. I strung one on either side, from the forward flotation compartment aft to the riggers. These hold a tremendous amount of gear and keep it handy. Everything else gets pushed into a pair of waterproof canoe bags, which are too big to slip under the deck and can be shifted about the boat to counterbalance the weight of water jugs, anchor, and the like.

My final modification to *Kavienga* was adding a dodger. Under certain conditions *Kavienga* could take a lot of spray, and a dodger seemed to be a good answer to the problem of water coming aboard. Since I sit low in the boat, the major consideration was that the dodger not block my view forward. After a little experimentation I found the optimum height.

The modifications to *Kavienga* have made her a far easier boat to live with. The addition of the permanently mounted bilge pump took less than two hours with a power drill, a knife, and a screwdriver. I had probably spent 20 hours cursing and attempting to bail, or wrestling with the hand-held pump before I got around to making the installation. The boat is not only safer, more comfortable, and more efficient, but I have the satisfaction of knowing that I made it that way.

WHEN John Garber made his trip along the Maine coast aboard the Phil Bolger-designed, H.H. "Dynamite" Payson-built 15-foot plywood skiff *Gypsy Girl*, he made some modifications even during his long row. He pulled into Camden, Maine and laid over for several days while canvas spray shields were built for the bow and stern of the boat. According to Garber, "They didn't do much but give me a feeling of safety." The first thoughts of a new boat started to germinate about the same time as the spray shields were being built. That trip was made on an inside course, but Garber began thinking about a boat that he'd be willing to take outside.

For the new boat, Garber's main design concerns were the same as for *Gypsy Girl*: he wanted a boat that could be rowed downwind. He discarded the idea of a dual-purpose, sailing-rowing craft, and thought more about a pure rowing boat. He built four half models and consulted with Phil Bolger twice and Ken Basset three times while the design process was going on. Finally he made his first attempt at drawing lines, a process he enjoyed. "There are really three designs for *Pogy*," Garber said, "the half model, lines drawing, and as-built. I relied entirely on Ken for construction details. She's built of plywood, and Ken's a wizard with plywood. As built, the boat has camber below the chine forward of amidships, and a slight hollow aft. She's three feet longer than *Gypsy Girl*, partially decked, with a V-bottom. She goes to weather—my son and I rowed her to weather in heavy chop and 25 to 30 knots and she only came out of the water once, and she came down soft."

Garber worked with Ken Basset for the last week of *Pogy*'s construction, and says they were in such a rush to finish her they never took the time to weigh the completed boat; he guesses she weighs about 200 pounds. With a single oarsman she balances well and the load can be shifted to make her balance equally well with an oarsman on each thwart. A pair of removable planks run from side to side to brace both oarsmen's feet. There are no foot straps, heel cups, or

John Garber's *Pogy.*

shoes, which allows them to change their position as they row. According to Garber, *Pogy*'s hull below the chine has "a codfish head and a mackerel tail—full forward and fine aft. She tracks perfectly. Of course the trade-off is that she's slow to turn. It makes her hard to bring alongside a float—but then she was designed as a cruising boat."

The first aspect of *Pogy* most people comment on is her handsome reverse transom. The idea for the stern was to provide a long waterline and cut weight. Garber estimates that reversing the transom saved 20 pounds, or 10 percent of the boat's weight, and he hopes it gives him a little extra windage going downwind. During the design period the transom received mixed reviews. "Ken Basset was really against that stern, and gave me a couple of long distance phone calls about it," says Garber. "He thought the pointed tip of the stern would drag. With beginner's luck the boat floated with that tip about an inch out of the water. Ken and other people felt seas would run up the stern into the boat. Bolger liked it. I had less rake in the early designs and he told me to increase the rake and it would look better. I did, and it did."

There is also the unique stern cleat over the transom. Garber designed it as part of his effort to show off the fact that *Pogy* was built from plywood, rather than conceal the fact, as many try to do. According to Garber, "It turned out to look like a fish. We put in the caudal sensors with copper nails and the eye with a punch, and that's how she came to be called *Pogy.*

Pogy rows beautifully, and there was not problem with seas washing over the reverse transom, as some expected. *Pogy* already has a lot of miles under her hull, and Garber is planning cruises along the east coast of Texas, and others in the Sea of Cortez, the Loire River, and the west coast of Ireland. *Pogy* is an example of what a dedicated endurance rower can do when he turns his mind to producing the ideal boat for his purposes.

I FIRST talked with Chris Maas about his plans to build a 24-foot single at a post-race party following the 1987 Tahoe North Shore Regatta. Based on recent race results, the writing was on the wall—if you wanted to be first to finish, you would have to row a 24. Maas wanted a boat similar to an Aero, but longer and leaner with less rocker.

At the time, Maas was also exploring the possibility of building a flat-water racing shell, and the idea of a 24-foot open-water boat was shelved temporarily. Meanwhile, Bob Jarvis and Gordie Nash were producing their long boats, and these boats were taking line honors in most races. Many competitive Aero rowers didn't like finishing behind other makes, and began badgering Maas to build a long boat. By 1988, the demand for a 24 was so great that Maas could not ignore it. He put the nearly completed flat-water boat on the shelf and turned his energies to a new open-water design.

Maas has always maintained he only designs and builds boats that please him; if other people want them, that's great. The success of his Vancouver 21, Aero, and Dragonfly double show that a lot of people want the same things in a boat that Chris Maas does. Though he received a lot of comments on what he should build, Maas followed his own instincts when it came to designing the 24: "I wanted a boat that was more challenging than the Aero. I wanted to design and build a boat that would be the fastest possible open-water single that could be rowed by skilled people in rough water." Obviously not a compromise boat.

"Twenty-four feet was a maximum length for open water, and 14 inches on the waterline was as narrow as you could make a boat and still have it stable enough to row in rough water," says Maas. Compared with the Aero, the 24's long, narrow hull has rounder sections to cut wetted surface—a Maas priority. For the same reason, there's a little less rocker forward and about the same rocker aft as on the Aero. This puts the knuckles at the waterline, and keeps the ends from having to be dragged through the water. Like other Maas designs, the 24 has a very fine entry to cut through rough water, and the maximum volume of the hull is abaft the middle of the boat. Maas locates the rower aft of the middle because he feels the catch is the most unstable part of the stroke in rough water, and he wants the rower to be over the bulk of the boat at that time.

The most noticeable design difference in the 24 is its wing, which Maas says is "a reaction to the width of the boat. We didn't have wide enough side decks to properly support outriggers, and I didn't want to put a wash-box on the boat and mount riggers in the traditional manner. The wing was the logical solution to the problem. I had rowed winged boats, and I didn't want a large, ugly wing; neither did I want a weak one. On some boats I'd rowed, the wings rose and fell at the catch rather than the oars going up and down. We built some prototypes and kept shaving weight and mass until we had one that was aesthetically pleasing and still stiff." The four-pound, carbon-fiber-and-foam wing actually shaved a couple of pounds off the weight of the boat, because Maas didn't have to add attachment points for trailing arms of conventional riggers or the framework supporting the forward riggers.

Maas built a prototype, rowed it, then revised the design. The deck and wing evolved during this process, though he says there were only minor changes to the hull. The Maas 24 was introduced to the public in February 1989 and nearly 200 were sold in the first 10 months. The 24 has done well racing: The design's finest hour came at the hands of Ann Donaldson in the 1989 Catalina race. In a rough year when no other class records were broken, Donaldson took nearly 34 minutes off the old record and beat the second place J-Shell by over 20 minutes.

After several thousand miles in an Aero, I was surprised at how unstable the 24 felt. It took me about 200 open-water miles I before I felt I had learned the boat's idiosyncrasies and was rowing to its potential. Finding out how to get the most out of a 24 in rough water was a steep learning curve, but one that was well worth it.

The ultimate example of boats designed and built for endurance rowing are not Gordie Nash's Pacific 30, John Garber's *Pogy*, or Chris Maas' 24—they are *Britannia II* and the boats she has inspired. Uffa Fox designed the 35-foot self-righting *Britannia II* for John Fairfax and Sylvia Cook to row across the Pacific. She was later used by Derek King and Peter Bird to row the Atlantic. Books have been written about both expeditions, and they are included in the Appendices. Gordie Nash recently finished a 34-foot single for a customer who plans to row the Pacific. It will take some time, but the trickle down from these expeditions will affect the average endurance rower. We won't be rowing massive self-righting boats designed to cross oceans, but these ultimate endurance rowers will challenge us to stretch our own limits.

- 13 -

Preparing Yourself

JUST AS modifying your boat to meet the demands of endurance rowing will make for a more successful race or cruise, so will properly preparing yourself. Sometimes getting yourself ready can easily slip down on the list of priorities. There are so many things to do getting ready for an endurance row, especially a cruise, that it's easy to forget about the single most important aspect of the trip—the oarsman.

Before you plan to go for a long row you *must* condition yourself, and the best way to get ready for a rowing excursion is to row. Rowing will get you in shape both physically and mentally. It's worth making the time for this preparation.

Rowing will also teach you to pace yourself. Especially if you are rowing sliding-seat, it's easy to burn yourself out after a couple of hours at the oars. You will have to develop a strong, slow stroke that allows the boat to work to its best advantage. This will move you along at a good rate, but not burn too many calories too fast. Since each combination of boat and oarsman is unique, rowing is the only way to learn this stroke.

Rowing has the added benefit of keeping you in touch with your boat. It will be easier to plan what gear and provisions you need for your trip if you are in the boat on a regular basis.

■ WORKING OUT

Any time you spend in the boat will be time well spent, but a planned or organized workout while rowing will best use your time. You don't have to row structured stroke or time pyramids, do interval training, or keep track of heart rate—but none of this would hurt. You will have to keep track of both what you are doing and how you are doing it. Whether you're racing or cruising, endurance is your first priority. For racing, strength and speed will come later. The old motor racing adage applies: "First you must finish before you can finish first." It doesn't matter if you do a horizon job on the fleet on the first leg, reaching the first mark five minutes ahead of your nearest competitor, if you fade on the next leg. Know your limits and strengths.

No matter what kind of workout you do on the water, start with some stretches, especially the hamstring and lower-back stretches described in Chapter 8. Once you're in the boat, warm up. Don't start pulling hard until your body is ready. Whether you're rowing sliding seat or fixed thwart, row for 10 or 15 minutes at quarter- or half-pressure. If you're rowing sliding seat and want to work on your technique while you're warming up, you can start with no-feather or no-leg rowing, but don't consider either your full warm-up. After a drill, do a few minutes at partial pressure before getting into the work-out itself.

Once you're underway you can follow any number of paths. Most rowers find they become bored if they do exactly the same workout each day. If you can put four days a week into your rowing, a great training regimen is to do one long row a week, say six to 15 miles depending on your endurance, and three shorter ones. The long row builds your endurance and breaks up the routine of the shorter ones. If you can row different courses for your short rows, so much the better.

When planning your workouts, consider the weather and water conditions you expect to encounter on your endurance row. The closer you can come to replicating those conditions during your workouts, the better prepared you will be when it comes time to race or cruise. You may not be able to exactly match conditions, but if you know your race or cruise will take you through exceptionally rough water, don't train in a protected harbor; go out when it's rough. Even if you don't expect to encounter adverse winds or steep chop, it's best if you know how to handle them. Always be prepared for the worst conditions—they will eventually find you.

■ ROWING SCHOOLS

There are several rowing schools around the country, but at this time few address the special demands of the open-water endurance rower. Most are interested in teaching beginners to row and in perfecting the strokes of flat-water scullers. There are two I know of that will take you past the beginner level in open water: Shirwin Smith's Open Water Rowing in Sausalito, California, is one. They train on San Francisco Bay and offer bimonthly rough-water seminars. Karen "KC" Carlson's W Dock Rowing in Santa Cruz, California, is the other. They specialize in ocean rowing. Both Smith and Carlson have thousands of open-water miles to their credit, have won their share of long races, and know what skills their students need to row well in exposed conditions. There may be other good schools for open-water rowing. Ask around.

If you find a rowing school in your area, or you plan to travel to attend one, there are some features to look into before you put your money on the line.

First check out the equipment; it can tell you a lot about a school. If the boats and oars are old-fashioned and poorly maintained, look around for another school. Find out if the school teaches the rowing disciplines you're interested in. If the chief instructor is a national or Olympic champion intent only on turning out other flat-water racers, look elsewhere. Then look for a tight student-to-teacher ratio. By the time you have reached the intermediate level you'll need individual attention. Some minor points you might look for are coaches who teach from shells, rather than from shore or a launch. If your coach is also rowing, you'll be able to watch his technique. If your coach isn't rowing, it's easy to develop a feeling of resentment. It's one thing to do a power-10 or power-20 if you know your coach is keeping up with you; it's another if all he's doing is twisting the outboard's throttle. I wouldn't select a school just because it offered videotaping, nor would I reject one because it didn't, but video can be a big plus. If you find a good school, a few hours of training there will be worth far more than the same amount of time training on your own.

■ SIX APPROACHES

Unfortunately we can't all find the time to work, be with our families, plan an extended rowing trip, and row two hours a day, four days a week in preparation. If you're planning a rowing cruise for early spring, or you want to kick some butt in the first regatta of the season, you'll have to train in the winter. If you can only make the time to get into the boat one or two times a week, or you live in a climate where you can't row year around, you still have to do something to get or stay in shape. In Chapter 8 we discussed compatible sports, the 22-minute drill, ergometers, gyms, and health clubs. This might be a good time to review that information. If working out is a bore, try to think of it as another stepping stone to your ultimate goal: A good exercise program will make you a more capable endurance rower.

Gordie Nash, Chris Maas, Shirwin Smith, Karen Carlson, Ann Donaldson, and Bill Berger—all endurance rowers with impressive credentials—have kindly consented to share some of their secrets. These are the training regimens of dedicated racers, but the cruiser can also learn from them.

Gordie Nash and Kevin Strain

Though he has retired from competitive rowing, for 11 years Gordie Nash was *the* open-water rower in the United States. In that span he not only built and designed boats that leapfrogged the fledgling sport into the 1990s, but he established a record of victories and course records that will probably never be duplicated. Though he is no longer racing, many attempt to emulate his commitment, and his records are still prime targets. To be able to say "I beat Gordie's time" will be a mark of honor for a long time to come.

Nash started rowing competitively in 1978, and through 1989 he won virtually every open-water race on both coasts, setting course records in many. When they paired up in early 1986, Nash and his rowing partner Kevin Strain made winning the Catalina to Marina del Rey race and setting a new record their long-term goal. They started training for the October race in the beginning of February. Their base was Nash's houseboat in Sausalito, California, on the western shore of Richardson's Bay, a large inlet on the northern shore of San Francisco Bay. Rowing the prototype Pacific 30, they started by going around Angel Island, a trip of 10 nautical miles. Depending on the current, they completed it in about 1 hour, 25 minutes, plus another 10 to 15 minutes to set up and warm down.

Their goal of setting a new course record meant that speed was as important to them as endurance. Their idea was to "get the boat up to its cruising speed, or a little higher, and the next day go a little faster." Each day they wanted to try to gradually improve both the boat's performance and their own physical performance. They rowed six days a week, with no set schedule of days off. As they neared the racing season they planned to take the day before a race as their rest day. If there wasn't a race on a given weekend, they would make their Sunday row 2 or 2 1/2 hours. Nash kept a training journal in which he noted distance rowed, length of time, average speed, weather conditions, data from the heart rate meters they wore, modifications to the boat, and any other information he felt was important. Along with providing a training log and a record of changes made to the boat, the journal told them the potential of both themselves and the boat under specific conditions. With this record they could monitor their performance over the course of the year.

Nash and Strain debuted the prototype Pacific 30 in San Diego's Bay to Bay Race. They won that race averaging 7.1 knots. Two months later, after a few changes in the boat and almost 60 more days training, they averaged nearly 8 knots in winning the Lake Tahoe North Shore Rowing Regatta.

Before the Catalina Race, Nash and Strain decided to add Alcatraz to their daily circle, increasing the total to nearly 15 nautical miles. If they encoun-

The finely-tuned Gordie Nash and Kevin Strain at work in the Catalina race.

tered severe weather they had another course, through Raccoon Strait (between Tiburon and Angel Island) and into the San Pablo Bay, the northern arm of San Francisco Bay. Nash remembers the summer of 1986 in San Francisco as being "pretty rough—even at six o'clock in the morning it was blowing at least 12, 14 knots, cold and wet." Their alternative course did not provide totally smooth conditions; Raccoon Straight can be the home of some vicious steep chop when the wind is blowing against the tide. In fact, Shirwin Smith uses the area for her rough-water clinics.

Two or three days a week Nash and Strain augmented their rowing workouts with trips to the gym, though Nash admits, "Kevin is more religious about it when it comes to working with weights than I am." Their workout was complemented with a high-complex carbohydrate diet, which included up to, but not over, 100 grams of protein per day. They didn't "do alcohol, smoking, drugs, or big heavy steaks."

Nash knows that not everyone has either the time or desire to train in such a manner.

Says Nash: "What we were doing was pushing ourselves and the boat above our real potential, and to do that you need an incredible amount of power. To go that extra two percent you really have to work, and we were into that range. We pushed it more than anyone else realistically, would or needs to. But that's what we wanted to do: we wanted to shatter that record and make it so it would stay for years. Rob and John [Jackson and Aranson, who also rowed a Pacific 30 in the 1986 Catalina Race] did it only eight minutes slower. Of course they're 10 years younger than we are, but they only trained an hour or so a day, three days a week. I think they could do it because they're excellent oarsmen who row well together and live clean, healthy lives, working out of doors in physically demanding jobs. You don't really need to do two hours a day to row competitively in open water, but you do have to know the boat, and the conditions. If you're an excellent oarsman in decent condition, you're going to do well."

Nash believes the sport has reached a point where the condition of the oarsman is the deciding factor. There are now enough good, proven designs available that anyone who is serious about his racing can have a state-of-the-art boat. It has turned into a race between the rowers—the engines—not the designers. "We're not racing Alden singles against Maas Aeros anymore," says Nash. "That difference no longer exists. You could put the biggest engine in the Alden and a good engine in an Aero and there's no contest—the Aero is just that much better boat. But you take two excellent oarsmen and put them in one of Chris's (Maas) boats and in one of mine, and you're going to have a horse race."

The message is clear: You can no longer make up for your own lack of condition by going out and buying the latest, fastest design. When you go to a race today, you see that everybody with a desire to win has a top-of-the-line boat under him, the only place left for improvement is in the rower.

Chris Maas

Chris Maas is the owner of the Maas Boat Company, designer and builder of the Aero, Dragonfly, and Maas 24, and a very competitive racer with a long string of victories to his credit. He keeps in shape during the winter by riding his bike six hours a week and spending an hour and a half working with free weights on a high-repetition, low-weight program. The only rowing he does during that time is boat and equipment testing.

As it gets closer to the first regatta of the season Maas switches into his race-training mode. This consists of a weekly regimen of 13 hours a week on his bike, four hours a week on his sailboard, which he considers "a really good workout if it's windy," and six hours of rowing. His rowing time is broken down into one hour of interval training, one hour of slow rowing (perfecting his technique), three hours of hard rowing, and one hour of boat and equipment testing. As far as his diet is concerned, Maas says, "I eat everything, and plenty of it." He doesn't smoke and rarely drinks.

After cruising in the Pacific Northwest, Maas developed some interesting insights into the type of training a person would want to undertake before going on an extended cruise. Assuming the rower was in relatively good shape—someone who rowed an hour to an hour and a half three times a week—Maas thinks they should start training two months before their intended departure date. He feels the most difficult part about cruising is soreness. "Your butt gets sore, your hands get sore, your back gets sore." You can overcome that with long rows, Maas says. "They don't have to be done at a fast pace. You don't have to be strong [to cruise] you just have to be conditioned to spending long periods of time in the boat."

Shirwin Smith

Shirwin Smith, founder of Open Water Rowing in Sausalito, rowed traditional boats when she was a child, then drifted away from the sport, only to come back strongly. In 1984, her second year of competitive rowing, she did the Catalina Race aboard Gordie Nash's stretched Alden Double, rigged as a triple. The following year she rowed the race in the Small Craft Double that Nash had turned into a triple. After her second season in a triple, she bought a Maas Dragonfly Double. In 1986 she and Mark Kelley rowed the boat in Washington's Great Cross Sound Regatta and set the fastest elapsed time. For the rest of the season, Smith teamed with her regular partner, Hillary Dembroff, and the pair won their class at Tahoe. In 1987, Dembroff was sidelined for part of the season with a work-related injury, and Smith rowed Catalina with Marie Hagelstein. The pair set a record for the women's doubles that still stands. In 1988 Dembroff and Smith took the Dragonfly across the Catalina Channel for the third time, again taking class honors. In 1989 Smith did her fifth Catalina Race, rowing a new Maas 24 single.

Before she got back into rowing, Smith worked for the National Park Service, where she had to meet the tough physical requirements of the firefighting crew. While she was with the Park Service she ran, "because you're out in the boonies and you have to do something with yourself." When she returned to rowing she found she was on the water four to five days a week. Smith won the first short race she entered, and started training regularly.

When she's racing, Smith weight-trains on alternate days using Keiser machines and free weights, and—not counting her teaching time—she rows at least five days a week, at least four miles a day—preferably eight—along with one long row. "When I'm planning for a long race I do one long row a weekend; if I'm planning for a 20- or 25-mile race, at least two months before that I do between 15 and 20 miles every weekend. Then, when the race comes, it's just one more long row."

Marie Hagelstein and Shirwin Smith, exhausted after setting the women's doubles record in the Catalina race.

Smith consulted with the same nutritionist who helped Gordie Nash develop his diet, and was pleased to learn that her diet was basically good: "I eat a lot of carbohydrates, a lot of breads and grain cereals, fresh vegetables and fresh fruits, a lot of dairy products, especially cheese, and fish or chicken three or four times a week. I can't eat rich things—I feel terrible afterwards. I don't smoke, and only have an occasional glass of wine." Smith claims she is not disciplined about her diet, eating "what my body wants me to eat."

Karen "KC" Carlson

Karen "KC" Carlson, owner of W Dock Rowing in Santa Cruz, has been competing in women's multiple-crewed boats for several years. Her sixth Catalina race was in 1989. Though fiercely competitive (no one could rack up a record like hers with out being competitive), Carlson says, "For me, rowing still has to be fun."

In 1984 Carlson rowed stroke in the Alden Double that Gordie Nash stretched into a triple for her, Shirwin Smith, and Hillary Dembroff. Over the next five years, Carlson teamed with Linda Locklin to row doubles—first a Small Craft, then one of Chris Maas' new Dragonflys. The first race on their competitive schedule each year has been the 26-mile Monterey to Santa Cruz Race at the end of July. With Catalina as their long-term goal they start their "serious, planned training" for the Santa Cruz race eight to 10 weeks before the event. Carlson says, "I used to just think I'd row and row and that would be enough, but I've found I need to train with weights to get stronger. I also officiate at basketball games and that keeps me running a lot. I reach a point with rowing where I just don't get any better. To go faster I have to gain strength, not endurance. On the other hand, Linda doesn't lift weights; she swims and runs."

Teaching rowing, Carlson finds herself in a boat as much as seven days a week, up to three to four hours a day, but she doesn't consider that serious training. As a team, she and Locklin try to "hit four days and vary the rowing between two eight-milers, a 15 and a 20." They don't row with electronics such as Strokecoaches or knotmeters, but they've started carrying a hand-held VHF radio for safety in the ocean off Santa Cruz. They have always carried PFDs, an air horn, and flares, but the radio has given them the extra confidence they needed to extend their training rows. Even without electronics, they time their pieces, keep accurate records, and compare times and sea conditions. By the time they've completed the Monterey to Santa Cruz Race, they "know what kind of time to aim at for Catalina."

After the Santa Cruz race, still with an eye on Catalina, they go into maintenance training. September brings a race every weekend and the trio cuts back on their full training regimen. Racing, they reason, will keep them in shape. They concentrate strategy and assessing their competition. Once September starts, Carlson stops lifting weights.

On the subject of diet, Carlson says that "hanging around gyms makes me think more about what I eat, but being a woman and having diets shoved at you all your life—I resent diets. I do take quite a few supplements, and if I do change my diet naturally, that's fine. I think I tend to have a better diet now than I used to."

ALL FOUR of the rowers above are members of the "rowing industry," but it's vital to understand that they are not good oarsmen because they are in the business, they are in the business because they are good oarsmen. The difference is subtle, but significant. There are people in the industry who are not very good rowers (all things being equal, I would not buy a boat from someone who couldn't row) and there are many, many superb oarsmen who have lives outside of rowing.

Ann Donaldson

Ann Donaldson burst onto the competitive rowing scene in 1989. In April of that year, rowing one of Open Water Rowing's Aeros, she entered her first race, Sausalito's Open Ocean Regatta, and won her division. The 34-year-old Minneapolis native had taken her first rowing lesson at Open Water Rowing in April of 1987. From that time on she had rowed almost three days a week. After the Open Ocean Regatta she ordered a Maas 24, which she took to the Tahoe North Shore Regatta. She placed second in her division. During the summer she rowed the 24 to a class win in San Francisco's Bridge to Bridge Regatta and a second in Seattle's Cross Sound Rowing Race. She also used an Aero to row to second place in the Masters' Nationals. She topped off the season in October, when she defeated four other women's singles to win her division in the Catalina race.

With an opening season like that, I assumed Donaldson had led a very healthy, athletic lifestyle before taking up rowing. She laughed and said, "No, I haven't been very athletic and I just gave up smoking a couple of years ago." So much for assumptions. Donaldson started her serious Catalina race training in July, rowing an hour and a half to two hours a day, nine to 12 miles, six days a week. Leaving from Open Water Rowing, her training rows took her across the bay to San Francisco, around Angel Island, or around Alcatraz and Angel Island—routes made popular by Nash and Strain when they first started their 1986 training for Catalina. She made many of her trips alone, but she also spent quite a bit of time training with others rowing out of Open Water

Rowing—Ken Robinson, Randy Hixon, Kevin Strain, and Shirwin Smith in their Maas 24's, and Bill Berger in a Maas Aero. Smith, who has probably rowed with and watched more competitive rowers than most of us, describes Donaldson as "an extremely determined woman."

Donaldson enhanced her ambitious on-the-water training program with a diet consisting of salads, pasta, fruit, bread, power bars and "lots of water." She augmented her diet with the Chinese herbs ginseng and dong quai. Discovering that dairy products made her dry when she was on the water, she gave them up. Her training and determination paid off, in a year that the Catalina race saw heavy chop in the middle of the channel, a year that no other class records were broken, Ann Donaldson crossed the channel in under six hours, taking more than half an hour off the women's singles record.

Bill Berger

In the late 1950s, Bill Berger rowed sweep at the University of California at Berkley, but drifted away from rowing as the demands of medical school ate up more of his time. In 1984, the 42-year-old anesthesiologist returned at San Francisco's Dolphin Rowing Club, where he rowed traditional (heavy) wooden Whitehalls. The following year he moved across the Bay, joining Sausalito Rowing Club, where he rowed a club-owned Vancouver 21 before buying his own Maas Aero.

In 1986, Berger made his racing debut at the Head of the Estuary Regatta. Since the organizers didn't have any other open-water entrants, Berger's Aero was classed with the racing shells and he finished seventh out of eight entrants. In 1987 he joined the central California group that annually makes its way south for the Catalina race. That year his 21-foot Aero placed second to Bob Jarvis' 24-foot J-Shell. In 1988, Berger suffered terribly from seasickness and retired after 20 miles. He brought his Aero back to Catalina for a third time in 1989 and finished third, the first boat in under 24 feet.

Having to be at work in the operating room at 7:30 every morning, Dr. Berger trains a little differently than most open-water rowers. Since he does most of his training in the afternoon, he spends more time in rough water than does his competition. He claims this is not all bad—the experience makes him a better open-water rower.

Rowing out of Open Water Rowing's Sausalito facility, Berger starts his Catalina training in January, developing what he refers to as "an aerobic base." Through March he "rows three or four times a week, totaling about 20 miles." In April and May he increases his distance slightly, and before the 10-mile Tahoe North Shore Regatta in June he does at least one 12-mile piece. In July and August he augments his usual training with a brace of 15-to 20-mile rows per month. September is his toughest training month—a 30-mile row, two 15-

to 20-milers, and his regular 20 miles per week. Berger estimates that 75 percent of his training is done alone, in the afternoon, but when his schedule permits he joins other competitors in group rows—loosely organized training expeditions where five or six rowers in doubles and singles do the same course, then regroup to eat together and evaluate the row.

Berger rows "the rare piece on the ergometer," adding that "at my age [48 at this writing] it's important to do a good warm-up and stretch out before rowing." Racing and training, Berger consumes vast quantities of water: "500 to 600 cubic centimeters an hour."

As for diet, Berger says he; "tends to go toward a salt-free, carbohydrate-intensive diet," though he admits to eating a steak now and then. After he starts his training in January, he limits himself to two glasses of wine per day, and abstains for two or three days before a race." In August he gives up wine altogether. Like Nash, Berger finds it both informative and important to keep an accurate training log. He keeps his on a tide log, and adds weather and sea conditions to the information already there.

SIX successful open-water rowers with six different paths to that success. I can add one more oarsman's training experiences—my own as a cruiser. When I decided to row a portion of the Sea of Cortez (see Chapter 17), I looked at my rowing program to see what I should change. I'm a little different from those mentioned above in that I'm not competitive. I row simply out of love of the sport, the feeling of peace it gives, and where it takes me. I rarely compete. Before planning the Sea of Cortez cruise I was rowing an Aero about an hour a day, six or seven days a week. My diet was nothing special, but it included very few sweets, and I don't smoke or drink. I didn't make any conscious changes in my diet, although I noticed the longer I prepared (I hate the word "train"), the fewer fats I ate. At the same time, I discovered I was eating more fruit. To increase my stamina, each week I stretched one day's row into two and a half hours. Depending on sea conditions, this meant about 15 to 18 miles. I made a serious mistake in my cruise preparation: I was lucky enough to have access to two boats at the time, a Maas Aero and my Appledore Pod. I did all my preparation in the Aero, simply because it was easier to move around and more fun to row. When I started the cruise aboard the fully laden Appledore, it felt like a barge. For all cruises since, I have rowed the cruising boat as much as possible in preparation.

Remember, there are no training absolutes. If you want to race or cruise, experiment with some of these regimens, but don't follow them blindly. Modify them to fit your needs or develop your own. Don't copy someone else just because you admire their results; it's your results that count. Remember to use the stepping-stone approach, set a long-term goal, and reward yourself as you attain interim goals.

- 14 -

Equipment and Preparation for the Endurance Rower

SEVERAL factors—including, of course, your own tastes—will influence how you plan a long row, and will determine what you *want* to take with you and what you ultimately *will* take: Is your row going to be a cruise, a long passage, or a race? Are you going for two hours or two weeks? Will you follow a route where supplies will be easy to pick up, or will you have to be completely self-sufficient? How reliable is your boat?

■ GEAR FOR RACING

If you're racing, the decision of what to take may seem deceptively easy. If you watch some experienced racers, it might appear that for a short- to medium-distance race, say up to 20 miles, you just have to grab a water bottle or two, get in the boat, and go. It's not quite that simple. Experience has taught these competitors to make a lot of decisions and do considerable preparation before they ever get to the launching site.

The seasoned racer's car or truck usually carries a complete selection of spare parts and tools. It's amazing how a boat can be rowed four or five days a week for months with no gear failures—but take it to a race and it seems to fall apart. If you race, you'll need to take to the launching area all the tools to adjust, fix, or replace, the oarlocks, foot stretchers, buttons and the riggers, and to tighten anything on the boat that could possibly come loose. Spare nuts, bolts, and screws will help if you drop something—and remember an axiom of Murphy's Law: You will lose or break the only part for which you don't have a spare. A spare fin and a pitch gauge or extras shims or bushings for your adjustable oarlocks should also be in your kit. Take along a can or bottle of Teflon-based lubricant for your sleeves, oarlocks, pins, and seat. Bring a spare seat, and, if you rely on one, a seat pad. A final, indispensable item endurance racers count on is duct tape. There's no way you can have too much of this valuable commodity with you.

The racer has to look intently at weather and water conditions. If the race is scheduled to start early it may be cold and he'll want to layer his upper body, making sure the clothes he chooses are easy to row in and to remove as the day—and the oarsman—gets warmer. If it's hot and sunny, you'll need a waterproof sunscreen and a cap or visor. Some rowers wear sunglasses. If you do, get a keeper that cinches them tightly to your face so they won't slip when you sweat. I strongly recommend a hat, sunglasses, or both; you need to protect your eyes on the water. If it's hot, or going to get hot, bring extra water bottles. Dehydration is one of the worst enemies of the endurance rower. Most middle- and long-distance races are so competitive today that no one can afford the time to stop and eat, but a few racers carry a banana or energy bar, something they can swallow quickly for energy.

Finally, there is the question of the three places the oarsman contacts the boat: hands, feet, and butt. Some rowers never wear gloves; they say they can't "feel" the oars. Some wear ³/₄-finger gloves, while others tape their hands with masking or adhesive tape. Many row barefoot; others keep a pair of socks to slip into once they are aboard.

Some oarsmen won't row without a seat pad, others can't stand them. However, the decision should be made long before the start of a race. You should row many miles both with and without a pad before deciding. Never

Be aware of the ripple effect: If you add a seat pad, you'll have to raise the height of your oarlocks.

change your mind about equipment at the start of a race—race with what you know, and make changes only after miles of testing. As mentioned before, most changes you make have a ripple effect: If you add or delete a seat pad at the start of a race, you will have to raise or drop the height of your oarlocks, which could prompt other last-minute changes.

Weather, too, may dictate how you tune your boat for the race. If it's flat calm, and predicted to stay that way throughout the day, set your oarlocks low and use a small fin, sacrificing tracking in favor of less drag and better turning ability. If it's rough, or local knowledge says it will be, raise your oarlocks to get some extra clearance, and use a larger fin for improved tracking. Tune your boat for the *worst* conditions you expect to encounter—it's easier to row a boat with high oarlocks and large fin in smooth water than it is to row a boat rigged for calm conditions when the weather kicks up.

Race instructions may mandate some special gear for the race. Most races require a PFD be carried aboard. Not only should you have one with you, you should know how to attach it. If you are rowing a traditional design, it's no problem—you can just toss it aboard. If you have a brand-new Maas 24, figure out how you're going to carry a life preserver before the start of a race. Many rowers duct-tape them to the deck aft of the cockpit or drill small holes in the hull/deck joint lip and run a shock cord across the deck so they can slip the PFD under that. Duct-taping a life preserver on at the last minute is one thing, but drilling holes and running shock cord can be far more time-consuming than it sounds, especially as the start of a race nears.

There are some wonderful stories of experienced racers who have had terrible experiences because they weren't properly prepared at the start of a race. I remember a boatbuilder dashing about before the start of a 20-miler, trying to borrow a seat pad—not a common spare in most rowers' gear bags. He ended up being a minute or two late for his start and did very poorly in the race, probably because his search for a seat pad (which he never found) took up all his preparation time.

Another oarsman ordered a brand new-boat to be delivered to him at the site of a 10-mile race. The builder delivered the boat, with the oarlocks properly pitched, and the oarsman, who had been training daily, arrived with his oars. The oar buttons were set, oarlock height and the stretchers adjusted. The oarsman should have been ready to finish well up in the fleet. He was in shape, he had the psychological advantage of knowing he had a brand-new boat, and every item was working for him, except one: His training boat had track shoes instead of clogs and he rowed barefoot. The new boat came equipped with leather clogs and plastic heel cups. The new leather was extremely stiff and the oarsman, who had never worn socks to row, hadn't even thought of bringing a pair. He got a good start and soon found himself passing boats, but after two miles the stiff leather and hard plastic had rubbed large blisters on the sides of his feet, the tops of his toes, and his heels. By the first turning mark, 2 $^2/_3$ miles into the race, the blisters were beginning to weep. On the next leg the blisters tore open and the oarsman finally had to stop as the leather chafed the raw skin underneath. When he finally rowed to shore, with his feet out of the clogs, the bottom of the cockpit was awash in his blood.

Experienced racers show up for the start of a race with far more gear than anyone could possibly imagine they would need. Gordie Nash always looks as if he has enough equipment to build a spare boat, and he probably does.

■ GEAR FOR PASSAGEMAKING

If you are doing a long-distance passage, you'll probably need more gear than the racer, but less than the cruiser. The shorter your passage the more your gear will parallel that of the racer; the longer, the more it will be like that of the cruiser. Always plan for the worst-case scenario.

When you start provisioning for a long-distance passage or cruise, you'll find that there is very little out there made with the rower in mind. This doesn't mean there aren't a lot of usable items, they just weren't made specifically for rowing. As you make lists of the things you need or want, you will discover you must look into equipment and supplies designed for other sports to fill your needs. Powerboating, sailing, canoeing, and kayaking will offer some very useful gear. Non-aquatic sports such as bicycling, camping, and mountain climbing will also be good sources of gear and provisions.

The more information you have about the area where you intend to row, the better equipped you will be to make decisions about what to take with you. Find out as much about your destination as you can. If you've chosen a place close to home it should be easy, but if you've decided to cartop your boat to some distant lake or shore, you'll have to do a little more research. Later we'll discuss some of the elements to consider when choosing a place to cruise and how to go about learning the area.

There are some oarsmen who prefer to plan everything before they leave on a cruise, feeling that it's part of the challenge and joy. Others feel it's a waste of energy to lug supplies for an entire trip, knowing they could resupply en route. If you *know* you will be able to resupply along the way, there's nothing wrong with this approach. Of course, if you arrive the day the store is closed or the day before it's expecting a big shipment from its wholesalers, you may be out of luck. Even if you are sure you're carrying everything you'll need, it's always wise to mark your chart with all possible resupply points.

▬ CLOTHING

Decide what it will take to keep you warm or cool, dry and comfortable. This may be your first excursion into the gear offered by other sports, and as we've said there is no company out there called "Rowing Clothiers" or anything remotely like it. Several specialized companies offer rowing shorts, special gloves and rowing jackets, but that's about it—not really enough to get you through a week or two in the wilds. We discussed some of the options available to rowers earlier.

Since by now you've learned your own comfort thresholds, you'll need to know about the conditions you can expect in your intended cruising grounds. Is it going to rain five days out of nine? Is it going to average 65 degrees, or 85? Is the average humidity going to be 45 or 95 percent? Finally, how much can you carry in your boat? Once you know all this, it's time to start looking at clothing.

In some areas you can get away with very little; in others you will have to plan for a variety of contingencies. Cruising California's Channel Islands in late summer, I took a good hat, two T-shirts, two pairs of shorts, a light jacket, and flaps for going ashore. This would be appropriate attire in that area six or seven months out of the year. In the middle of winter (yes, there is winter in Southern California) a pair of long sweatpants, a heavier jacket or vest, heavier shirt, and some rain gear would have been necessary.

There are some special factors an oarsman must take into consideration when buying clothing for use on his boat. The most obvious is whether he can row in them. There are a lot of great clothes that may keep you warm or cool or dry, but you just plain can't row in. You might want to review the clothing chapter before you go shopping for new rowing clothes.

One final note on clothing, don't take brand new gear on a long row, be it cruise or race. Be sure you've rowed in everything you take before you go. Twenty-five miles into a trip is not the time to find out you can't go into the catch position in your new rain gear, or your thumbs snag in your jacket pockets each time you initiate a recovery.

▬ CLOTHING STORAGE

No matter what clothes you take, you'll want to keep them dry when you're not wearing them. If you've rowed all day in wind-driven spray, and reach camp only to discover the warm, dry clothes you've been thinking about for the past two hours are wetter than what you're wearing, you'll understand what the word "disappointment" means.

The conditions where you row, and the type of boat you own, will dictate how you keep clothing and other gear dry. If you're rowing an open-water shell, you'll have to use canoe or kayak bags strapped to the hull. These are very dry, but virtually impossible to get into while underway. They can also be used aboard traditional boats and are great in extreme conditions. I once used a body (coroner's) bag on *Kavienga*. It was large, had a rugged full-length plastic zipper, and was perfectly watertight. Enough people told me it was "gross" and "disgusting" that when the bag wore out I finally shifted over to a pair of small Bone Dry kayaking storage bags. The two small bags are better than the one large one because they can be shifted around the boat for better weight distribution. For shorter trips in good weather I just toss gear into a knapsack. The day pack is water repellent and keeps everything together.

Kyle and Suzy Collins of Salt Lake City, Utah, who row a 17-foot Whitehall in the Sea of Cortez where they don't have to worry about weather other than heat, pack all their extra clothing, toilet articles, provisions, and camera in four Grade IV canoe packs. These packs have watertight roll tops and keep everything compact, together, and easy to handle. Their camping equipment is all kept in the self-contained bags it came in, and the bags and packs allow them to shift gear as required to balance the boat. With everything in water-tight bags they don't have to worry about keeping special items dry.

■ CAMPING GEAR

If you haven't looked into camping equipment for some time you will find there have been great strides made in the efficiency of the gear available today. Gone are the days of heavy canvas tents and thick, heavy sleeping bags that once wet, stayed wet forever.

If you are going to be sleeping aboard, or the climate is mild and there aren't a lot of bugs, you won't need a tent. (It would almost be a shame to miss out on using a modern tent—there are so many great ones available.) If you need one and don't know about them, talk to knowledgeable salespeople, or campers and hikers whose opinions you respect. While these tents are good, they are also expensive, and you won't want to spend more than you have to.

Unless you already have one, I wouldn't recommend the dome tents—they look sexy and have plenty of room, but most are designed for major expeditions into heavy snow country. They're not light, and would be overkill for the average rowing excursion. I have used an unorthodox shaped tent by North Face called the Bullfrog. It has netting that keeps out bugs but lets in cool breezes. It also has a rain flap for protection when the weather turns nasty. It packs into a tiny space and weighs only six pounds. If this is too heavy for you, a new model called the Tadpole weighs only four pounds. Moss Tents, of Camden, Maine, also offers some interesting equipment.

Sleeping bags, too, have made giant strides in the past few years. If you have a moldy old bag in your basement or attic, you can certainly air it out and use it, but if it's down rather than synthetic you should probably think about a new one. There's a great variety to choose from. Like today's tents, modern sleeping bags are made for specific conditions. Sleeping bags are rated according to the lowest temperature the bag can handle. If a 20-degree bag is ample, you will only be spending extra money and burdening yourself with extra mass by buying a minus-10-degree bag. North Face and Moonstone are both well-known brands, and offer a good selection. A good bag will probably weigh between 2 1/2 and 3 1/2 pounds.

An inexpensive, inflatable air mattress that weighs almost nothing and folds to store in no space at all is one of the most important comfort items you can take with you. It's more comfortable and easier to store than a foam pad, which usually has to be rolled up and tends to soak up and retain water. When you pack your air mattress, be sure to include a patch kit. If you don't have the patch kit with you, you'll be sure to hole the mattress.

A good stove is essential. Sure, you can eat cold food directly out of a can, and do without a warm cup of coffee or tea in the morning, but there are some wonderful camp stoves that weigh very little and burn either propane or white gas. Friends who spend more time camping than I recommend white gas, saying that propane is not cost-efficient.

I tend to stay away from stoves that require pressurization. I was once at Bahia de Santa Maria, a beautiful bay 25 miles south of San Felipe on the Sea of Cortez. The bay is about a half-mile long and the tidal fluctuation is so great that the entire bay is dry at low tide. It's a wonderful place to explore. I spent more time trying to pressurize an old Coleman stove I'd borrowed than exploring the bay.

Before buying a stove, consider what it weighs, how fast it will boil a quart of water, and how fuel-efficient it is. A company by the name of MSR makes some good ones. Most camping stoves come with a neat little package of lightweight cooking utensils that are easy to store and make a lot more sense than raiding your kitchen cabinets.

Aside from providing light to read or eat by, lanterns can be a major safety factor. If you're sleeping aboard and there's even the slightest chance of other craft moving in your vicinity, keep a lantern lit. Aboard *Kavienga*, I place an oar upright in the mast partner and hang a lantern from it. You can achieve the same effect by resting one oar athwartships in the oarlocks and lashing the other to it vertically. In the interest of safety, I prefer a battery-powered lantern, rather than one with a flame. Be sure to start with a fresh battery, and pack a spare battery and an extra bulb. If weight and space considerations permit, carry a spare lantern.

If your cruising area offers an ample supply of fresh water, you can save a lot of weight and space in your boat by taking freeze-dried food. There is lots of great stuff available; it is easy to store, and most of it quite tasty. If you have the space, don't care about the weight, or aren't going to find freshwater streams, your alternative is canned food. Even if you pack your cans in a watertight bag, take the time to mark each one with a grease pencil so you know what it contains. Just a little spray can do considerable damage to a paper label. Also be sure you take *two* can openers—and be sure you take the empty cans home with you or dispose of them properly.

No matter which type or combination of foods you take, be sure you have plenty. You'll be doing a lot of work out there and food, along with being necessity, is a great reward. A good meal on a secluded beach after a long row can be a wonderful experience. Try the foods at home before you go, and take ample snacks that you can eat easily while rowing. I like apples, bananas, dried apricots, and a variety of trail mixes while I row; others prefer a candy bar, and still others like to gnaw on beef jerky. Take what pleases you, but take something—you're going to burn up a lot of calories while you row.

If you enjoy fishing, use your catch to augment your diet. Just don't arrange your entire diet around what you *hope* to catch. One summer I rowed a beautiful mountain lake in Idaho. The water was gin clear, and scores of large trout were visible. Not one could be tempted to take a lure, bait, or a fly. I sat in the boat eating a sandwich, watching the fish congregate in the shade of the hull.

No single provision is more important than water. Rowing is exhausting, and dehydration is a very real concern. Be sure you have more than enough water and that you store it carefully. A friend who rows the Sea of Cortez, where fresh water is virtually unattainable, has some marvelous collapsible water jugs. When they're empty he can flatten them and store them out of the way. He has also started taking a solar still with him. Borrowed from life rafts, this contraption uses condensation to turn salt water into fresh. He keeps it as an emergency backup in case he runs into trouble and has to stay out longer than planned. The water produced by the still doesn't taste as if it came from a mountain stream, but if he needs it, it will save his life.

I prefer to carry water in half-gallon plastic bottles, the way it comes from the store. The bottles are small and easy to handle, each bottle is sealed, and if one is holed, only the water in that one is lost. By distributing the bottles around the boat I can balance her. Storing the empties doesn't bother me, and they can be refilled or disposed of (properly) along the way. If you've found a good anchorage and plan to use it again that day, you can tie one of these empty jugs to the anchor line to mark it.

After food, clothing, and water, there are still first aid, navigation, and safety gear, along with toilet articles, dishes, and eating utensils. Some people can happily get by with a single pan, using it for both cooking and eating. Others prefer plastic, metal, or paper plates, and some just have to have their morning coffee in a special insulated mug.

One item expedition outfitters can supply is a waterproof toilet paper container—a good investment. Personal items such as toothbrush and toothpaste take up only a little space. You might also think about adding a small transistor radio and a good paperback. Both make pleasant camp companions, but need to be stored where they will remain dry. A camera is fun to have along, but will require some special care. No matter how good your watertight storage bags are, I would not recommend taking a brand new Canon F-1 on a rowing expedition. Take either a "disposable" camera or one of the new "sports cameras" designed to stand up to conditions around the water. Remember that the film should be kept cool, not allowed to bake all day in a sealed bag.

If the racer has to bring a truckload of tools to the start of an event, the cruiser has to take his tools with him. Weight and available storage space demand that the cruiser be selective about what tools and spare parts he finds necessary. A lot of space and weight can be saved by doubling up. For instance, several open-end or box wrenches can be replaced by a single crescent wrench. Don't agonize over a single tool; if you might need it, take it. There isn't a lot to break on a rowing boat, but anything that does can ruin your trip.

Always keep a high-quality knife on board—either a heavy sheath knife or compact pocket knife, or both. Don't scrimp on either, a good knife will last a lifetime, and each day you will find uses for it.

If you're rowing fixed-seat, take a spare oarlock—you never know what you might drop. If you're rowing sliding-seat, take an extra pin, and be sure you have the wrenches you need to make the change. Depending on the length of your trip, you might want to take an extra sliding seat. They don't weigh much, and are not the kind of item you can easily repair or replace on a cruise.

The question of an extra oar, or even a pair of oars always comes up. I've broken only two oars in my life, and both were snapped in the surf. But this doesn't mean I won't break a third on a cruise. I think if I were contemplating a cruise in an Aero I would also choose to leave the spare at home. When cruising aboard *Kavienga* I do carry a spare oar.

An anchor is another item you won't be worrying about in an open-water shell, but it's something that could come in very handy in a traditional design. The beauty of traditional boats is that they are light, with low windage, when compared with a motorboat or sailboat, so it doesn't take much to anchor them. Your choice of anchor will depend on the size of your boat and the bottom where you most often anchor. Aboard *Kavienga* I use a 12-pound modified mushroom (the long shaft common to these anchors was cut down to make it more manageable aboard), which works very well in sand and gravel, and moderately well in rock. It's equipped with five feet of $^3/_{16}$-inch chain and 60 feet of $^3/_8$-inch nylon rode. This gear is all a little heavy for a 16-foot peapod, and breaks my minimalism rule. My excuse is that it's left over from a small sailboat I once owned and I haven't been able to bring myself to spend money on lighter ground tackle. In case of emergency the nylon rode could be used as a tow line, or streamed as a warp in heavy seas.

If you're rowing a traditional design and plan to haul out at night, think about how you'll slide the boat up the beach. Both sand and rock can damage the bottom of your boat, and the boat, fully loaded, can be extremely heavy. Before you go, experiment with loading the boat and see if you can move it easily. You may need to look into rollers; there are some good inflatable ones that will take up little space, but you'll have to blow them up first.

Once you have a list of all your clothes, food, tools, safety gear, and navigation equipment, take a long, hard look at it. Remember, you'll have to share the limited space in your boat with its mass and propel its weight every foot of the way with the power of your muscles. Of his long row along the Maine coast, John Garber says he started out, "overloaded and overequipped." The line between over-equipped and underequipped is a fine one, which each oarsman must draw for himself. Most often that line is best recognized in hindsight, but the line you scribed after your last voyage will make the one you draw before your next journey that much easier. If it comes down to a choice between being overloaded or underequipped, err on the side of conservatism: It's usually easier to get rid of gear along the course of a trip than to acquire new gear.

Whether you're going out for a 20-mile race or a 100-mile cruise, after you've practiced storing all your gear, go over your boat. Examine everything, and make sure it's in top working order. This is no time to procrastinate—a squeaking seat isn't going to suddenly stop squeaking 15 miles offshore; a cross-threaded nut on an oarlock gate is not going to repair itself. If your bailer has been hard to open or hard to close, you can be sure it won't lubricate itself on a beach 30 miles from home. Take it apart and fix it before you leave. If the thwart's varnish is lifting and there's a possibility of splinters, sand it down and add three coats of good varnish. Take the time to do repairs properly—it will save a lot of time and inconvenience on the water. No matter what the problem is, it's going to be easier to work on at home, where you will have more tools and be closer to suppliers you know and trust.

- 15 -

Choosing a Cruising Ground

Y OU'VE modified your boat, you've decided what to take with you, and you've worked yourself into good shape. Now what? If you're a racer, it's simple—you look at the racing calendar and select the events that mesh with your schedule and abilities. If you're not a racer, it gets a little tougher. First you have to decide whether to make a long-distance passage or a cruise.

For our purposes a long-distance passage can be defined as more of an endurance test, getting from point A to point B, and not caring too much about what we see along the way. On a long-distance passage, the destination is more important than the journey. A cruise, on the other hand, is more a voyage of discovery, where the object of the exercise is to explore the territory, and learn what it has to offer.

The biggest complaint I've heard from cruisers who feel they have "failed" is that they tried to tackle too much, too soon. Remember the stepping-stone approach to long-distance rowing: If you've never tackled an overnighter in your boat, it is probably best not to set your sights on a 100-miler as your first cruise. Try spending a full day in the boat. You won't have to make any modifications to your boat or assemble much gear. Just pack some dry clothes, your safety equipment, a lunch, and some water. Row up or down the coast or lake shore, making your goal a particular cove or point. Have lunch at your destination and row back. This first day-cruise can teach you quite a bit about yourself and your boat, and it will probably whet your appetite for longer cruises.

If you've opted to challenge yourself with a long passage, you'll find it easier to plan than a cruise. A round trip is nice, say 20 to 30 miles out and back, because you don't need to cope with the logistics of getting you and the boat home from your destination. A friend's first long-distance row was up and down the length of Lake Tahoe. The lake is 26 miles long; he took provisions to be out two days, rowed from North Shore to South Shore on the first day, camped out overnight, then rowed back.

If you are choosing a cruising ground close to home, you'll probably already know quite a bit about it. Still, there may be some aspects you will have to look at from the special perspective of a rowing boat. It's one thing to think of the beauty of a coastline or lake shore as seen from a speeding powerboat or a well-equipped sailing boat, or even from the road paralleling it; it's quite another to row along that same shore. Before you start out consider currents, tides, surf, beaches where you can land, wind, fog, and the locations of bottoms with good holding ground for anchoring. To be on the safe side, do all the research you would do if you knew nothing of the territory. What you learn may surprise you, and also save you some problems during the cruise or passage.

If you choose an area to cruise because it has always intrigued you, there's no doubt that you will need to learn about the territory—especially the weather conditions. You may hear that "it's nice there that time of year—you'll love it." But what may be nice to a vacationer staying in a motor home or hotel may not be equally "nice" for the oarsman sleeping in his boat. Dense night and morning fogs may slip the mind of the tourist with a comfortable bed in a room with a thermostat, but the same conditions could make your trip cold, damp, and dangerous.

Learn about the range of temperatures, average rainfall, and force and direction of the winds. Know also about the strength and extreme ranges of the tides, the force and direction of the currents, the direction of the surf, and a dozen other specifics. To find out, talk to boaters who have cruised the area. Unless they too are rowers, remember the differences between their craft and yours. If you don't know many people who have traveled your intended course, or even if you know hundreds, augment what they tell you by reading the local and regional boating magazines and newspapers and, most importantly, an authoritative, up-to-date cruising guide.

Good cruising guides are marvelous books. They will provide you with just about everything you need to know about an area. They are full of small charts, photographs of natural and man-made landmarks, and information about weather, currents, and tides. Harbors and marinas and their entrances are described in great detail. The history of the area is discussed, and that can add considerably to the enjoyment of a cruise. The authors' personal observations can be very helpful, and usually their anecdotes make important points. A cruising guide will inform you about subjects as diverse as holding ground for anchoring and seasonal storms. Before leaving for the Santa Barbara

Channel Islands I read in my cruising guide that "Anacapa is suicidal in a strong Santa Ana wind." That was a bit of information that stayed with me through the cruise, and I listened very carefully to my radio for the slightest mention of the strong desert winds.

Before memorizing your cruising guide, check your book's publication date. What may have been very true in 1981 may no longer be true in 1991. There is also the problem of focus; cruising guides are written for sailors and powerboaters, not rowers. You may need to read between the lines occasionally—there's a big difference between pushing the throttle forward half an inch to deal with an adverse current, and trying to row against it. Cruising guides are available through ships' chandleries and nautical bookstores, many of which offer mail-order service.

For your cruise you will need to know about both natural and man-made sources of supply. For instance, when Chris Maas and Greg Shell cruised the Pacific Northwest, they discovered scores of freshwater streams. On the other hand, when I cruised the Santa Barbara Channel Islands, there was no fresh water at all. It's one thing to start a cruise with three gallons of water you don't need and quite another to arrive at a deserted, dry landfall with none.

If you investigate an area carefully and learn of factors that will obstruct your cruise or passage, think about changing areas. Don't allow yourself to become locked into a destination because it was your first choice. If you're committed a particular vacation time slot and find that your first choice of a cruising ground is too hot, cold, humid, dry, or windy at that time of year, look around for another. There are so many interesting places to cruise that none of us will ever have time to try any more than a small percentage of them.

When you look at charts of your intended cruising grounds, or the area you will be passing through on an endurance row, plan for contingencies. Make careful note of beaches where you could haul out in an emergency, and towns or marinas where you might be able to pick up some necessary supplies. Even look for places where you could cancel your cruise or passage. There's no disgrace in cutting a trip short, and there can be a hundred unforeseen reasons for doing so. Remember, Gordie Nash completed only one of his three round-trip attempts from San Francisco to the Farallons. If you quit your trip early, remember why you stopped and apply that knowledge to your next attempt.

Kyle and Suzy Collins have approached cruising in a different and fascinating way. For several years they had a 17-foot, 95-pound WEST System fixed-thwart Gunning Dory, which they carried on top of their four-wheel-drive pickup truck. They loaded the bed of the truck with camping gear and headed for Mexico and Baja California. Whenever they found a likely looking beach or cove they unloaded the dory, shifted the camping gear to the boat, and went rowing.

With the truck they had the maneuverability to explore a wide area and cruise those that interested them. On their last three-week trip, after seeing some of the mainland coast and exploring the coves between San Jose del Cabo and Cabo San Lucas, they ended up with a four-day row through Bahia de la Concepcion. They loved the bay's wonderful beaches, spectacular scenery, and fishing, and planned to return for a longer cruise.

The year after their Bahia de la Conception cruise, they built a 17-foot Whitehall. The Whitehall gave away a bit of seaworthiness in rough conditions, but in four years of rowing the dory they had never experienced anything approaching survival conditions. The Collinses felt the Whitehall's speed-producing longer waterline more than compensated for any loss of rough-water handling. When I last spoke to them they had just returned from a month exploring the Midriff Islands in the Sea of Cortez, and were planning their next voyage.

If you don't want to make modifications to your boat or do all the planning a cruise requires, there's a new option to consider—professionally planned rowing excursions. In England you can rent a traditional Thames skiff, fully equipped with camping gear, and spend several days rowing the historic old river. The same type of service is being offered in Germany. In Baja California there are planned group tours led in sailing-rowing Drascombs. Small businesses like these are sure to come and go, but they provide an alternative to spending the time and effort of doing everything yourself. Some also offer the security of a group and an experienced leader. Look into these—one of them could be the ideal first rowing cruise for you.

- 16 -
Safety and First Aid

THE endurance rower, whether going solo or with others, must accept responsibility for safety. Even if you've rowed thousands of miles, review Chapter 7. Many of us become too comfortable rowing our local waters and fall into poor, slipshod habits, like forgetting to file a float plan before setting out on a long-distance row.

■ SAFETY EQUIPMENT

While competing in a race, a PFD will usually be a sufficient precaution. Racing, there will be other competitors around you, and frequently, chase or escort boats. When you go off on your own, for a long-distance passage or a cruise, you will be at the mercy of the elements and *must* be equipped to get yourself out of any trouble. It's one thing to forget your PFD on a three-mile row inside the harbor; it's another entirely to leave it behind when starting off on a 50-mile cruise. Preparation, planning, and forethought based on experience can help you avoid trouble, but sometimes, no matter how well prepared and careful you are, trouble will find you.

In Chapter 7 we discussed PFDs. I strongly advise getting a Type I vest before attempting a cruise or long-distance passage. Tie a whistle to it, and a small hand-held strobe light or flashlight to help rescuers locate you at night.

When you start rowing long distances, avoiding collisions may become more important than when rowing in your home waters. There is some gear you can carry aboard that *may* make you more visible to other boaters, either to avoid collision or facilitate rescue. In Santa Barbara there's a dory with a six-foot mast made from a $1^1/_2$-inch dowel. The owner fixes a small radar reflector to the masthead and lashes the mast forward. I have my doubts about its effectiveness, but it seems to make him feel better. You can also fix battery-pow-

A PFD with strobe and whistle securely fastened in the stern of *Kavienga.*

ered running lights or "shake and break" chemical light sticks to your boat, but I wouldn't count on many other boaters spotting them. Use anything you think will help, but do keep a good strong flashlight handy so you can shine it at the helmsman of an approaching vessel. Gina Billings uses a pair of Tekna lights—they are small, light, and throw a powerful beam. She keeps two because it's easier than carrying spare batteries and a spare bulb, and if she drops the light overboard the spare batteries and bulb would do her little good.

Again, bailers are vital for both comfort and safety. If you're rowing a recreational shell and your suction bailer locks up you can always bail the small cockpit with your cupped hands; if you're rowing a traditional design keep at least one conventional bailer tied securely to the boat.

For all their apparent strength, stainless steel oarlock pins have proved to be somewhat vulnerable. If you're rowing long distances, take a spare pin, complete with nuts and spacers, and the wrenches you will need to replace it in the field.

If your cruise or passage takes you far from shore you might want to look into an emergency position-indicating radio beacon (EPIRB). When activated, an EPIRB automatically sends out a radio beacon on which a rescuer can home in. The Class-A EPIRB is stored in an inverted position and activates automatically when turned upright. This is great on a larger boat, but not too practical aboard a rowing boat. A Class-B EPIRB has to be turned on by hand and is probably a better choice for a small boat. Both units are designed for use more than 20 miles offshore, where their signals can be picked up by aircraft and military search-and-rescue facilities. The Class-C EPIRB is intended for use closer to shore as it uses the VHF/FM frequencies received by marine radiotelephones.

▬ MEDICATIONS

Many row, or started rowing, for health reasons. If you have a health problem, see your doctor before tackling an endurance row. Even if he was the one who originally suggested you take up rowing, a 100-mile cruise or 20-mile race may not be what he had in mind. If you are taking any form of prescription drug the condition you're taking it for won't go away just because you decide to go for a long row. Be sure to take enough of your medication to see you through a longer trip than the one you plan. You might even want to take twice as much, divided between two different bottles and stored in different places on the boat as a precaution against loss or damage.

▬ FIRST AID

Since most of us row by ourselves we have to be able to give ourselves any first aid we might need. As in safety, prevention is better than practice, but you must know what to do in case of emergency. Don't assume, because you bought it at a marine hardware store, it has a red cross on it, and it says "Nautical First-Aid Kit" that the little plastic box contains everything you need. The box itself, especially if it has a good O-ring seal, may be perfect for your needs, but do a careful inventory of the contents and make changes as needed.

With a little help from those who have rowed log distances before, and a doctor, each of us is best suited to figure out what we really need. How long you are going to be out, and where you are going to be rowing will determine how you want to fill your first-aid kit. If you're rowing the Connecticut coast from Stamford to Guilford, exploring the Norwalk and Thimble Islands, you probably won't need to pack much. It's a populated area with all the modern conveniences and you will never be far from help. On the other hand, if you're cruising the Baja peninsula, you'll be on your own in a largely uninhabited area. You will need to carry quite a bit more, including a snake-bite kit.

The following is not intended as a complete list, but it will cover the basics:

First-aid manual	Aspirin (or equivalent)
Pepto-Bismol	Assorted Band-Aids
Sterile gauze pads/roll	Finger and toe splints
Adhesive tape	Antihistamine tablets
Ace bandage	Hydrocortisone cream
Eye drops	Rubber bands
Waterproof sunscreen	Polysporin (or equivalent)
Scissors	Tweezers
Chemical hot and cold packs	Q-Tips

There are many other items you may want to take. For instance, you might want to have someone teach you how to sew yourself up and include a suture kit. Tell your doctor what you plan to do and ask his advice; he might suggest additions and write prescriptions for a painkiller or antibiotic.

If you're ready for a long-distance row, you've already faced the problem of seasickness. If over-the-counter medications haven't helped, ask your doctor to write you a prescription for Transderm Scop. Many people swear by these little Band-Aid-like patches, but be sure you try one or two before your long-distance row. A few people have bad reactions, and you don't want to find out you're one of them when you're 15 miles offshore.

Cuts, burns, and blisters of varying severity will be the most common complaints you will have to deal with. Read your first-aid manual before you go—it will be easier than when you are sitting in the boat dripping blood on it from a badly cut index finger. Learn to recognize different types of burns and bleeding, know about ways to clean and protect a wound, use splints, and find pressure points. Taking a Red Cross first-aid course would be a wise precaution, even if you never injure yourself while rowing.

Heat can be a killer. Since you will be both doctor and patient, read your manual and learn the *early* symptoms of heat cramps, heat exhaustion, and heatstroke. Find out what to do for yourself as soon as you even think you're beginning to suffer from one of these ailments.

At the other end of the thermometer, extreme hypothermia can kill you; even relatively mild hypothermia can cause weakness and loss of concentration. Read your first-aid manual on the causes and treatment of hypothermia, paying particular attention to prevention. Take care to keep warm and dry, because even mild water, especially in combination with a chilling wind, can lower your body temperature significantly. Know your rowing area, know the temperature of the water, and plan your clothing ahead of time.

If you go overboard, get out of the water quickly and, unless you and the boat are in danger, concentrate on yourself. Hypothermia is best treated by warming the body *slowly*, this avoids overstimulating your system and pumping lots of cold blood from extremities to vital organs. If you can get to shore without any problems, do so. If not, you will have to take care of yourself in the boat. Strip off all your wet clothes and lie down in a sleeping bag or wrap yourself in a warm blanket. If you can't do either, bundle up in the warmest, driest clothes you have. If you have to row, take it very easy—exercise, too, can overstimulate the flow of blood. Avoid drinks with caffeine or alcohol.

Fatigue can also be a very real problem, but it's easy to deal with if you are aware of it. Don't chase last-minute details until the moment you leave; get a good night's sleep before you shove off—it will carry you quite a way. Setting realistic daily goals will help, as will eating well and getting plenty of sleep. If your trip is scheduled for a week or more, and you begin to feel fatigue, cut back on your daily goals. Spend more time on the beach or at anchor, and get more rest.

None of this is intended to frighten the prospective long-distance rower, but it's a fact that you will be entering a potentially hostile environment, and must be able to take care of yourself. With the proper planning and fore-thought your trip should be a safe one. I'm a real klutz around the house: I stub my toes on doorways, chairs, and table legs, I trip over the dog, and if I go out to the garage to do any work with tools the chances are very good that I'll come in with a bloody finger. However, I've never suffered a major accident while rowing. Rowing is a safe sport if you take the time to anticipate problems and use common sense.

- 17 -

A Cruise

THIS chapter and the next are provided to remind us why we're learning to row, to tell how damn much fun it is out there, and maybe teach a little at the same time. This chapter illustrates the type of experience available to the cruising oarsman.

I HAD made no long distance cruises in *Kavienga* in two years. Something told me it was time to start planning more than a daily row. I had the boat—now I needed to figure out when and where to make my cruise. Early spring seemed like a good time to take off, for no other reason than I was making my plans in February and it would take about that long to get ready.

For some time, three destinations had been vying for my attention. Every day the bulk of Catalina stood on the horizon and I thought about circumnavigating the 19 1/2-mile long island. The most popular offshore destination in Southern California, Catalina is crowded in summer, but virtually deserted at other times of the year. Its rugged, untouched landscape reminds one of what California must have been like before freeways, malls, and housing developments. Thinking about Catalina didn't progress further than a simple plan. I postponed the Catalina trip—the weather would be better in late September or early October. April still sees the occasional front bringing wind and rain from the northwest.

The second possible destination was Lake Powell, on the Arizona-Utah border. Lake Powell was created when the Colorado River was dammed at Page, Arizona. Before the Glen Canyon Dam the area was a mini-Grand Canyon. Now it's a mini-Grand Canyon with a floor of water. I postponed the Powell trip when I discovered the weather was less than ideal in early April. A friend who had taken his powerboat to the lake the year before, told me the nights could be freezing. Besides, he wanted to row the lake as well, but couldn't get away until early June. We decided to make the trip together, and I opted for my third destination.

■ A BAJA CALIFORNIA CRUISE

To many in the West and Southwest, Baja California is a handy playground. Windsurfers, dirt bikers, surfers, fishermen, four-wheel-drive fanatics, and others regularly flock to the rugged, unspoiled desert and its pristine shores. For some time I had entertained the idea of a cruise on the Sea of Cortez. My ultimate goal was to explore some of the Midriff Islands, near the center of the 800-mile-long sea. But before going that far afield I thought it best to experience the northern end of the sea. Conditions there were similar, but it was closer to home.

I had been to Baja several times and knew some people who had rowed there, but I felt the need for more research. For several weeks I read, planned, read some more, and changed my plans. Lists of needed equipment kept growing, but *Kavienga*'s volume did not increase accordingly. The more I read, the more I felt as if I was taking my life in my hands venturing into Baja. Each book stressed the lack of facilities and desolation. The books weren't exaggerating the remoteness of the area, but neither were they presenting an optimistic picture. One mentioned the possibility of bandits.

I had spent enough time in Baja to know that the guidebooks were presenting Baja in a way to make travelers think twice, but that they were accurate in advising people to bring everything they would need. There are no convenience stores on the coast of the Sea of Cortez. As items were checked off my lists, the garage seemed to bulge with gear. I repeatedly went through the pile, giving each piece of equipment second and third thoughts, discarding some, but adding others. In final weight- and space-saving moves the anchor chain was taken out of my ground tackle, and my tent was set aside. I copied appropriate pages from Baja guidebooks. I talked to others who had rowed the same area. I needed car insurance, a Mexican fishing license, and a tourist card.

While reading and planning, I trained, spending more and more time in the boat each week. I felt strong enough for the trip, but needed to put in hours just sitting in the boat, acclimating my body. I rowed five or six days a week, four or five 5- to 6-milers and one 15-miler. As my departure date neared I carried a pair of sand bags in the boat to simulate the weight of my provisions.

Planning and anticipating a cruise can be both challenging and fun, but eventually you have to move from the mental to the physical and actually get in the boat. San Felipe, my jumping-off point, is a long way from Southern California. I left for Mexico the day before the planned start of my row. *Kavienga* and three sculls were securely tied atop my truck; the bed was full of provisions and gear. Four hours of driving got me to the border crossing at Mexicali, where I picked up Mexico Highway 5, a two-lane road through the desert ending 130 miles later in San Felipe.

At a general store on the sandy main street I bought some fresh shrimp and some wonderful local sweet rolls called pan dulce, corn tortillas, and a jar of salsa. Then I drove back up Highway 5 and turned off on a rough dirt track leading to a rugged campsite on the coast just above town. For a fee, the caretaker said he would watch my truck for me, and I saw no choice but to trust him.

I spent the afternoon transferring gear from the truck to the boat and carefully storing and re-storing it. Then I took a bearing on Punta Estrella, the only major point of land between me and my first day's destination. I did my reciprocals and made a note of the first course I would row. Once everything was set I made a small fire with wood purchased from the caretaker and barbecued the shrimp. Night fell as I enjoyed my shrimp and salsa and reviewed plans for the cruise. If I'd attempted to use my borrowed Coleman stove that night I would have discovered a problem that was to plague me for the entire trip. Even so, I don't know what I could have done about it.

The schedule for the cruise was quite open. I anticipated being out for six days, and carried provisions for seven. These could be stretched if the need arose. I gave my then-wife a float plan and told her to expect to hear from me in eight days. The rough strategy was to head south for three days, hugging the coastline, then turn around and come back. If I made it as far as the tiny fishing village of Puertecitos, 51 miles down the coast, fine. If I didn't that was fine too. If anything caught my interest I would stop and explore for as long as I wanted. The goal of the trip was to get away and experience the desolate coastline to prepare for a more ambitious cruise later, not to reach a destination. I put out the fire and turned in early. The next day was going to be a busy one.

On the Sea of Cortez, a rower's schedule is dictated by the tides. Spring tides can range up to 20 feet and they're tricky. Part of the sea can be experiencing an ebb while other areas are seeing a flood. The University of Arizona produces a very good tide table for the area, but careful observation is still important.

My goal for the first day was ambitious. I wanted to spend the night at Bahia de Santa Maria, a bay 20 miles south of San Felipe. The plan was to leave camp just before high water, figuring it would be better to row against the tide early, when I was fresh, than at the end of the day. Bahia de Santa Maria is a large, shallow bay that empties at low tide, putting the beach where I intended to camp a mile from the water. I hoped to arrive at the entrance to the bay just as the tide was turning and ride it to shore.

Kavienga seemed almost hopelessly loaded down as I pushed her off the beach just before sunrise. The heaviest single provision was water. The Baja coast is not beach as most know it—it's desert—and I wanted to be prepared. Eleven half-gallon plastic water jugs weighing 44 pounds were scattered around the boat. They were augmented by seven pint containers of grapefruit juice. I was allotting myself three and a half quarts of liquid per day and did not feel overprepared. In my first-aid kit were some Halizone tablets to treat any questionable water picked up en route. Along with 51 pounds of liquid was the mountain of food and gear I had lugged down with me, all carefully stored in Bone Dry bags. *Kavienga* sat low in the water.

I breakfasted on a large pan dulce with Australian tinned butter and a pint of grapefruit juice, reducing the load by just more than a pound. After a few stretches I climbed aboard and slid out the Concept IIs. *Kavienga* moves best when rowed at a relatively low stroke rate. At 18 strokes per minute (spm) she felt sluggish, but this was no race. If I didn't make Bahia de Santa Maria it didn't really matter; I'd plotted a fallback camping spot.

A few shafts of light were spearing the sky over the horizon as I passed Punta de Machoro at the north end of San Felipe. Moments later the whole eastern sky turned a bright reddish gold, and a beam of light found Cerro el Machoro, the 940-foot peak of Punta de Machoro. Three miles later, with the swollen, reddish orange ball of the sun hanging above the horizon, I passed Punta San Felipe. By this time *Kavienga* was more than two miles offshore, heading out to round Punta Estrella south of the town. *Kavienga* felt less sluggish, and it seemed that landmarks on shore were passing faster—the tide had evidently turned and was giving me some assistance. I passed the harbor where shrimpers rafted up and pangas were dragged ashore, then the hotels at the south end of town.

It may have just been the exuberance of the first day's row, or the extra push of the ebbing tide, but *Kavienga* cleared Punta Estrella well ahead of schedule and I set my course for Bahia de Santa Maria. Some gulls checked us out, but when it was apparent there was no bait for them, they departed. Terns dove on small fish, and a huge flock of brown pelicans, flying single-file, glided past silently, their long wingtip feathers nearly brushing the surface of the water. Except for the birds, *Kavienga* was alone on the sea.

A light northwesterly came up and combined with the ebbing tide to give me a little extra push, making 18 spm feel like a very easy pace. I knew landfall at Bahia de Santa Maria would be a snap.

Kavienga actually reached the entrance of the bay too soon. The tide was still ebbing when I got there. A white-brown line of breaking water caused by the tide boiling over the bar at the bay entrance greeted us. A single bright sail cruised slowly off the mouth of the bay—a boardsailor also looking for a way back to shore. A mile away, on the clean white sand of our goal, I could see a half dozen bright sails and two vehicles beside a pair of tents.

The boardsailor ghosted over, dropped his rig, and sat on his board while we discussed our shared dilemma. He guessed that the bay was less than a foot deep, too shallow for his daggerboard, so he planned to beach his board at the south entrance to the bay and walk to camp. He told me the bar at the entrance was soft sand and mud, and I decided to try it. The foot of water inside was enough, and I only had to row a mile against the current to get where I wanted to be.

While he headed for a beach below the wide entrance to the bay, I looked for low spots in the wall of frothing water, theorizing they would mark deeper channels. I shifted a few water bottles and my kayaking bags aft, trimming *Kavienga* in a bow-up mode, and drove for a promising spot. For a moment it was like rowing through a washing machine as the boat, even heavily laden, bounced around like a cork. Then the peapod was across the bar and into flat water.

Once inside the bay I had the feeling I was rowing at eight or nine knots—the water was speeding by, but I wasn't putting much distance between myself and the bar. I was getting pretty tired, and not making any significant progress, when my starboard oar scrapped bottom. My low stern dragged, telling me there was no way I was going to reach shore before running out of water. It was more important that I stop the tide from washing me back across the bar. I pulled in the oars, grabbed the anchor and tossed it as far ahead of me as I could. While *Kavienga* rode the tide back toward the Sea of Cortez I hastily shortened up on the anchor rode and made it fast. The anchor skipped along the bottom for a few yards, then caught and held. I sat panting as the tide rushed out of the bay. After rewarding myself with a long hit on a water bottle I watched the retreating water as some dark shapes raced for the sea—stingrays. The shallow bay would be full of them at high tide, something to remember if I went wading.

Half an hour after crossing over the bar, *Kavienga* was high and dry on the sandy bottom of Bahia de Santa Maria. I had almost made it—I was only a mile short of my destination. My first thought was to unload some of my gear and carry it to the beach. Then I remembered I was in Mexico, the land of manana: The tide would come back, and in three or four hours I would be able to row to shore the easy way. I adjusted my broad brimmed straw hat and looked around.

The boardsailor I had met at sea was walking toward me from where he had landed, and six other figures were approaching from the beach. I had not expected a welcoming committee. We introduced ourselves and fanned out, exploring the bottom of the bay. We discussed their wind safari and my rowing adventure as we picked up sand dollars and other shells. We found a small ray trapped in a pool and gave it a wide berth. By the time we reached their camp we were all hot and tired. They had two vehicles, a Chevy van, which was stuck to its hubs in the soft sand, and a 4X4 Toyota pickup. A large awning was rigged off the van and we all rested in the shade.

One of the boardsailors kept checking the condition of the water at the bar through a pair of binoculars and finally announced that the tide was coming in. They invited me to camp with them and I accepted, then started the long walk out to where *Kavienga* waited patiently for me and the water.

I mistimed my walk out to the boat. With no idea how fast the tide would flood into the bay I took my time, pausing to look for shells. I was just halfway to *Kavienga* when I realized the water had already reached her. With her anchor securely dug in, I wasn't worried that she would float away, but I didn't want to swim to her, or wade through water with rays on the bottom. I started to jog. When I reached the water, or the water reached me, I broke into a run. The water quickly rose to my calves and forced me into a slow shuffle, which at least cleared any rays from my path. By the time I reached *Kavienga* the water was waist deep and she was bobbing happily with nearly three feet of water under her. I climbed aboard and rowed to the beach.

The northwesterly had filled in to a pleasant 12 to 15 knots, providing some relief from the heat. The boardsailors hit the bay while I laid out some of my gear and relaxed in the shade of their awning. One of the books I had read while planning the cruise was the Southern California Auto Club's guide to Baja California. The book had described Bahia de Santa Maria as a "rustic campsite." If "rustic" means there's nothing there, then the guidebook had hit the nail squarely on the head. There were some round brick houses with thatched roofs, evidently owned or leased by Americans, and were unoccupied. That was all. The boardsailors had even brought their own firewood. One thing they hadn't brought was a radio or a tape-player, seeming to know intuitively that any kind of loud music would have been out of place in that primordial land.

That night I learned about the problem with the Coleman stove. A week before leaving on the trip, I had started to clean my own stove and discovered it was broken. I borrowed the Coleman from a friend and thought I was set. I should have checked before I left. At first it wouldn't pressurize, and when I finally got it going, it went out almost immediately.

The boardsailors let me share their campfire while they told horror stories of the dirt road down from San Felipe and tried to decide if they would pull out the following day. While we ate and talked everyone took a try at fixing the borrowed stove. After two hours, and several applications of Crazy Glue and duct tape, the stove was declared "fixed."

We had finished dinner and I was thinking about heading back for my sleeping bag when we heard the unmistakable sound of a rattlesnake. I had never heard one in the wild, but there was no doubt in my mind as to what it was. We all scattered as fast as we could. While the boardsailors went back, armed with sticks and flashlights, I cautiously lifted my sleeping bag into *Kavienga*. After convincing myself a rattler couldn't slither over her sleek glass sides, I finally fell asleep.

I woke before dawn, debating what I would do on my second day. Bahia de Santa Maria was interesting, and I had an urge to explore, but if *Kavienga* missed the morning high water I would have to wait to leave until late afternoon, when it was hotter. I had no real goal for my second day, though I had penciled a tiny question mark at Punta San Fermin, 20 miles farther south. I had no idea what I'd find there except that Arroyo Matomi met the sea at the point. Making 20 miles would mean that Puertecitos would be an easy row the following day.

As the sun exploded out of the eastern horizon and the tide flooded the bay, I loaded *Kavienga* and watched a great blue heron stalk the shallows. By the time the sun was up *Kavienga* was ready to go. Two of the boardsailors were awake and I shared the last of my pan dulce with them and had a cup of tea heated on their camp stove. (The "repaired" Coleman wasn't tested.) As I was leaving, I discovered that the previous afternoon's northwesterly had left a layer of grit on *Kavienga*. I took the time to clean the seat tracks and oarlocks, then shoved off.

The second day's row was peaceful. I passed two small camps where 4X4s were parked, and saw another boardsailor, but I didn't speak to a soul. After three hours in the boat I came into shore at a wide sandy beach that didn't look as if it had ever seen a human. I stretched my legs, had a light lunch sitting on the sand, slathered up with sunscreen, and watched pelicans, gulls, and terns work over a school of small fish just offshore.

The activity in the water reminded me of the fishing pole stowed aboard. I quickly assembled the short pole and spinning reel and tied a feathered jig to the line.

I'm a passive fisherman. My idea of fishing is to troll the lure and, if it happens to pass a fish, and if the fish chooses to bite, then I'll try to reel him in. I pushed off, put out what I thought was an appropriate amount of line, and I took up the oars. I hadn't taken 10 strokes when the line sang off the reel. I dropped the oars, set the hook, and tightened down on the drag. Less than five minutes later a nice bonito was splashing alongside. I passed a line through its gills to tow it aft, then cast out again. The oars were still trailing when the line once again began to sing out. Five minutes later two bonito bobbed in *Kavienga*'s wake and the rod was stowed. I had more than enough fish for dinner.

Kavienga was moving easily, but rowing had become hot and tiring. I'd about had it for the day and was ready to find a spot to camp. With the oars pulled in, I was half twisted around in the seat, looking for Punta San Fermin, when *Kavienga* gave a terrible lurch. I slid the oars out for stability and looked around to see what had caused it. We seemed alone on the sea, a mile and a half from shore. A swirl of water aft caught my eye and a black scimitar pierced the surface. Through the sun-dappled water I saw the body of a shark. It's tail flicked gently, driving it at our stern. The boat twisted and bobbed and I realized the shark, about a five-foot blue, was eating my dinner. I grabbed the trailing line and yanked the bonito aboard. The line came easily, bringing the head of one fish and about two thirds of the other. The shark made another slow pass and rolled over on its side, looking up at me with one large, unblinking eye. I had the disturbing feeling I was being warned.

After the incident with the shark I headed *Kavienga* toward shore. I went in stern first, looking for landmarks on the featureless shore. Punta San Fermin was still down the coast. Like the day before, I was about a mile short of my goal. It didn't matter—the beach was a good one, clean and untouched, backed up by some magnificent cholla cactus. The tide was out, and the high-water mark was about a quarter of a mile inland, but I was getting used to that.

My dining plans had changed twice that day. Originally the plan had involved a can of beef stew; then it became fillet of bonito. Now, thanks to the shark, I was back to beef stew. But there was enough bonita left to make an appetizer of seviche. I cut up the fish, put it in a shallow pan, squeezed in the juice of two limes, added a cut-up tomato, diced onion, and half a diced green chili. I didn't have any cilantro, but was I camping and figured I had to rough it. While my appetizer marinated in the shade of the dodger I went exploring, keeping a careful eye on the incoming tide. Later, when the tide lifted *Kavienga*, I rowed to the new shore and set up camp. That night I learned my stove was not really "fixed." The only way it would maintain a flame was with constant hand-pumping.

There is a small bay just north of Puertecitos where some native pangas were moored well out, near the entrance. I reached it early in the morning the third day. *Kavienga* had just passed this bay, her course set due south for the point protecting Puertecitos, when I heard the roar of an outboard. A Boston Whaler's blunt bow appeared from among the pangas I had just passed. Two Americans in their early teens were aboard. They did a high-speed doughnut around *Kavienga* waving and shouting, then applied full power and headed south. I was left rocking violently in their wake, thinking unkind thoughts.

I reached Puertecitos well before noon. The small town wraps around a shallow, southeast-facing bay. The tide was still high enough to allow me to row almost all the way to shore before grounding on the sand and pebble bottom. The Boston Whaler used by my welcoming committee was tied near the rough concrete launching ramp on the eastern side of the bay.

My guidebook described Puertecitos as "an unpolished resort." Looking around I felt the book was being unnecessarily generous. It seemed that much of the town was made up of trailers and ramshackle bungalows, vacation homes for Americans. There was a restaurant on the beach in front of me and, I knew from the guidebook, there was an airstrip behind it. The book had also revealed the existence of some natural hot springs on the eastern point, out past the launching ramp. I had reached my goal and was disappointed. The most interesting place on the trip had been Bahia de Santa Maria.

With *Kavienga* on the hard I took a few minutes to organize the boat and take inventory. There was a general store in the town, and I could I could stock up if anything was low. There was still food for four and a half days, though I seemed to have been drinking my water and juice a little faster than planned. Consuming the water had the advantage of making the boat lighter, but I decided to add a gallon—the eight pounds was nothing compared with the safety factor.

By the time inventory was finished the bay around me had dried out, and I heard the high-pitched whine of motors. Adjusting my wide-brimmed straw hat to block the sun, I saw three Quad Runners approaching across the shoal. The four-wheeled motorcycles, each with a beer can in a holder bolted to the handlebars, and one with a huge tape player strapped on the luggage rack, carried Americans in their middle teens. I could hear their music over the collective noise of the three motors. They split into two groups, passing on either side of *Kavienga* and kicking up a wake of wet sand and pebbles. They made my decision for me: I would shove off as soon as the tide would permit.

I didn't like leaving *Kavienga* unattended, and kept my eye on her while walking the half-mile up to the shore. I found the store, quickly bought a gallon jug of water, a cold can of orange juice, jar of salsa, and some fresh flour tortillas. I then hurried back to *Kavienga*, drinking the juice as I went. My peapod had attracted a small knot of young Mexicans, all standing at a respectful distance. My Spanish is practically nonexistent, but I smiled and they smiled. They watched while I stored my gear, then an older man with the weathered face of a fisherman arrived to shoo them away. He spoke quite a bit of English and we chatted briefly about my boat and his town.

The sliding seat rowing rig fascinated him, as did the carbon-fiber sculls. I told him about enjoying Bahia de Santa Maria, he smiled and told me a long story about sailing on a shrimper out of San Felipe when he was younger and being stranded at Santa Maria for two weeks with a broken engine. He, too, had enjoyed the bay's quiet peace.

The three young Americans on their Quad Runners stormed back past us, their motors and music stopping conversation for the duration of their passing, and my new friend suggested his town was more pleasant to visit during the week. I had lost track of time and not realized it was Saturday. I thought he had been eyeing my five empty plastic water jugs and asked him if he had any use for them—he did, the fishermen used them as floats. I gave them to him, gaining some space in the boat, and he thanked me profusely. Finally he told me he had to go to work in the restaurant and ambled away.

I was trying to decide which of my canned delicacies would be the least offensive cold, as I had no desire to wrestle with the stove to prepare lunch, when a small boy ran across the shoal towards me. He stopped running about 10 yards away and approached shyly, offering a paper bag. I smiled at him and took the offering, and he was off like a shot. The bag contained a ripe avocado, a tomato, and a foil-wrapped bundle. I peeled away the foil to find half a dozen large shrimp, sauteed to perfection, and two soft flour tortillas. I waved in the direction of the restaurant, though I was too far away to be seen, and quickly made two huge shrimp tacos. The trip to Puertecitos had been worth it after all.

I didn't make it to Punta San Fermin that afternoon, and camped at the base of an unnamed arroyo five or six miles north of Puertecitos. Just before beaching I landed another bonito. After battling the stove I dined on fish tacos—not as good as lunch, but far better than my canned option.

With high tide around 9:30, I decided to rise early and row a few hours, beach the boat while the tide ebbed, and maybe row again after it turned. My internal clock woke me at 4:00. I wanted a cup of tea, but not enough to face the stove. After a pint of juice I struck camp and was on the water a half-hour later. Another brilliant sunrise silhouetted two shrimpers working several miles offshore, and not long after I caught a long, lean barracuda on my trolling jig.

By 9:30 I had reached an area of "rustic campsites" with four or five trucks parked on the beach. I rowed on, fighting the ebbing tide for several miles because I still felt fresh and didn't want to beach right at high water. Finally I rowed to shore between two of the camps and anchored in shallow water a quarter of a mile below the high-water line. When the tide left us aground I cleaned the barracuda, struggled with the stove, and once again made fish tacos. Having tacos three meals out of four was a bit much, but it used up the tortillas, tomato, and salsa (the avocado had gone with the shrimp). The beach offered very little of interest so I rearranged *Kavienga,* allowing me to siesta with my head in the shade of the dodger.

The incoming tide woke me, and by the time *Kavienga* was afloat I was ready to press on. I entertained no hope of making Bahia de Santa Maria that afternoon, but another 10 miles of rowing would put the bay within easy striking distance the following morning.

That night I came in on a deserted beach somewhere south of Bahia de Santa Maria. I hadn't been there 15 minutes when a tired old jeep with no muffler arrived. What caught my attention was the shotgun in a leather scabbard on the driver's side. Remembering the warnings about bandits I smiled broadly. The driver, a local in his early 20s wearing cowboy boots, faded jeans, a purple western shirt, and a red baseball cap, told me I owed him two dollars for using his "camp." I paid and settled down to fight the stove and make dinner.

The tide was still flooding and the sun was well up when I pulled into Bahia de Santa Maria on the fifth day. I had a strange feeling that I was coming home. It was Monday morning, there were no vehicles on the beach, and no sign of habitation around the brick houses. Seeing the bay full of water, I realized there was a small island, really just a high sand dune, near where I'd camped before. I steered *Kavienga* toward it, figuring it should be free of snakes.

It was a delightful little islet—which reminded me of a whale's back. At high water the white sand mound was about 40 feet long and 20 feet wide, with it's high point three feet above the water. I buried *Kavienga's* anchor in the dry sand, then pushed her back out so the tide would reach her well before high water.

The tide quickly ebbed, leaving *Kavienga* aground 70 feet from the high-water line on the island. I carried some of my gear ashore, then went exploring. If you didn't look at the round brick houses it was easy to imagine that no human had ever set foot at Bahia de Santa Maria. I walked out to the sea and watched terns diving on small fish, then walked slowly back to the island, now iust a hill ded by drying mud and sand.

ken on a certain odor over the past few days—an odor made climbed in the sky and the heat intensified. She was begindead fish. While the tide was out I transferred all my gear and the rowing rig to the shore, and when the tide came in I used my bailer to wash her down. After I sponged her out and restowed all the gear and provisions she smelled better and was ready to go. There was plenty of food and water left, so I decided to extend my cruise and spend another day at Bahia de Santa Maria. It would give me time to do some exploring. Besides, my butt was sore.

In the late afternoon a 20-knot northwesterly blew across the desert, bringing sand and grit with it. At sunset it subsided and I cleaned the oarlocks and seat tracks, then battled the stove to make a simple dinner. It was pleasant waking up the next morning and not having to jump into the boat and row. I stayed in my sleeping bag and read, then made a light, cold breakfast and followed the ebbing tide out to the sea, picking up seashells as I went.

By the time the tide started to flood in late afternoon I'd decided that if I stayed any longer I might never leave. I loaded up *Kavienga*, took in the anchor, and stepped aboard, waiting for the water. When she was finally afloat I rowed against the tide to the entrance of the bay, drove across the fast water at the shallow bar and headed north, riding the tide. San Felipe wasn't my goal—I wanted to do 10 miles and camp somewhere between Punta Diggs and Punta Estrella so that the row back to the truck would only be 11 or 12 miles the following morning.

That night I camped on a rocky beach in the shadow of Punta Estrella and ate a huge dinner. I was three rowing hours away from my truck, and rationalized that it would be easier to carry food in my stomach than in *Kavienga*. There was plenty of food left—the fish and shrimp had stretched my rations considerably. I was, however, glad for the extra gallon of water I'd bought in Puertecitos. By extending my trip I'd used up all I'd brought with me.

Kavienga's hull ground onto the sand in front of my truck at 8:00 on the seventh morning of the cruise. It had been a nearly perfect trip. I know some sailors who almost hope something will break on their boat so they can show their ingenuity by making repairs at sea. That is not my idea of fun. To me, a well-planned and executed cruise is one where nothing goes terribly wrong. I get nearly as much joy from planning and preparing correctly as I do from experiencing the cruise. Everything had gone well, I had learned a lot, and I was looking forward to planning my cruise to the Midriff Islands.

- 18 -

The Great Catalina to Marina Del Rey Rowing and Paddling Derby

ANYONE who persists in referring to our branch of the sport as "recreational rowing" has never witnessed California Yacht Club's annual ultramarathon. Almost since its inception, The Great Catalina to Marina del Rey Rowing and Paddling Derby has been known as "the Catalina race," or, among competitive rowers, simply "Catalina." It is open-water rowing at its most challenging, and has become the ultimate goal of long-distance rowers on the West Coast. There's a saying in motor sports that, "racing improves the breed." That's also true in open-water rowing, and nowhere is it more obvious than in the Catalina race.

The demanding 32-nautical mile course was inaugurated in 1976 by long-time oarsman and Cal Yacht Club member Charles Hathaway when he rowed a traditional (read "heavy") dory across the channel to celebrate his fiftieth birthday. The row quickly became an annual event, the goal being to finish. It didn't take long to develop into a major race, with its own traditions.

Steve Hathaway, Charles' son, set a singles record in his Martin Trainer in the 1983 race. That record held until 1986, even though most top open-water oarsmen took a shot at it. *Millennium Falcon*, a three-man, high-performance wooden dory equipped with Oarmasters, was designed and built specifically for the race. *Falcon* won the extremely rough 1981 event, then came back as a quad in 1982 with four Oarmasters and won again. Some intriguing triples from Santa Cruz and San Francisco have come south with mixed results. Gordie Nash's California Wherry, an old design with a new life, earned a niche in rowing history by winning its class in the 1984 race.

Through the years, the race has both mirrored and influenced the dramatic change of attitude and design in the sport. Karen "KC" Carlson, who made her sixth trip across the channel in 1989, credits California Yacht Club with being the first to recognize women rowers by giving them their own class, and now,

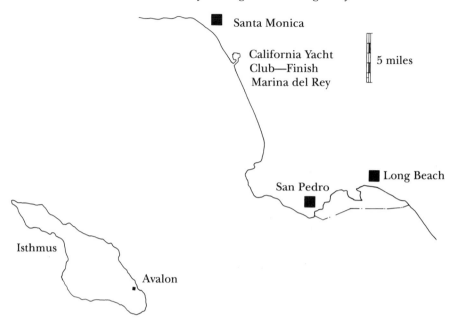

Catalina Island and the mainland, the venue for the California Yacht Club's Great Catalina to Marina del Rey Rowing and Paddling Derby.

classes. The goal is no longer to finish—it is to win, and set a new record. The boats are no longer tricked-out traditional designs or Aldens; they are state-of-the-art racers, developed specifically for open-water conditions.

Certain individual races have developed mystiques of their own, adding to the history of the event. The 1981 race is remembered as a rough one, when most failed to finish. The 1985 race was notable not just for the escalation of the design and building race, which saw Nash's modified ARS battle Hertig's super-trick Laser, and the tremendous battle in the triples class. Shirwin Smith and Hillary Dembroff recruited Dolly Stockman, an East Coast sculler with no open-water experience, and added her to the Small Craft triple Nash built for them. Their only competition that year was Craig Rogers, Bill Simpkins, and George Blackwell in another triple. After nearly six hours the women finished four seconds behind the men to a great cheer from the committee and spectators alike. Rowers remember 1986 as "the year the records fell," and 1989 as "the year of the women."

Gordie Nash first discovered the Catalina race in 1977 and has done 12 crossings—384 racing miles and untold thousands in training. The Catalina race, and the training he has done to prepare for it, have taught Nash a lot about open-water rowing. This knowledge influenced not only the boats he has modified and helped design but the sport as well. The Small Craft Double was a direct result of Nash's association with Small Craft, and of his win in the 1983 doubles class, rowing an Alden Double he had modified. Earlier, we saw how Nash modified a Small Craft ARS and turned a Small Craft Double into a triple for the 1985 event; how Tad Springer of Laser took a giant step forward, turning a double into a lightweight single for Per Hertig to win the singles class. We also learned how Nash designed and built his own new-generation double for 1986, and recruited Kevin Strain as his rowing partner with the announced goal of smashing the existing doubles record.

Nash was not the only person working on a new boat or getting ready for the 1986 Catalina race. Chris Maas was developing his own Dragonfly Double at the same time Nash was working on the Pacific 30. These two designs represent the new generation of high-performance, open-water doubles— doubles that are faster than singles. This is not as strange a statement as it might sound: Until the introduction of these two new 30-footers, recreational doubles were relatively slow boats. There was considerable potential in doubles, but it was never fully tapped. Doubles were too short (before the Small Craft Double was introduced they were all 20 feet or under), and they were too heavy, well over 100 pounds. Builders seemed to have thought that the boats had to be short for people to move around, and heavily built to withstand the strains of two people rowing. Short, in any kind of a boat, means slow, and heavily built and strongly built are not the same thing. Doubles seemed to be an afterthought, put together by builders to meet the demand of a small segment of the market. The builders erroneously viewed this portion of the market as a couple, or parent and child, out for a leisurely row in quiet water—not serious rowers interested in open-water racing or cruising. The Small Craft Double may have been the first step away from this design philosophy. But if it was a step, the boats by Nash and Maas were a leap. Both the Pacific 30 and the Dragonfly are long, lean, light, strong boats designed to be at home in open water.

One of Maas's Dragonflys was to be rowed by the women's team of Linda Locklin and KC Carlson from Santa Cruz. Another Maas design, the Aero, was entered by Mark Steffy, Director of the Tahoe Rowing Club, a Maas dealer at his Rower's Boathouse, and organizer of the Tahoe Regatta. Before the start of the race, Maas and Steffy made some minor modifications to the sleek Aero, adding a small splash guard forward of the cockpit and replacing the standard fin with a large Dragonfly to keep the boat tracking in a heavy cross-sea.

Bob Jarvis of Santa Cruz had recently acquired the prototype Robinson/ Knecht and the rights to produce the boat as the J-Shell. The design appears on Nash's graph as a "stable racing shell." At $23^1/2$ feet the J-Shell was not the longest open-water single around, but at 15 inches wide she is by far the

Linda Locklin and KC Carlson at work in their Maas Dragonfly.

narrowest. Her 40-pound weight was close to the Aero and the Pacific 24. The boat was originally designed as a trainer for scullers, but Jarvis added some internal stiffness and modified the cockpit to take an Elvstrom bailer. He won all five races he entered while training for Catalina.

The day before the race—the day the boats are loaded aboard their escorts and taken to the island—found Bob Jarvis working frantically in the California Yacht Club parking lot. Though he had driven thousands of miles with the boat on top of his car and experienced no problems, his unique seat had blown out on his drive down from Santa Cruz. The original seat had 14-inch axles and was designed to ride on a lip inside the splash box. The designers had done this to allow them to shorten the seat deck, so the rowers would not bang their calves at the finish. The seat deck had been reduced to a tiny step to use while boarding the boat. Replacing the seat on short notice was impossible—there just aren't that many seats around with 14-inch axles. Therefore Jarvis had to buy tracks and a standard seat and build a new seat deck out of plywood.

The stage was set. Gordie Nash and Kevin Strain had trained for a year and had visualized setting a new record. Now they just had to do it. Mark Steffy and Bob Jarvis were set to do battle in boats they both believed in. KC Carlson and Linda Locklin had only one competitor that year—the clock. There were 18 other competitors, all with their own goals.

Early October may very well be the ideal time to visit Catalina Island. The weather is good, and most of the tourists have gone back to the mainland. The escort boats made passage over glassy seas and took moorings in Isthmus and Fourth of July coves. As soon as the mooring wands were picked up, many of the competitors put their boats in the water for a brief afternoon row while their supporters listened attentively to marine weather forecasts.

The early morning clouds and fog that sometimes blot out the Southern California sun for a week at a time in early summer are long gone by October. The winter storms are still four or five months away, but the Santa Ana winds— the hot dry winds that whip off the inland deserts at up to 50 knots—are a seasonal threat. The air had a certain "Santa Ana feel" to it, warm and dry, and everyone waited anxiously for the weather report.

While Gordie Nash secluded himself, most of the competitors, the owners and crews of the escort vessels, and the organizers enjoyed a huge dinner ashore. The weather news was not good—possible Santa Anas were predicted for the following day. Chuck Wright, event chairman, quietly circulated among the competitors, polling them about an earlier start to avoid the strong headwinds. The traditional early-morning starting time had been moved up so that competitors would cross the shipping lanes in daylight. Starting later was a welcome change, but might be a mistake if the Santa Ana developed during the morning. The decision was made to stay with the later starting time, and it turned out the decision was a good one.

Soon after every one was asleep, the Santa Anas whipped across the channel and battered the island. With the winds ricochetting off the island and venturing around the sheer rock cliffs it was hard to tell their true strength, but the escort fleet rocked in the normally placid waters. By the time people began to launch, the winds were gone and the sea was down. Competitors breathed a collective sigh of relief as they taped hands, slipped on gloves, and readied themselves and their boats for the ordeal to come.

Gordie Nash and Kevin Strain were among the first to launch, one hour before their scheduled start. While their competitors started and rowed off into the darkness, Nash and Strain rowed, warming up. According to Nash: "In our minds we knew what we wanted to do, we had trained all summer, we had a new boat and all the equipment. We knew exactly how fast the boat could go and how fast we could go; we knew in our minds we could do it, we visualized going across the finish line in $4^1/2$ hours. Now we just had to show everybody else that we could do it."

Boats started individually, with the boats that the organizers thought would be the slowest going off first. Nash and Strain started last. Marked by "shake-and-break" light sticks on their oars, or single lights on their sterns, the small boats left the starting line and their escorts slipped into their wakes.

Game plans, which had been laboriously worked out on the trip over, took some time to be put into operation. Some worked better than others. Most of the rowers had not met their escort skippers until the day before, and the navigation problems, which seemed so easy in the daylight, had to be worked out in the darkness. Many rowers couldn't see their compasses in the dark, and responsibility for navigation shifted to the escorts. Rowers who had thought the escorts would simply be following them had to learn how to read navigation lights and place themselves directly in front of their escorts, adjusting their course to match that of the larger boat.

Bob Jarvis may have suffered the most from a communication breakdown. Navigation responsibility belonged to his escort vessel, *Andrea*. After Jarvis started, *Andrea* had to maneuver through some heavy traffic around the line and Jarvis, watching her running lights, thought she was trying to indicate that he should alter his course. Due to a bend in the California coastline and the way Catalina Island lies, the course from the Isthmus to Marina del Rey is almost due north. Jarvis headed off strongly in a northeasterly direction, outdistancing his escort.

For the first hour, Nash and Strain rowed at over eight knots. With the exception of Jarvis, who appeared headed for Long Beach, Nash and Strain were on the most easterly course. Next came Mark Steffy, then Carlson and Locklin, with the rest of the fleet spread out to the northwest. After the race, when Nash was asked about their seemingly low course, he laughed and said, "We were right on my course. There's a secret to crossing that channel—after nine years I've learned it, and I'm not telling what it is!"

At sunrise a school of dolphins surged through the fleet, briefly pacing some of the rowing boats. Jarvis realized the entire fleet was well north of him and swung through almost 90-degrees to head up to them. Mark Steffy, rowing his first long-distance ocean race had started in almost a sprint and was flagging. He would, though, get his second wind.

Bob Jarvis overcorrected and wound up high of the course, just above Carlson and Locklin in their double. He finally rejoined his escort boat and got back on course. Suddenly, he was in the water. One of his foot stretchers had pulled loose and he pitched out of the boat. Jarvis spent 20 minutes in the water, trying to fix his boat while *Andrea* hovered nearby. Finally he climbed aboard and again took up the oars. The stretcher broke again, and he was doomed to finish the race using just one leg to drive him through the stroke.

The water stayed mercifully smooth, and the winds remained light as the fleet converged on the Marina del Rey entrance. The radio net announced, "Gordie and Kevin are approaching the breakwater. Gordie's screaming for grapefruit juice. We can't tell if he's delirious or not."

Nash and Strain crossed the line in an elapsed time of 4:37:23, taking 43 minutes off the old record. Margie Cate and Craig Leeds, rowing Nash's prototype Pacific 30, set a mixed doubles record at 5:10:51. Rowing against the clock, KC Carlson and Linda Locklin brought their Maas Dragonfly in at 5:28:26, setting a new women's double record. After all his problems with a broken boat and poor navigation, Bob Jarvis still managed to set a new singles record when he finished after 5:27:02 on the water, beating Mark Steffy by 23 minutes.

A combination of ideal conditions, a year of commitment to training and design, and building evolution produced records in five out of the six rowing classes. The 1986 Catalina to Marina del Rey Rowing and Paddling Derby not only went into the record books—it rewrote them.

■ THE 1987 RACE

All those who played a significant role in the 1986 Catalina Race returned in 1987. One might have thought Nash and Strain's record-shattering 1986 performance would have scared away competition in the men's doubles class, but it seemed to have had the opposite effect: Six other teams showed up to row against the record-holding pair in their Pacific 30, including the father/son team of Charles and Steve Hathaway. Both men had held singles records, but this was to be the first time they would combine their skills and experience. After the 1986 race the Hathaways ordered a double from Nash, then spent the summer racing in some of the tough central California races.

The always-tough team of Jim Flack and Scott Ellsworth made the long haul down from San Francisco with their well-campaigned Maas Dragonfly. In preparation for Catalina, they had entered and won both the Tahoe event and Sausalito's Open Ocean Regatta. No one expected to see Nash and Strain's 1986 record broken, and several knowledgeable observers said that breaking the 4:37:23 time would require a new design.

Bob Jarvis was back, this time with one of his production J-Shells. After his navigation and gear problems of the previous years, he knew his own record was "soft" and was intent on bettering it. His competition also promised to be better—a second J-Shell, three Maas Aeros, a Maas Vancouver 21, a Pacific 24, and a 24-foot Laser double, rigged as a single. There would be no slack in the men's singles class: No one rowing a poor course or suffering gear failure could hope to win in a class with that depth.

Margie Cate and Craig Leeds were back with a Pacific 30 to defend their 1986 mixed doubles record against the Sausalito team of Kate Erhart and Mark Kelley in a Maas Dragonfly. The class that many were expecting to provide the closest racing was the women's doubles. KC Carlson and Linda Locklin returned with their Maas Dragonfly, but this time they would not just be rowing against the clock: Shirwin Smith had planned to enter her Maas Dragonfly with regular partner, Hillary Dembroff. Early in the season the pair had won their class at Tahoe, but Dembroff had subsequently injured her back. Smith recruited Marie Hagelstein, who regularly dominated the women's singles class in her Maas Aero, as her new partner. Before joining Smith in the double, Hagelstein's impressive 1987 record included class wins at Tahoe, Open Ocean Regatta and the Bay to Bay Race, giving her a virtual lock on the annual class trophy. But injury continued to plague Smith's team: Two days before Catalina, Hagelstein jammed her finger into the side of a pool while swimming. Undaunted, she bent the finger to fit an oar grip and taped it in place. A third Maas Dragonfly was entered for C'Anne Cook-Steffy and Vera Strock, both of Tahoe Rowing Club.

Significantly, of the 20 rowing boats entered, 19 represented the modern open-water design and building methods of the central California boat-builders. Eleven entrants came from the design board and shop of Chris Maas; six were built by Gordie Nash, and Bob Jarvis' brace of J-Shells rounded out the 19. Designed and built independently, the boats from these three shops share common evolutionary traits. They're long, light, stiff, and strong, de-signed to be rowed safely in open water conditions. They all have hard decks and small, sealed cockpits. The sole exception among the 1987 entries was the Laser double rigged as a single—similar to the boat Per Hertig rowed in 1985. In terms of open-water boat design and construction, 1985 seemed like light years ago.

With the strongest fleet in the history of the regatta, and a hurricane off Baja California threatening to spin wind and rain into Southern California,

Gordie Nash in a familiar situation—the winner's circle.

race chairman Chuck Wright wisely compressed the starting sequence, sending the boats off at two-minute intervals. First to start that morning, at 5:00, was Skip Lind in his Laser. Last away were Nash and Strain.

The 1987 trip across the channel was rougher than the year before, but not dangerously so. Margie Cate and Craig Leeds led the boats across the finish line—20 minutes ahead of Erhart and Kelley—winning their class and beating their own 1986 record time. Bob Jarvis once again won the men's singles class. Rowing a straighter course than the year before, and suffering no breakdowns, he set a new record and bested second-place finisher Bill Berger by more than 20 minutes. In the women's doubles, Shirwin Smith and Marie Hagelstein smoked across the channel, winning their class and setting a new record. The only class that didn't see a record set was the men's doubles where, predictably, Nash and Strain won.

■ THE 1988 RACE

The 1988 race is the story of one man and four women. Rowing a Maas Aero in the 10-strong men's singles class, Steve Hathaway smashed the record, posting a time of 5:18:52. He averaged nearly six knots, finishing more than 23 minutes ahead of second place finisher Bob Jarvis—and this with a sprained wrist!

A new category—actually an old category resurrected—was introduced. The *Santa Cruzer* harkened back to the early days of the race, continuing the tradition of weird and wonderful designs from central California (Santa Cruz to be precise). A Pocock quad with coxswain, she was decked over fore and aft and fitted with a Plexiglas splash guard, and equipped with bailers and a bilge pump operated by the cox. Her goal was Nash and Strain's 1986 record. Slowed by chop, she missed the time set by the double, but set a class record of 5:01:34. Margie Cate and Craig Leeds again won the mixed doubles and Kathy Grant won women's singles.

Nash and Strain took their Pacific 30 across the Channel for the third time, but not as planned. During the winter, Nash had built a 33-foot, V-bottom, wooden double for Strain and himself. While building, the pair had continued to race and train in both the Pacific 30 and a new Empacher flat-water double. The new boat was finished in time for the race, but the custom riggers failed to arrive from the East Coast in time to get the boat assembled and tuned. When it became obvious that they were going to have to call on the 30 for a third trip across the Channel, Nash shifted his efforts to the old boat. He ripped out the digital compass and its battery, replacing it with a standard compass, saving eight pounds. They also switched positions, Nash moving to the bow to navigate while Strain took the stroke seat. They started fast, blasting along at 28 spm on their usual course, four degrees below the rhumbline. Nash had developed this course over the years through experience and by studying wind and wave patterns and bottom contours. His course is designed to take full advantage of the seas fanning around the end of the island and, nearer the finish, a shallow spot where the boat can gain a bit of a push from the surf. After an hour, they slowed their stroke rate to 26 and posted their third class win.

The tightest race was the match race in the women's doubles class. Shirwin Smith was reunited with her partner, Hillary Dembroff, and they were up against their regular competition, KC Carlson and Linda Locklin—both teams in their well-rowed Maas Dragonflys. The speed differential for the race was .001 knot, with Smith and Dembroff winning by just five seconds. At the awards luncheon nobody knew the 1988 race marked the end of an era.

■ THE 1989 RACE

When the faithful gathered at California Yacht Club in September, 1989, there were serious changes in the fleet's makeup. The previous race had seen a shift away from doubles to singles and 1989 continued that trend. Fourteen singles showed up compared with five doubles teams. The *Santa Cruzer* was back with a new crew, and this time she had competition—the old *Millennium Falcon* was ready for her third trip across the channel.

Gordie Nash, for the first time in 11 years, was not racing. Sidelined by an injury, he was serving on the committee boat. Kevin Strain, Nash's partner for the last three class-winning trips across the channel, had entered a new Maas 24 in the nine-man singles class. Shirwin Smith, who had successfully rowed doubles and triples in her four previous crossings, was also in a Maas 24, competing in the rejuvenated, five-strong women's singles class. Also in the class was Margie Cate, who held the mixed-doubles record, and Ann Donaldson who, in her first year of competitive rowing had cut a wide swath through the women's singles class at venues as diverse as Sausalito's Open Ocean Regatta, the Tahoe Regatta, the Cross Sound Race and the Master's Nationals. After reclaiming the men's singles record the year before, Steve Hathaway had recruited Craig Leeds, Margie Cate's former partner, to help him attempt to break Nash and Strain's record. Some things never seem to change: KC Carlson and Linda Locklin returned with their Maas Dragonfly, aiming at Shirwin Smith and Marie Hagelstein's 1987 record.

For competitors waking up at Catalina's isthmus, Southern California's gray marine layer is comforting. One thing they don't want to see is the lights on the mainland: A clear sky usually presages wind in the channel. In 1989 the lights of Palos Verdes Peninsula beckoned brightly. The wind was southerly for the start, pushing the competitors toward their destination, but that didn't last long. Shortly after dawn it went easterly and began kicking up a short, steep chop—and the worst was yet to come.

Rowing a Pocock double, Dennis Murphy and Joe Hammond found themselves in trouble, taking on more water than they could void. They were finally forced to accept a short tow from their escort while they bailed. Once the boat was empty, they cast off to finish under their own power and disqualified themselves for accepting the tow. Halfway across the channel, while leading the men's singles class, Kevin Strain broke a pin. While Strain struggled to change the pin, his escort's swim step smacked the Maas 24, breaking a huge chunk out of the hull and deck, forcing Strain to withdraw. Peaking at 15 knots, the wind took a slight northerly swing, sending a confusing cross-chop down on a race course already made sloppy by the easterly.

Starting last by virtue of the organizers' assumption that they would post the fastest time over the course, Steve Hathaway and Craig Leeds charged through the fleet, rowing their Pacific 30 at more than 6.5 knots. Rowing a low course similar to the one rowed the past three years by Nash and Strain, Ann Donaldson was passing all the women who had started ahead of her.

Once in the lee of Palos Verdes Peninsula the sea lay down. Many had worn themselves out, and the flat water allowed them to finish; those who still had reserve power were able to lengthen their stroke and drive toward the finish. California Yacht Club is located at the very foot of crowded Marina del Rey, so after 30 mind-numbing miles of open-ocean rowing, with fatigue blurring their vision and their thinking, the competitors negotiated the twists and turns of the harbor, along with a moving maze of sail and power boats.

Hathaway and Leeds came in first, with an elapsed time of 4:49:09, just 11 minutes and change off Nash and Strain's 1986 record, a remarkable feat, considering the conditions. Craig Rogers rowed his J-shell to a 5:31 victory in the men's singles, again less than a quarter of an hour off the class record. Everyone who started the race turned in a credible performance, but the nod for performance of the year would have to go to Ann Donaldson in her Maas 24. Winning the women's singles class with a time of 5:59:04, she took 34:21 off the old record.

THE Catalina Race isn't for everyone. Many serious open-water competitors with long, successful histories in the sport have never entered the ultramarathon, but we have all benefited from those who have. Even if you never enter an open-water rowing race, if you row one of the new breed of open-water shells—a light, stiff boat with a rigid deck, a small, sealed cockpit and a bailer—you can thank the Catalina competitors.

- 19 -
Reflections

ROWING, like life, can be as much as you are willing to make it. It's not always easy, but worthwhile accomplishments rarely are. The intent of this book has not been to get every reader to buy a Maas 24 and attempt to set a singles record in the Catalina race, or to have a customized cruising boat built for long rows along the Maine coast; it has been to make rowers aware of their options.

No matter what level oarsman you are, each time you slip your boat into the water you have a choice to make: Do I just do my regular row, or a little bit extra? If you normally row four miles inside the harbor or along the lake shore, why not add a mile or go out into the open water? The more you put into rowing, the more rewarding you will find it.

Once you've made the commitment to get more out of your rowing, remember the stepping stone-approach. Set long-term goals, but back them up with interim, realistic goals you can reach along the way. As you reach each interim goal, you will not only be advancing toward your ultimate goal, but you will be learning about the sea, your boat, and yourself. The training and the interim goals will not only make you a better oarsman—they will make you a fitter, healthier, happier person.

Rowing can be a lifelong sport. One of its beauties is that it changes constantly, always challenging the participant. There are oarsmen who have been rowing 50 years who freely admit they still don't have the perfect rowing stroke—yet they go out day after day, enjoy the sport, and try to achieve their goal.

When you reach your ultimate goal you will probably find you have established a new, higher goal to strive for. *Go for it!*

Appendix 1

■ **SUGGESTIONS FOR FURTHER READING**

SOME of the books listed here are no longer in print. Try libraries or used-book stores; the books are worth the search.

The Annapolis Book of Seamanship, John Rousmaniere. Simon & Schuster (1989). Written for sailors, this very detailed work contains a wealth of vital information. Read the chapters on first aid, anchoring, weather, and navigation, if nothing else.

Boatbuilding Manual, 3rd Edition, Robert M. Steward. International Marine Publishing Company (1987). Considered the classic text in its field. Covers the latest techniques, materials, and products in wooden boat construction.

Building Classic Small Craft, Volume 1, and *More Building Classic Small Craft*, John Gardner. International Marine Publishing Company (1977, 1990). Full of information on the design, history, and use of traditional rowing boats.

The Dory Book, John Gardner. Mystic Seaport Museum (1987). The definitive work on this classic rowing boat, also a wealth of information about wooden boat building.

Dr. Cohen's Healthy Sailor, Michael M. Cohen, M.D. International Marine Publishing Company (1983).

Emergency Navigation, Revised Edition, David Burch. International Marine Publishing (1990). Essential navigation techniques for anyone venturing offshore.

Fiberglass Boat Repair Manual, Allan H. Vaitses. International Marine Publishing Company (1988). An encyclopedic source covering everything from fixing cosmetic dings and scratches to major repairs.

Lightweight Camping Equipment, Gerry Cunningham and Margaret Hanson. Charles Scribner's Sons.

Medical Emergencies at Sea, William Kessler, M.D. Hearst Marine Books (1986).

Oars Across the Pacific, John Fairfax and Sylvia Cook. W. W. Norton & Co. (1973). The story of a transpacific row.

Piloting and Dead Reckoning, H.H. Shafeldt and G. D. Dunlap. Naval Institute Press (1981).

Practical Pilot, Leonard Eyges. International Marine Publishing Company (1989). A commonsense approach to coastal navigation.

Rowing Machine Workouts, Dr. Charles T. Kuntzleman. Contemporary Books, Inc. (1985).

Sail and Oar, John Leather. International Marine Publishing Company (1982). A survey of designs, mostly traditional.

Sailing America, Larry Brown. International Marine Publishing Company (1990). Capsule views of North America's waters, with tips on trailering.

Small Boat Against the Sea, Derek King and Peter Bird. Paul Elek (1976). Story of the first attempt to row around the world.

Appendix 2

■ GLOSSARY

Arc: The path of an oar blade during the pull-through.

Back: To move the boat backward by rowing with the face of the blade turned to face the bow.

Blade: The wide outboard end of an oar.

Bow: The forward end of a boat.

Bucket (to): Allowing the body to come forward too soon during the recovery portion of the stroke.

Buck the oar: Bringing the body forward to the oars at the end of the pull-through, rather than bringing the oars to the body.

Button(s): An adjustable flange or stop placed on the sleeve or loom to prevent the oar from sliding through the oarlock. The buttons also set the amount of overlap.

Catch: Placing the oar in the water to begin the pull-through. Also known as "taking the water."

Clog: A wood and leather sandal used to hold the foot on the stretcher in some boats.

Cockpit: The area where the rower(s) sit in a boat.

Crab (to catch a): Trapping an oar in the water at the release.

Double: A boat sculled by two people.

Drive: The pull-through portion of the stroke.

Feather (to): Turning the blade face parallel to the water on the recovery portion of the stroke.

Fin: A skeg, either wood, metal or plastic, attached to the bottom of the hull to help the boat hold a straight course.

Finish: The portion of the pull-through just before the release.

Foot stretcher: See Stretcher.

Gate: A bar across the otherwise open top of an oarlock.

Grip: The rubber or plastic sleeve over the inboard end of the oar, held by the oarsman.

Handle: See Grip.

Heel cups: Plastic or metal units for supporting the heels on the stretchers of some boats, usually used with clogs or straps.

Height: The distance from the highest portion of the seat to the bottom of the oarlock.

Knife in: To take the catch with the blade under-squared, allowing it to dive too deeply into the water.

Layback: The rower's backward lean (toward the bow) at the release.

Leather: See Sleeve.

Loom: The shaft of an oar or scull.

Oarlock (or lock): A U-shaped fitting that holds the oar while rowing. On a sliding seat boat, it swivels around a pin.

Outrigger (or rigger): A framework that places the oarlocks outboard of the hull.

Pin: A vertical rod attached to the sill, upon which the oarlock swivels.

Pitch: Deviation from the vertical expressed in degrees. In the rower's usual context, the total pitch is the sum of the pitches of the oar back and the oarlock face.

Port: The left side of the boat when facing forward.

Puddles: Swirls or disturbances left in the water when the oar blade emerges.

Rate: Number of strokes per minute.

Recovery: The portion of the stroke between release and catch.

Release: The portion of the stroke at which the blade is lifted from the water.

Rigger: See Outrigger.

Scull: To row with a pair of oars.

Sculls: Oars (usually 9′9″ or 9′10″ inches long) used in pairs.

Sill: The plate at the outboard end of the riggers on which the oarlock is mounted.

Sleeve (or leather): The covering of the loom that prevents wear at the oarlock.

Sliding seat: A seat that rolls fore and aft on wheels.

Splay: The angle between clogs or shoes on the stretcher.

SPM: Strokes per minute. See Rate.

Spread: The distance from pin to pin, measured at their centers.

Starboard: The right side of the boat when facing forward.

Stretcher: An angled plate or framework that provides support for the feet.

Tholepin: See Pin.

Wash out: To have the blade leave the water before the release.

Appendix 3

■ SOURCES: GEAR AND INSTRUCTION

Rowing is almost an underground sport; it seems you have to know someone who knows someone to find a shop or a school. This appendix is an attempt to ease you into the underground. Most rowing-related companies, be they schools, boatbuilders, or equipment manufacturers, are small businesses. As such, they come and go at an alarming rate. Some simply move, others change ownership and management, and still others go out of business. The following list of companies was put together shortly before we went to press; it is as complete as possible, but by the time you read it there may have been changes.

Boathouse Row Sports, 1021 Ridge Ave., Philadelphia, PA 19123 (215) 236-1883: Clothing.

Coffey Racing Shells, 918 Addison Rd., Painted Post, NY 14870 (607) 962-1982: Ergometers.

Concept II, Inc., RR1, Box 1100, Morrisville, VT 05655 (802) 888-7971: Dreissigacker oars, ergometers, oarlocks.

Dana Book & Navigation, 24402 Del Prado, Dana Point, CA 92629 (714) 661-3926: Books, charts, navigational supplies.

Gordon Nash Boat Builders, 10 Liberty Ship Way, #39, Sausalito, CA 94965 (405) 332-1489: Traditional rowing boat designs in fiberglass.

Little River Marine Co., P.O. Box 968, Gainesville, FL 32602 (904) 378-5025: Little River Boats, hardware, accessories.

Maas Oar Co., P.O. Box 28117, Seattle, WA 98118 (206) 723-7601: Maas composite sculls.

Maas Rowing Shells, 1453 Harbour Way South, Richmond, CA 94804 (415) 232-1612: Maas Boats.

Martin Marine Co., Box 251, Kittery Point, ME 03905 (207) 439-1507: Martin and Alden boats, oars, Oarmaster.

Nielsen-Kellerman Co., 201 E. 10th St., Marcus Hook, PA 19061 (215) 495-0602: Strokecoach.

Open Water Rowing, 85 Liberty Ship Way, #102, Sausalito, CA 94965 (405) 332-1091: Maas boats, instruction, rentals, clothing, hardware, books, used shells.

The Rower's Bookshelf, P.O. Box 440, Essex, MA 01929 (508) 468-4096: Rowing books. FAX: (508) 468-6388.

Rowing Northwest-Seattle, 3304 Fuhrman Ave. East, Seattle, WA 98103 (206) 324-5800: Maas and Graham boats, rentals and instruction.

Rowing Northwest-Spokane, North 10711 College Place Dr., Spokane, WA 99218 (509) 466-8158: Maas and Graham boats, instruction.

Small Craft, Inc., 59 Brunswick Ave., Moosup, CT 06354 (203) 564-2751: Small Craft boats.

Sew Sporty, 653 Third St., Encinitas, CA 92024 (619) 944-7300: Clothing.

Sparhawk Sculling School, 222 Porters Point Rd., Colchester, VT 05446 (802) 658-4799: Maas boats and instruction.

Thunderwear Inc., 930 E. Calle Negocio, San Clemente, CA 92672: Gloves.

Trimline by Graham, 2351 Highway 28, Quincy, WA 98848 (509) 787-1225: Trimline boats.

Woods Cove Rowing Shop, P.O. Box 1905, Laguna Beach, CA 92652 (714) 494-6476, FAX (714) 494-2669: Maas boats.

Appendix 4

■ OPEN-WATER RACING RULES

Definition of Open-Water Racing
In open-water racing the competitor races over a designated course of no less than three miles on water not subject to prescribed standards. The sculler must take the water as he/she finds it and be prepared to handle rough water, floating hazards, and windy conditions.

General Regulations
Competitors
- All competitors must be current members of the United States Rowing Association (USRA) when competing in any open-water race that is sanctioned by the USRA.
- In offshore open-water races over 20 miles, entrants must have a proven background of open-water racing or other experience deemed equivalent by the race committee.

Categories
Open-water races may be run in the following categories:
OP = open water; 1D = one design; FS = fixed seat
Men (OP1, OP2, OP3, OP DBL 1, OP DBL 2 1D, FS, FS DBL)
Women (OP1, OP2, OP3, OP DBL 1, OP DBL 2 1D, FS, FS DBL)
Mixed (OP DBL 1, OP DBL 2, 1D, FS DBL)

The one-design class may be used whenever five or more of the same-design boat are entered in the men's, women's, or mixed categories.

Classes and Building Rules
Limitations
Following are the specifications for the OP classes.

	Maximum Length	Minimum Weight
OP1:	19 ft.	40 lbs.
OP2:	22 ft.	38 lbs.
OP3:	25 ft. 2 in.	38 lbs.
OP DBL 1:	24 ft.	80 lbs.
OP DBL 2:	30 ft.	80 lbs.

Measuring

If the equipment safety officer is unfamiliar with a boat entered in any category, the following methods should be used to measure and determine within which category the boat belongs.

- The length should be measured from bow to stern along the deck.
- The appropriate template should be used to determine whether the beam at water-line meets the minimum requirements for the class indicated by a boat's length.
- Boats should be weighed dry, fully rigged, with all equipment needed to operate the boat excluding electronics, safety, and personal gear.

Organization of the Competitions
Officials

Competitions will be held under the supervision of the following officials: race organizer, race secretary, starter(s), finish line judge(s), timekeeper(s), equipment safety officer.

If necessary, and circumstances permit, one person may function in two of the above positions. The overall management of the competition is handled by a race committee consisting of the race organizer, race secretary, and equipment safety officer.

The race committee must:

- organize the race and supervise its arrangements;
- postpone and reschedule the race due to inclement weather or other unforeseen circumstances that make it impossible to safely stage the race;
- hear any protests that may be made and settle any disputes that may arise;
- decide matters concerning disqualifications in cases where the regulations have been broken during the race. Decisions of the race committee will be based on the Open-Water Racing Rules;
- before any decision is made regarding an alleged infraction of the rules, hear the opinion of the officials who were in direct control of the race, if it is necessary to clear up the alleged offense.

The race committee may disqualify any competitor who behaves improperly or who, by his conduct or speech, shows contempt toward the officials, other competitors, or onlookers.

Duties of the Officials

The race organizer is responsible for the preparation for and running of the competition. The organizer will decide all matters arising during the actual contest that are not dealt with in these rules.

The race secretary is responsible for the organization of entries, recording the results, preparing lists of final times, and notifying all contestants of the race results. The secretary must keep the minutes of any protest meetings.

The starter decides all questions concerning the start of the races, and alone is responsible for decisions as to false starts. The starter's decision is final.

The finish line judge decides the order in which the competitors have crossed the finish line. If, with more than one judge, there is a disagreement about finishing line position, the disagreement shall be decided by a simple majority.

The timekeepers are responsible for recording the times. Before each race the chief timekeeper shall be satisfied that the watches or other timekeeping equipment is working satisfactorily.

The equipment/safety officer ensures that the dimensions of the boats conform to the Open-Water Racing Rules and that the required safety equipment is carried by each competitor. Should any boat not conform to the Open-Water Racing Rules requirements it will be excluded from the race.

Race Announcements
A race announcement will contain:
- time and place of race;
- plan of the course;
- classes and distances of races;
- sequence and start times of races;
- nature of the course, water conditions, and degree of difficulty;
- safety equipment required;
- racing experience required, if appropriate;
- bad weather alternate course, if appropriate;
- bad weather alternate race date, if appropriate;
- entry fee and deadline;
- address where entry should be sent.

Entries
In offshore open-water races over 20 miles, the race committee may require every entrant to list prior open-water race experience to show ability to complete the course.

Every entry form will include a waiver to be signed by each competitor.

Acceptance of Entries
Applications of entries must be acknowledged within 48 hours of receipt.

Withdrawals
The withdrawal of any entry fee is considered final. Entry fees will not be refunded.

Alteration in Course or Event
The sequence of races and courses set in the announcement are binding on the race committee unless severe weather forces a postponement or change in the race course. Alternate race courses will be those published in the race announcement.

Marking Signs
All flags marking the open-water race courses, for the start, finish, and turns, will be international orange, at least 2 feet by 3 feet. The start and finish lines will be marked with one flag at each end. The flags for the finish may be set closer together than the flags for the starting line if the competitors have been informed of that change prior to the start of the race.

For the start and finish lines, large orange buoys may be substituted for flags. If conditions or current does not allow the placement of one of the flags or buoys, a flag on shore or aboard a stationary vessel may be substituted.

Courses
The categories for courses are:
- Short: 3 to 5 miles
- Standard: 5 to 10 miles
- Long: 10 to 20 miles
- Marathon: more than 20 miles

The bodies of water and numbers of turns used in any race are up to the race committee. All turns shall be negotiated as directed by the race organizer.

In any race with turns, the angle between course lines approaching and departing from a mark must be at least 30 degrees to avoid collisions on opposing courses.

Boat Numbers
All boats must carry a number attached to either the boat or oarsman as directed by the race organizer.

Instructions for Competitors

Each competitor will receive printed instructions at least an hour before the race start, containing the following:

- detailed information on the courses and marks;
- starting times and procedures;
- configuration of start and finish lines;
- competitor's race number;
- safety equipment requirements;
- bad-weather course alternates.

Protests

A protest made during the competition relating to an incident in the race must be brought to the race organizer's attention not later than one hour after that competitor has completed the course or been forced to retire from the course.

The protest outcome will be decided by the race committee. Information will be gathered from the competitors involved and any other race officials who observed the incident.

Racing Regulations

Starts

Competitors shall be at the start at the time specified in the racing program. The start will be given without deference to any absentees.

The position of the boats at the start is such that the bows of the competing boats are on the starting line. If the starting line is not wide enough to accommodate all the entrants in any one class, those competitors whose race records show them to be among the first to finish will be brought forward to the start line with all other competitors lining up as closely behind those competitors as space allows.

The starter will give the following sound signals to start the race: 3 long at 3 min.; 2 long at 2 min.; 1 long at 1 min.; 3 short at 30 seconds; 2 short at 20 seconds; 1 short at 10 seconds; and a countdown from 5 seconds and a long signal to start. If any competitor begins rowing before the last long signal, that will constitute a false start.

Any competitor who starts before the last signal (a false start) will be given a time penalty of two percent of his/her total elapsed time.

Where strong tides or currents render a stationary line-up impossible, a rolling start—where the boats line up at least 50 yards behind the start line—may be used. The starter will use the same sound signals as in a stationary start; no boat may cross the start line before the start signal. Those competitors crossing early are given a two percent time penalty.

Turns and Right of Way

When a race is run on a course with turning points, these shall be passed to port (i.e. to the rower's right side) unless otherwise directed.

Within three boat lengths of a turning mark, the outside boat shall give each boat **overlapping** on the inside (between that boat and the mark) room to round. **Overlapping** means that the bow of the overtaking boat is level with a line extending through the sternmost oarlocks of the leading boat, perpendicular to the long line of that boat. When two boats are on **converging courses**, the boat to starboard (i.e. the rower's left side) has the right of way. If two boats are on converging courses and the courses are **dead ahead and opposite**, both boats must alter course to avoid a collision.

Overtaking

The leading boat has the right of way and the overtaking boat must keep clear. The leading boat shall not alter course in such a way as to prevent the overtaking boat from passing.

Penalties

If, during any part of the race, competitors lock oars, the boat to starboard shall be allowed to row free while the other boat(s) involved remain stationary.

A boat that collides with or causes a right-of-way boat to alter course may be disqualified unless it completes one full 360-degree turn as soon after the foul as possible. A boat in the process of a 360-degree turn has no right of way and must stay clear of other boats.

Any competitor who attempts to win a race by other than honorable means, or who breaks the racing rules, or who disregards the honorable nature of the racing regulations will be disqualified from that race.

Should a competitor have completed a race in a boat that is shown upon inspection not to fulfill the OWRR classifications, that competitor will be disqualified from the race.

Assistance

In the marathon category of open-water races, competitors may receive assistance from their designated escort boats. Such assistance is limited to first aid, provision of food, drink, and clothes, replacement of faulty equipment, including oars, and help with repairs, but not replacement of the boat itself. While providing assistance the escort boats may not move the competitor or his/her boat forward on the race course.

In any race where the entrants are required or allowed to have a designated escort, the competitor must always be positioned ahead of the escort. Competitors will not be allowed to ride the wake of an escort vessel during a race.

No exchange of boats is permitted during a race. All competitors must use the same boat throughout the race.

Open-water racing may put participants in dangerous situations. Any competitor seeing another in real danger shall render all assistance in his/her power. Failure to do so may involve disqualification from the race.

Safety Measures

Each boat must carry sufficient buoyancy material to keep it afloat when filled with water, one PFD for each rower, and for the OP categories, a self-bailer.

Other safety measures may be required by the race organizer, such as a compass, water bottles, tool kit, lights, or high visibility vest. Required safety equipment will be noted on the race entry form. Any competitor failing to observe the safety requirements shall be refused the right to start.

Competitors participate at their own risk. The race organizers and race committee cannot be held responsible for accidents or damage that may occur during a race.

Every official is required to observe that the safety measures are being adhered to, and prevent boats or competitors from starting or continuing if they fail to meet requirements laid down in the rules.

Finish

The finish line is reached when the bow of the boat has passed the line between the finish line flags. If two or more boats reach the finish line at the same time, they receive the same finish position.

It is best to have two finish line judges, two timekeepers, and a video cameraperson to record race finishes. The judges should be positioned one above and behind the other, in line with the two finish line flags. For smaller races, one judge and one timekeeper can be similarly positioned.

January 30, 1990

Index